T0330145

Women and Market Societies

Women and Market Societies

Crisis and Opportunity

Edited by

Barbara Einhorn and Eileen Janes Yeo

Research Centre in Women's Studies
University of Sussex, UK

Edward Elgar

Aldershot, UK • Brookfield, US

Published by
Edward Elgar Publishing Limited
Gower House
Croft Road
Aldershot
Hants GU11 3HR
England

Edward Elgar Publishing Company
Old Post Road
Brookfield
Vermont 05036
US

British Library Cataloguing in Publication Data

Women and Market Societies: Crisis and Opportunity
    I. Einhorn, Barbara II. Yeo, Eileen Janes
    305.42

Library of Congress Cataloguing in Publication Data

Women and market societies: crisis and opportunity / edited by
    Barbara Einhorn and Eileen Janes Yeo.
      256p. 23cm.
      Includes index.
      1. Women—Economic conditions—Cross-cultural studies.
    2.Women—Social conditions—Cross-cultural studies.
    I. Einhorn, Barbara. II. Yeo, Eileen Janes.
    HQ1381.W626 1995   95–15672
    305.42—dc20   CIP

ISBN 1 85898 317 7

Printed in Great Britain at the University Press, Cambridge

Contents

Notes on Contributors

CRESCY CANNAN
Crescy Cannan is Senior Lecturer in Social Policy and Social Work at the University of Sussex. She has previously worked as a social worker. Her research interests include ideologies in social work and welfare, with experience in India, Germany and France. She is interested in social and community development approaches to promoting women's and children's welfare and is currently working on a comparative study of Britain and France. Her publications include *Changing Families, Changing Welfare: Family Centres and the Welfare State* (1992); and (with Lynn Berry and Karen Lyons), *Social Work and Europe* (1992).

STEPHANIE DONALD
Stephanie Donald is currently a Teaching Assistant in Media Studies at the University of Sussex. Her doctoral research is on Chinese cinema and civil society. Earlier she worked as a professional actress in film, theatre and radio. She has also written and directed in radio and theatre for young people. Forthcoming publications include articles in: *Diatribe, Women – a Cultural Review, Screen, Britain-China*.

CLAIRE DUCHEN
Claire Duchen is Senior Lecturer in French at the University of Sussex. She has published widely on women in France and on feminism. Her latest book is *Women's Rights and Women's Lives in France 1944–1968* (1994). She is African and European Editor of the journal *Women's Studies International Forum*.

BARBARA EINHORN
Barbara Einhorn is an Honorary Research Fellow in the Research Centre in Women's Studies at the University of Sussex. She is interested in the impact of the transition to market societies on women's rights in East Central Europe and China. Her publications include 'Where Have All the Women Gone?' (*Feminist Review*, 1991); and *Cinderella Goes to Market: Citizenship, Gender and Women's Movements in East Central Europe* (1993). She is Associate Editor for Eastern Europe for the *European Journal of Women's Studies*.

MAGGIE GÜNSBERG

Maggie Günsberg is a Lecturer in Italian at the University of Sussex. She is the author of *Patriarchal Representations: Gender and Discourse in Pirandello's Theatre* (1994). She is currently working on a book entitled *Gender on the Italian Stage: From the Renaissance to Rome.*

MARIA JASCHOK

Maria Jaschok is currently based in Henan Province, China, where she is completing a two-year research project. She has participated in developing China's first International Women's College (Zhengzhou University) and its affiliated Women's Museum. Her publications include *Concubines and Bondservants* (1988) and (co-edited with Suzanne Miers), *Chinese Patriarchy and Women* (1994).

KIM KYUNG-AI

Kim Kyung-Ai gained her DPhil, on 'Married Women's Labour Force Participation and Status in South Korea', in 1994 from the Institute of Development Studies at Sussex University where she has recently been a Visiting Fellow. She has also worked as a researcher for the Korean Women's Research Institute of Ewha Women's University in Seoul, South Korea. Her research interests are women's participation in politics and the feminist movement, and violence against women in Korea. Her writing includes 'A Study of the Thought on Sexual Equality of *Donghak, Chundokyo* (a Korean School)' (unpublished MA thesis, 1984); and *A Woman's Fate is a Gourd's Fate: Labour and Sexuality of Korean Married Women* (Brighton: IDS Discussion Paper, 1995).

LISA LEUNG

Lisa Leung is a final year DPhil student at the University of Sussex. Her thesis examines the parameters of and tensions involved in, the production of franchised magazine editions in Hong Kong and their impact on representations of femininity. In it she reasserts the need for local media to appeal to local cultural specificities. She has also been writing on the aspects of diaspora and disjuncture within the globalization of culture.

LIU BOHONG

Liu Bohong is Associate Fellow and Director of Theoretical Research on Women at the Women's Studies Institute of China. Her main fields of research are women in employment and the media. Her publications include *Words of Celebrities on the Family* (1992); and the sections on employment and culture in *Ten Years of Research on Chinese Women* (1992). She was chief editor of a *Report on the Investigation into Women's Employment in Beijing, Guangzhou and Hong Kong* (1994).

SHEILA ROWBOTHAM
Sheila Rowbotham is a Research Fellow at Manchester University. She has published widely on women's history and is currently working on a history of women in the twentieth century in Britain and the US. Her books include *Hidden from History* (1973); *The Past is Before Us* (1989); and *Women in Movement* (1993).

GILLIAN SCOTT
Gillian Scott is an historian with a special interest in working-class feminism. She is a Senior Lecturer in the School of Historical and Critical Studies at the University of Brighton. Gillian is the author of 'A Trade Union for Married Women: The Women's Co-operative Guild 1914–1920', in Sybil Oldfield (ed.), *This Working-Day World: Women's Lives and Culture(s) in Britain 1914–1945* (1994); and is currently completing *A Smouldering in the Hearth: Feminism, Femininity and the Politics of Working Women – The Women's Co-operative Guild 1880s to World War II* (1996 forthcoming; working title).

JENNY SHAW
Jenny Shaw is a Lecturer in Sociology at the University of Sussex. She is interested in gender, education, time, shopping, the pace of life, mass-observation and the application of psychoanalytical ideas to social issues. Jenny is the author of *Education, Gender and Anxiety* (1995); and has co-edited *Making Gender Work* (1995).

SUN RONG
Sun Rong is Assistant Professor at the Women's Studies Institute of China. Her research interests include: women's social status in Chinese society, re-production and family planning, marriage and family life. Her publications include chapters on social interaction, the utilization of time, childbirth and family planning in *General Review of Women's Social Status in China* (1993); a chapter on unmarried youth in *The Situation of Marriage and the Family in Beijing* (1994); and chapters on women's social status and lifestyle, and reproduction and health in *Research on Women's Social Status in China* (1995).

XU MIN

Xu Min is Deputy Director of the Women's Studies Centre at Hangzhou University, China. Her main publications are a textbook on *Principles of Sociology* (1988); *Views from Eden – The Essence of Sex* (1991); and 'Modern Girl Students' Sense of Identity and Social Expectations of Their Role' (*Zhejiang Study Journal*, January 1994). In 1991 she made a television series for Zhejiang television entitled *A Dialogue between Men and Women*. She also hosts a radio hotline talk show, and writes a weekly newspaper column entitled 'Female Viewpoint' in the *Hangzhou Daily*.

EILEEN JANES YEO

Eileen Janes Yeo is an historian, who researches into British class. She is a member of the Research Centre in Women's Studies at the University of Sussex where she offers a course on 'Women in Society: America, Britain, Nazi Germany and Revolutionary China'. Her publications include *The Contest for Social Science: Relations and Representations of Gender and Class (1995)*. She has lectured in China and took part in the 1994 summer school 'Women Working Together' sponsored by the All-China Women's Federation and the Great Britain-China Centre.

ZHAO WEIJIE

Zhao Weijie is an Associate Research Fellow at the Academy of Social Sciences in Shenzhen, China. Her main research interests are on gender issues, particularly marriage and the family in China's Special Economic Zones. Her most recent publication, prepared for the fourth UN Conference on Women (Beijing, September 1995) is *The Enigma of Shenzhen's Venus* (1995). She is also co-author of *Deng Xiao Ping's Theory and Practice on the Special Economic Zones* (1995).

Preface

The editors wish to acknowledge the support of the Research Development Fund at the University of Sussex in the preparation of this volume for publication. Their thanks go to all the students and faculty of Women's Studies who have participated in the discussions leading up to this book and given comments on individual draft chapters. Individual authors are to be congratulated on their cooperation with the tight schedules which the goal of publishing the volume in time for the Fourth UN World Conference in Beijing in September 1995 necessitated. We would also like to extend particular thanks to Pilwha Chang for her substantive comments and help with the jacket design. The editors are particularly grateful to their Chinese colleagues who made the cross-cultural study possible by their long-distance participation in the project. We hope that this cooperation will continue as the research underlying this book progresses.

Special thanks are due to Andrew Proctor whose professionalism, patience, and close interest in the content of the chapters made the preparation of camera-ready copy a pleasure. Without the prompt and constructive responses of Dymphna Evans and Julie Leppard at Edward Elgar, this volume could not have been produced in the short timescale. Finally, personal thanks are due to David Evans for his practical and emotional support, and particularly for his comments on Barbara Einhorn's drafts.

Barbara Einhorn and Eileen Janes Yeo

Introduction

Barbara Einhorn

Current trends towards marketization have far-reaching gender implications which present both a crisis and an opportunity for women worldwide. The collapse of old structures and certainties in the East and in the West has opened the possibility of new international dialogues among women who have much to learn from each other's experience. It is in this spirit that members of the Research Centre in Women's Studies at the University of Sussex have brought together their individual work and joint discussions with the research of Women's Studies colleagues in East Asia. The direct impetus for producing this volume was the Fourth United Nations World Conference on Women (Beijing, September 1995). The aim is not to come to definitive conclusions, but to create an agenda for ongoing research and discussion.

The book collects together essays which explore the problems and possibilities for women which arise from the dismantling of state socialism in East Central Europe, from the transition to a 'socialist' market economy in China and from the current restructuring of the older capitalist economies and welfare states in Western Europe. The authors were conscious of the need for a perspective which keeps both similarity and difference in view. Mesmerized by current discourses on difference, it can be all too easy to overlook the fact that the creation of a global market economy affects women in their different locations in similar ways. This insight informs the present collection of essays which encompasses the theoretical approaches of different disciplines and the specificities of different cultures.

International capital appears to favour female labour in its global search for cost-cutting and profit-maximization. However, the search for ever cheaper supplies of labour sets up international competition between women workers: high female involvement in the labour market in East Asia is bought at the expense of increases in part-time, temporary and home-based work and the degradation of working conditions in Western Europe, and high female unemployment in the countries of East Central Europe which formerly boasted unparalleled levels of female labour force participation. In these situations, where there is a 'preference' for female labour, it seems to go hand in hand with worsening and unprotected working conditions, with low-paid jobs for women without training or career prospects (ILO, 1994; for an examination of the effect of these trends in the global division of labour, see also Gittings, 1995). And within most societies, forms of unequal gender relations reinforce inequalities between men and women in the market, at home, and in society at large.

The construction of a global market economy according to the currently dominant neo-liberal paradigm is characterized by a dual process of marketization and the withdrawal or contraction of the state sector. The market is posited as the sole and sufficient regulator of economic and social development. In Western industrialized countries this is expressed as a drive toward privatization and contraction of the state sector, as owner, employer and provider of formerly public services. In the (former) state socialist countries of East Central Europe and China,[1] the stagnation of centrally planned economies is being replaced by the dynamism of the market. In these contexts too, the process involves privatization and withdrawal of the state as arbiter of working conditions and provider of welfare.

The global trend towards marketization has significant repercussions for women, since it is the state which has traditionally set minimum labour standards, been responsible for the provision of facilities such as childcare which underpin women's ability to participate in the public spheres of work and politics, and in part regulated their reproductive labour in the private sphere. In the West, this process has been characterized as the elimination of what has been called a 'dependency culture' (Cannan, Chapter 11) in favour of a culture of individual responsibility based on the family unit. Western practice shows that this in effect means devolution onto the unpaid work of women. In East Central Europe and China too, individual enterprise is being raised to the level of a socially worthy activity, displacing notions of equity or social justice as a collective goal.

This dual process has some common implications for women in different societies: on the one hand it cuts loose the social supports for their role as workers; on the other it constructs them on many levels as consumers. What is interesting is precisely the historically and culturally specific ways in which these processes are appropriated, internalized and resisted by women in different cultures. Nor are women within any one country or culture a homogeneous group, as many of the chapters show. This volume offers analyses of the economic, social, and cultural impact of marketization on women in Britain, the US, China, South Korea, Hong Kong and East Central Europe, both historically and at the present time. It poses questions about gender relations, the contradictions between private and public spheres, and women's space for self-definition and implementation of their rights as citizens.

The Chinese character for 'crisis' means 'danger' and 'opportunity'. Opportunities for self-development offered by a liberal democratic paradigm based on individualism are, for women, always modified by the predominant systems of gender relations which tend to disadvantage them. In East Central Europe, for example, marketization has been seen as synonymous with democratization, but the introduction of Western-style liberal democracy has been predicated, as it was historically in Western capitalist societies, on a male subject making contracts in the marketplace.

Now the neo-liberal market paradigm is itself in crisis. Recent studies point to the market's negative potential (Lasch, 1995; Rowntree, 1995). Lauded as the single most efficient route to development, the global market has over the past 15 years shown its destructive potential in a spectacular growth in inequalities, both between the countries of North and South, and within countries: between men and women, between classes and ethnic groups. Inequalities within one society are most starkly evident in industrialized countries like Britain which have most rigorously applied deregulatory market policies, coupled with a roll-back of the welfare state (Gray, 1995). The 1995 report of the Joseph Rowntree Foundation Inquiry into Income and Wealth claims that the neo-liberal 'trickle-down' theory of economics does not work and that market mechanisms by themselves are inadequate providers of investment in human capital. This volume seeks to explore the specifically gender-based dimensions of some of these market processes and their social consequences.

The focus on the impact of the market – especially in times of transition – on women's choices and opportunities, enables the authors of this volume, from their very different research perspectives, to highlight some of the central questions which need to be addressed if women's rights are to become a priority. The multi-disciplinary and comparative approach, slicing across different historical periods, different countries and different issues, is not only an asset characteristic of Women's Studies, but also operates as a source of new and creative insights into some of the still unresolved questions of feminist political theory and research as well as gender policy questions.

The volume concentrates on issues around whether and in which way the market constrains and/or empowers women. How do transitions to and within the market, both historically, with the introduction of capitalist modes of production, and currently, in East Central and Western Europe, and in East Asia, affect women's employment opportunities and prospects? And what is their impact on the complex way in which the relationship between the family and the wider society, between women's productive and reproductive roles, is constructed? What policy decisions underlie such transitions and how do they alter women's opportunities to operate as autonomous subjects, as citizens within the public sphere? How has the role of the state and social welfare provision been affected by the transition to the market in East and West, at different points in history? How do images transmitted by global media conglomerates or marketed by multinational companies influence women's sense of self in varying cultures? And how do local cultures modulate such internationally marketed images of femininity?

The chapters in this volume focus on the contradictions which must be addressed in order that women can help create societies based on a paradigm of social justice and gender equality. Neither of these goals is central to much currently fashionable discourse; yet it is only a matter of time before they come on the agenda again. The authors in this volume take as illustrations those sites in which the market relegates women to an ostensibly passive role as consumers (shopping for the family, reproducing the workforce from their dominion in the kitchen, watching films and buying products and magazines which in turn inculcate the social norms around femininity) as well as their more active participation in the labour market itself. It shows that there is a need for political resistance to market forces, but also that this resistance can come from unexpected quarters.[2] The public/private divide, and the unequal gender relations operating in both, have often been seen as the main sources of women's subordination in society. Many of the chapters in this volume pay tribute to women's creativity in transcending the boundaries of public and private, or in using their very role as wives, mothers, consumers as a basis for effective political activism.

Always highlighting women's active role, the chapters in Part One assess two early cases of women in the older market societies of Britain and the United States who have successfully used their role as consumers to intervene in mainstream politics. Gillian Scott (Chapter 2) focuses on the work of the Women's Co-operative Guild in Britain between 1883 and 1920 to highlight the tension between the market's tendency to reproduce traditional gender roles and relationships, and feminist efforts to contest them. Sheila Rowbotham (Chapter 1) looks at the United States over a similar, slightly longer period (1880–1940). She focuses on working-class and middle-class women's cooperative projects – combinations of labour organizing and community action – as examples of the use of consumer power for legislative reform and of direct action to control the market.

That key site of women's work, the kitchen, is the focus of Part Two, which highlights the paradoxical effects of modernizing housework in widely differing social and cultural contexts in Western Europe and China. Claire Duchen (Chapter 3) examines the relationship between domesticity and modernity in France between 1920 and 1960. She takes the kitchen as both locus of women's domestic labour, and emblem of the ideology of a 'woman's proper place'. Post-war periods – particularly the years immediately follow-ing World War II – have shown raised expectations that women might play a full part in rebuilding public life. Yet, in France the woman in the kitchen symbolized a particular notion of 'home' that appeared as the location of women's fulfilment within an emerging consumer culture. Xu Min's chapter (Chapter 4) is based on interviews with four generations of women from one Chinese family. It provides an illuminating picture of social change on two levels: the physical improvements in kitchen facilities during this century on the one hand, and changes in women's attitudes to working in the kitchen, attitudes driven by differing social mores and political projects in different periods, on the other.

The first two chapters in Part Three look at constructions of the social roles available to women in films from two different cultures. Opportunities for women in both consumption and active participation are ostensibly opened up by the market but in fact constrained by traditional mores in Italian neo-realist cinema. In Chapter 5, Maggie Günsberg examines *Ossessione, Ladri di Biciclette* and *Ladri di Saponette* to explore the depiction of domestic space in pre- and post-boom Italy. She sees the differing relationship of female characters to domestic space as contingent on the historical and socio-economic context of the production of each film, a context which can also be seen to interface with varying cinematic practices. Two films made shortly after the introduction of market reforms in China indicate in Stephanie Donald's view (Chapter 6) that the new ideology brings its own problems of representation. She looks at feminism and dominant culture, and the use of women's stories as part of an historical project, in her readings of *Sacrifice of Youth* and *Yellow Earth*. Both these chapters also consider issues of female spectatorship in relation to the projected images of women.

The power of the media, advertising and market sales techniques to create new female images and role models, and the possibilities for embracing or resisting these representations in self-definition and the formation of female identities, concern two further chapters in this section. Lisa Leung (Chapter 7) analyses the fractured and contested transmission of images (of femininity and sexuality) within the global cultural economy. She illustrates this using the example of franchised women's magazines, in particular *Cosmopolitan Hong Kong*. Maria Jaschok's study (Chapter 8) explores China's development into a market economy from within the subjectivities of women of different ages and stages in their life cycle, as they seek to maintain, adapt or contest notions of appropriate femininity. Material for it comes from interviews she conducted in Henan Province, China with two different generations of women. The first, with Avon ladies and their clients, explores the power of imported images in a time of transition and cultural confusion. The second, with young women aged around 20, shows the strength of local patterns of identity formation, including the role of generational emulation and distancing, which lessens the impact of the imported images, at least for younger women. The paper suggests that by foregrounding the multi-layered process which intervenes between commercial representation and its reception by the consumer, greater understanding may be attained of the engendering of a culture-specific female identity.

The final two parts focus on the labour market itself, and on tensions in the articulation of women's paid and unpaid work between public and private spheres. They also examine the extent to which Eastern or Western legislative frameworks about rights and benefits have eased or exacerbated these tensions, and hence the role of the state in relation to women's rights. Eileen Janes Yeo (Chapter 9) gives an historical overview of the difficulties both working-class and middle-class women have faced in moving from a domestic to a market economy, a move which historically often entailed the concealment of one or other half of women's lives. She details the continuation of contradictions between women's dual roles in the export of traditional forms of the 'feminization' of work to the global level. Focusing on time as the ultimate scarce resource, Jenny Shaw (Chapter 10) looks at the way women manage the contradictions between public and private, paid and unpaid work. She points out that the price they pay for thus mediating between market and non-market sectors is high, and is set to increase further in future. Both chapters see new forms of exploitation resulting for women from the development of a global market economy.

The profoundly gendered outcomes of the contemporary restructuring of Western welfare states and labour markets in the name of marketization is explored by Crescy Cannan (Chapter 11). She asks what are the limits and possibilities of the new enterprise cultures for women as workers, as welfare recipients, and as citizens. Using examples from welfare regimes in the UK, France, Germany, Scandinavia and the United States, she argues that it is possible to modify the effects of marketization by espousing new kinds of social protection for, and promotion of, individuals, families and their communities.

Social change brings disorientation and a need to construct new identities. Recent analyses of the transition to market societies in the (former) state socialist countries have pointed out that this process involves a triple set of conflicting models: that of the previous 40 years of state socialist conformity which constructed women as workers and mothers contrasts with market pressures which tend to displace women as workers in favour of women as consumers, and/or to increase their labour force participation under disadvantageous working conditions. Underlying this change, however, there is a third layer which is seeping to the surface: that of traditional peasant cultures in East Central Europe and of revived Confucian morality in China, Hong Kong and South Korea, both of them deeply patriarchal cultures advocating a hierarchy of gender-divided separate spheres.

In the case of South Korea the state socialist experiment is present only as the negative example of North Korea. Nonetheless, Kim Kyung-Ai (Chapter 12) demonstrates that despite the contradiction between traditional norms of behaviour as prescribed by Confucian ideology and women's paid work, the number of married women entering the labour market is growing fast in response to labour shortages. However, there is a 'marital division of labour' in the gender-segregated South Korean labour market, in which married women take up those jobs abandoned by male and single female workers, occupying the lowest rung of the occupational ladder and experiencing the worst working conditions.

China's transition to a 'socialist' market economy is exposing contradictions between the shrinking state sector and a fast expanding private sector. Liu Bohong and Sun Rong (Chapter 13) show that the development of a labour market has introduced choice into women's working lives. Yet at the same time, the state is increasingly unable to control the development of sub-standard working conditions for women. The rush to new wealth which is especially evident in the Special Economic Zones is accompanied by a crisis in social mores. Zhao Weijie (Chapter 14) sees the pattern which is emerging as the traditional system of concubinage in modern guise: some newly rich men shed family responsibilities or acquire multiple wives. Reinforced by new Westernized marketed images of the ideal woman, this development creates an acute sense of anxiety in the middle generation of Chinese women, accustomed to perceiving themselves as their husband's equals and working partners.

In the final chapter, Barbara Einhorn (Chapter 15) looks at entitlements as a basis for citizenship rights in East Central Europe. This provides the context for an analysis of women's economic, social and reproductive rights which are under attack by a powerful combination of global market forces and local conservative and/or nationalist discourses.

Existing analyses of women's experience both East and West have provided us with critiques of *both* market-based and centrally planned economic systems. This book begins to construct a vision of new social structures which could empower women as citizens in a broader sense. The present historical conjuncture presents a unique opportunity to rethink the theoretical and policy issues surrounding questions of gender equality. State socialist and Western democratic societies operated with very different paradigms with regard to women's rights. State socialism granted women 'emancipation' from above, but within a development strategy with a 'productivist bias' (Young, 1993, p. 135). Hence the issue of women's rights remained largely invisible. Western capitalist democracies by contrast have historically viewed women as a 'reserve army of labour'. Domestic responsibilities have been regarded as their primary role, and such legislative and political change as there has been, has been achieved by activist struggle from below. Indeed it could be said that women's opportunities in both systems were subject to economic and demographic imperatives.

Although there has been significant change in most of the societies with which this volume is concerned, it can be argued that neither the capitalist nor the socialist paradigm have delivered the goods in terms of creating a society characterized by gender equality. The state socialist paradigm favoured women as workers, but turned a blind eye to gender inequalities in the household. Nor have Western feminist successes in forcing what went on behind the closed door of the private sphere into the realm of public jurisdiction fundamentally altered those intra-household power relations. This very lack of change within the household or in the public/private divide, against a background of far-reaching changes in the world economy, provides the incentive for an exciting dialogue around what might be the route to women's empowerment in the societies of the future.

NOTES

1   It is of course necessary to distinguish between East Central Europe's full-speed drive towards the market and China's attempt to balance the two systems with the introduction of a 'socialist market economy' (White, 1993). The chapters in this volume lend illustration to Gordon White's contention that this attempt is fatally flawed, and that its inherent contradictions, especially the attempt to maintain an authoritarian political grip on the liberalized economic development, must eventually cause the experiment to explode (or implode).
2   In Russia through the 1960s to the 1980s, for example, the kitchen was seen as 'a front of massive resistance to the totalitarian regime' (Lissyutkina, 1993, p. 276).

BIBLIOGRAPHY

Gittings, John (1995), 'West Cries "Piracy" While Pillaging Chinese Labour', *The Guardian*, 17 February.
Gray, John (1995), 'Beggaring Our Own Neighbours: The Gulf Between Rich and Poor is Not the Only Factor to Destroy Communities', *The Guardian*, 17 February.
ILO (1994), *Productive Employment: Women Workers in a Changing Global Environment*, ILO Contribution to Chapter II of the *1994 UN World Survey on the Role of Women in Development*, Geneva: International Labour Organization.
Lasch, Christopher (1995), *The Revolt of the Elites*, mentioned in 'Markets and Other Monsters', the Leader of the *Independent on Sunday*, 5 February.
Lissyutkina, Larissa (1993), 'Soviet Women at the Crossroads of Perestroika' in Nanette Funk and Magda Mueller (eds), *Gender Politics and Post-Communism: Reflections from Eastern Europe and the Former Soviet Union*, London and New York: Routledge.
Rowntree (1995), 'Growing Inequality Means the Poor Keep Getting Poorer', Will Hutton sums up the Findings of the Joseph Rowntree Foundation Inquiry into Income and Wealth, *The Guardian*, 10 February.
White, Gordon (1993), *Riding the Tiger: The Politics of Reform in Post-Mao China*, Basingstoke: Macmillan.
Young, Kate (1993), *Planning Development with Women: Making a World of Difference*, Basingstoke: Macmillan.

PART ONE

Consumption and Women's Politics:
Past Experiences

1. Consumer Power: Women's Contribution to Alternatives and Resistance to the Market in the United States 1880–1940

Sheila Rowbotham

INTRODUCTION

Though the market is frequently abstracted as a timeless economic force, markets are social structures which have been shaped and reshaped historically. The period after World War I in the United States saw a dramatic transformation in consumption. During the 1920s the rapid expansion of goods and services began to change the pattern of daily life. The depression in the 1930s, followed by the war, put restraints on the consumer boom, but by the 1950s the United States was producing domestic products on a mass scale. It was never just a matter of selling goods; advertisers promoted the good life. During the Cold War the superiority of American society in terms of individual consumption was an important ideological weapon.

The particular pattern of consumption set by this era of optimistic faith in the capacity of the commodity to fulfil human needs, was to have an international impact economically, socially and culturally. It has both met needs and generated new wants; made many aspects of life – including housework – more convenient, while creating new forms of inequality and deprivation. On the whole this approach to consumption has been better at providing things for those who can afford to buy than meeting human needs which require social reorganization. It has neglected the well-being and social rights of the poor, devastated the environment and failed to attend to the importance of care and nurture.

The structuring of markets does not just happen. Powerful vested interests backed by capital fought both economically and ideologically for the market values which came to predominate in America. Retrospectively the focus on individual consumers in individual homes buying individual products might seem a foregone conclusion. However the form which prevailed was not the only approach which existed historically to meeting human need. There were alternative associative visions of how American society might develop, there were cooperative projects and movements which sought social control over consumption.

Ingenious schemes for reshaping consumption and production, reorganizing daily life, including housework and childcare, had their roots in a long tradition of 'perfectionism' which had influenced American radicalism in the nineteeth century. Religious and secular utopian communities had sought to change relationships and desires in the here and now. Some of these social experiments located needs which were to form the basis of domestic technology as well as theories of child rearing and interest in nutrition.

In the late nineteenth century enthusiasm for utopian communities was beginning to wane but utopian thinking persisted and the link between improving the conditions of labour and consumption continued in the trades unions and among rural populists who were demanding social reform. This was the era when social science had a pervasive influence. Middle-class reformers in the cities aimed to reach the immigrant poor through self-help community work based in social settlements. By the early twentieth century these centres for investigation and research not only encouraged mutual aid but became bases for a wide range of campaigns with a progressive political agenda. The sheer scale of the problems they encountered led progressives to demand state intervention through legislation and municipal reform to improve both working and living conditions. The state as well as cooperation was thus increasingly seen as the means of creating social forms of meeting needs.

Black Americans however were to remain outside this process of social integration. Much less likely to benefit from state intervention, they created their own systems of cooperative self-help and social improvement through education, settlements, social projects and economic institutions. Black women took part in the suffrage movement and in movements against racial injustice. They also played an active role economically within black communities.

The cooperative alternatives did not of course all originate in the United States. Foreign immigrants brought a wide range of cooperative ideas and projects in which mutual survival combined with glimpses of a cooperative society. These interacted with traditions of social unionism which continued to exist in some parts of the American labour movement.

Efforts to intervene in consumption have not only involved visions of a cooperative society and actual cooperative projects producing goods or providing services. There have also been attempts to improve the conditions of work and collective resistance to high rents and prices.

Social forms and social intervention thus coexisted with the market and were regarded by many Americans, both working-class and middle-class as containing an alternative possibility. With hindsight this hope, which was strenuously assailed along with labour organizing and other radical movements, can be seen to falter by the mid-1920s as a general conception of society. It was never completely destroyed as an underground oppositional aspiration however and the tradition of individual cooperatives and consumer action has survived.

Both middle-class and working-class women have contributed to co-operative schemes and projects. Women have also been active in consumer-based pressure groups and in collective resistance. Their participation raises much wider issues about gender and economic development and social policy. It also suggests that the scope of class consciousness needs to be extended to include the circumstances of daily life. A broader view of social relationships would enable us to consider how differing kinds of gendered class consciousness have taken divergent political forms and have been affected by the specific cultural circumstances of race, ethnicity and region.

The history of the efforts to reorganize the circumstances and gain access to resources in the reproduction of daily life is less known than the history of production. Consumption is usually assumed to be an individual affair, but it has a social and collective history too. This needs to be considered in relation to action around production and demands made on the state, rather than compartmentalized as a separate zone. In real life all three were intercon-nected. Many questions have simply not been asked and there are many gaps. For example the cooperative forms brought by the immigrants to the United States remain to be researched; so does the revival of interest in cooperatives in the 1930s.

What follows is an outline of various attempts to reshape consumption and daily life evident in utopian writing and in cooperative schemes; examples of the organization of consumer power for legislative reform and of direct action to control the market; combinations of labour organizing and community action, a social unionism running counter to the emphasis on the wage.

UTOPIAN SCHEMERS AND PRACTICAL ACTIVISTS

Alternative utopias abounded in late nineteenth and early twentieth century America. Writers of novels as well as treatises sketched out their answers to the problems of capitalism with confident enthusiasm and were not afraid to propose radical restructuring. This faith in the possibility of altering not only labour conditions but daily life was not confined to the left, it had a wider influence through the growth of social science. Middle-class social reformers, women as well as men, investigated social problems and debated the differing solutions presented by utopian writers. The cooperative alternatives ranged from decentralized communities to centralized state collectivization. Production was returned to the household and developed into mass-scale industry. Individual consumption was both socialized and supplemented by private commercial services. Though they disagreed on the specifics, the utopians shared a conviction that the existing social structure was far from ideal and in need of drastic change.

One of the most famous and influential works was Edward Bellamy's *Looking Backward* (1888) in which the author imagined that by the year 2000 domestic activities would be done by public services. Another book called *The Golden Bottle* by Ignatius Donnelly in 1892 argued for consumer power as a means of improving the working conditions of women. Charlotte Perkins Gilman, an evolutionary socialist and feminist influenced by Bellamy, was wary of utopian communities because of unhappy childhood experiences of collective living. Instead she advocated apartment houses in which people could enjoy privacy, accompanied by the provision of laundry and cooking services. She presumed that the residents would be professionals who could afford to pay for these private services and believed, like Bellamy, in technology, which she thought would eliminate housework. She was concerned to emancipate middle-class educated women like herself; it was not clear how poorer women would benefit. However Charlotte Perkins Gilman's writing, both her fiction and her theoretical works, presented a view of economics which recognized that production and consumption were linked and considered how values and wants might evolve in cooperative rather than competitive ways. She had a profound influence, not only within the United States but internationally, upon socialists, feminists and radical social reformers; in Dolores Hayden's words she 'synthesized the thinking of suffragists, home economists and utopian novelists on the question of the home' (Hayden, 1982, p. 183).

Activists in a wide range of movements were also inspired by a vision of a cooperative society and their commitments frequently spanned several causes. For example in the late nineteenth century ideas about cooperative reorganization were present in the rural populist movement and in the Knights of Labor which advocated that trades unionism be combined with cooperation. The National Woman's Alliance founded in 1891 brought together women from both groups and was committed 'to aid in carrying out the principle of co-operation in every department of human life to its fullest extent' (The National Woman's Alliance quoted in Buhle, 1983, p. 88).

Their view that social needs could be reshaped and redirected was shared by Frances Willard, who was a leading force in the Woman's Christian Temperance Union and in the suffrage movement. Inspired by Bellamy, she belonged to a significant strand among women reformers who sought to reorganize domestic activities by making demands for public services, declaring that her aim was 'to make the whole world homelike' (Frances

Willard quoted in Buhle, 1983, p. 65). Women, it was argued, could bring special skills and values to the wider reform of society. Frances Willard also argued that the suffrage was necessary if women were to secure temperance and other moral and social reform.

Another suffrage and temperance reformer, Jane Addams, settled in the immigrant area of Chicago in 1889 and drew together a group of middle-class professionals at the settlement Hull House. Social settlements in American cities sought to adapt the cooperative vision to the problems of the urban poor. The middle-class settlers researched conditions in direct contact with workers and their families and sought solutions through a variety of strategies. Florence Kelley, for example, tried to secure legislation to curb the sweated homework that she found in the neighbourhood of Hull House. The settlements thus combined cooperative projects with political campaigns for state intervention and municipal reforms.

Professionals attracted to settlement work tended to assume that remedies could be found by applying enlightened reason to the problems of the working class. The results were mixed. They tended to equate reason with their own view of what was best and this could cause resentment. For instance, attempts to Americanize working-class immigrants through cooperative restaurants based on the new theories of 'home economics' met with little success, proving more popular with the middle-class social workers themselves. On the other hand the settlements did enable middle-class reformers to learn about conditions and many social projects were generated through these social laboratories.

The settlements also provided a basis for a critique of competition and the market which drew on imagery rooted in women's experience as housewives and mothers. Jane Addams described the process of making domestic values social as 'city housekeeping' (Jane Addams quoted in Hayden, 1982, p. 175) and Caroline Hunt, a Hull House resident and pioneer home economist, argued that housewives' role as guardians of the home carried responsibilities for the conditions under which commodities were produced. This idea of mobilizing consumer power for reforming the workplace was developed by Florence Kelley in the National Consumer League.

Black communities, who were neglected by white settlements, established their own networks of self-help action to care for people's welfare, and began to think about how to direct social consumption. Some of these turned to wider political organizing and debates about how to secure economic and social well-being in the urban ghettos. Women played an important role in these, linking the demand for political rights with social rights. Stephanie Shaw shows how black club women helped to set up girls' homes, nurseries, public health clinics, orphanages and care for the elderly (Shaw, 1991, p. 10–19).

Alternative approaches to consumption were thus not only utopian conceptions but were embedded in several practical reforming initiatives. Women played an important part in these social and cooperative alternatives, contributing understandings from their specific experiences and seeking different ways of organizing daily life. Ideas of cooperative housekeeping which had been developed in mid-nineteenth century communities persisted.

COOPERATIVE HOUSEKEEPING

Utopian theories of cooperative housekeeping found some pragmatic protagonists in rural areas in the late nineteenth century. Susan Strasser notes how 'some Midwestern dairy co-operatives utilized the water supplies and the steam plants already operating in their creameries to do laundry for the co-operating families' (Strasser, 1982, p. 113).

These economies of scale saved considerable time. In a period when washing took a housewife a whole day the Milltown Co-operative Creamery Company in Wisconsin could do fifty families' clothes in forty-five minutes. Cooperative services became part of rural life; in Wisconsin and Minnesota, for example, the cooperative laundries were extremely successful and there was interest in developing cooperative methods further. There were still signs of interest in cooperative housekeeping in the early twentieth century. Farm women in 1913 asked for guidance from the US Department of Agriculture (USDA) about setting up systems of cooperative housekeeping. USDA encouraged cooperative methods of agricultural marketing but regarded the individual home as a private sphere. Katherine Jellison notes that 'pressures from the business community' (Jellison, 1993, p. 37) because they wanted to sell 'products to individual families' (Jellison, 1993, p. 37) influenced the Extension Service policy against cooperation between households.

In the towns and cities too there were many small-scale schemes, community kitchens and dining halls, cooperative dwellings and cooperative home service clubs being set up in the early twentieth century in middle-class circles. Indeed the *Ladies' Home Journal* and Ethel Puffer Howes' *Woman's Home Companion* were still advocating cooperative housekeeping in the 1920s. When Howes went off to investigate a series on community kitchens, cooperative laundries, bakeries and cafeterias, Dolores Hayden describes how the *Woman's Home Companion* received two thousand letters about 'housewives' isolation, overwork, and depression' (Hayden, 1982, p. 270) which led Howes to conclude 'homemaking as at present conducted is a sweated industry' (Hayden, 1982, p. 270).

Cooperative domestic activity was not only a practical labour saving measure; it was socially important in improving the quality of daily life and relationships.

Some working-class immigrant women also created cooperative structures.

In New York City a group of Finnish domestic servants clubbed together to rent a small apartment so they could have some independent space on their days off. Maxine Seller observes:

> Within a few years the Finnish Women's Co-operative Home, as it was called, grew into a four-storey building with sleeping accommodation for forty, lounges, clubrooms, a library, a restaurant and an employment bureau ... still owned and operated by the women themselves. (Seller, 1991, p. 66)

These cooperative services grew up in an *ad hoc* manner as a way of responding to immediate needs. They were encouraged by some social settlements which instead of seeing Americanization as being about a private family and a home isolated from the community, encouraged communal and collective endeavours. The cooperative housekeeping of the Jane Club for women factory workers at Jane Addams' Hull House in Chicago is one example. A less well-known project was established in Buffalo; a club of immigrant Jewish women in a settlement house bought and remodelled an old home where they established a daycare centre.

The settlements retained elements of the utopian impulse of the communities of an earlier era providing a space in which needs and relationships of the future were prefigured. However settlements were also engaged in campaigns for resources and intervention from the state. 'City housekeeping' cost money for it soon became evident that many problems could not be solved simply by reorganization. Municipal services and the demand for a money allowance from the state, in the form of Mothers' Pensions, were ways of redistributing resources through the state. The shift to state intervention tended to reduce the transformative element of the cooperative projects; progressive social reformers came to accept existing social relationships as given.

There was moreover an ambiguity in the maternalist vision of making the world homelike. It ignored the fact that poor women, especially black women, had to work and it dismissed the demands many middle-class women were making for the right to work. Social reformers who put the emphasis on women's different qualities as nurturer and housekeeper assumed that domestic activity would still be done by women, even when it was turned into socialized services. By the early twentieth century more radical perspectives were being advocated by left socialists and feminists. Henrietta Rodman and Crystal Eastman, two Greenwich Village feminists, for instance, argued for cooperative housekeeping to be shared between the sexes so women could go out to work on equal terms with men. The left-wing union organizer, Elizabeth Gurley Flynn thought housework ought to be mechanized so women would be able to earn money as workers.

Demands for cooperative forms were continued by Ethel Puffer Howes who supported cooperative housekeeping, laundries, food services and nurseries and argued for part-time jobs for mothers at her Institute for the Co-ordination of Women's Interests at Smith College in the 1920s.

However, the cooperative transformation of daily life was soon to vanish completely from the agenda of home economists. Consumption was indeed being reshaped but not on cooperative lines. Dolores Hayden points out that by 1920 advertising and marketing firms were spending one billion dollars persuading consumers to buy private domestic goods. This considerable material pressure was to intensify during the 1920s (Hayden, 1982, p. 274). It was accompanied by a compelling ideological offensive asserting individuality, freedom and personal control. Domestic existence was too valuable as a market to be left to cooperators. Vacuum cleaners promised cleanliness and individual control. House cleaning products symbolized power, fast food provided speed. Frequently the private market moved in to meet needs which had been identified through communities and mutual self-help projects. Domestic technology was pioneered in utopian communities; mass-scale cheap prepared food was provided during strikes before it was exploited commercially.

Home economics lost its pre-war commitment to the social reorganization of domestic needs and was redefined in the twenties by Christine Frederick's and Lillian Gilbreth's vision of scientific management in the home. Instead of taking the activities of the individual household into the community, they brought products into the individual household. Private consumption found an ethical basis in self-help and propagated faith in modernization instead of association. The Taylorized works canteen was to be the unlikely survivor from the planning zeal of the utopian communities.

CONSUMER POWER

Consumer pressure for social purposes in the form of boycotts already had a long history in the United States when a young clothing worker from a rebel Irish family, Leonora O'Reilly who was a member of the Knights of Labor, became involved in a small cross-class organization, The Working Women's Society, in 1886. The Society investigated the conditions of women workers in shops and, deciding that unionization was not feasible, aimed to reach middle-class women as consumers.

Applying the ideas of John Ruskin about political economy to women's sweated labour, the Society asserted: 'It is the *democratic demand* for cheapness that keeps alive this sad condition of things. It is *our* needs and *our* desires that regulate a large part of production' (Working Women's Society quoted in Tax, 1980, p. 98; emphasis in original). This ethical questioning of needs and desires formed the basis for the Consumer League in 1890 which sought to improve working conditions through moralizing the buying power of middle-class women in order to help working-class women. Eileen Boris also shows that there was a link to an alternative aesthetic in the Arts and Crafts Movement – better working conditions meant beauty in utilitarian and craft products.

In 1899 Florence Kelley left her work with Jane Addams at Hull House, to become the president of the Consumer Leagues. The National Consumer League, which, at its height, had 60 branches in 20 states, was to become a powerful force in the struggle for protective legislation and the banning of child labour, working closely with the Women's Trade Union League.

Self-help welfare projects which combined education with a broad vision of social reforms had a long tradition among African-American women. Racial oppression made many black women activists aware of the link between social injustice and political rights and some were prepared to connect to a wider struggle for human rights. For example, at the World's Congress of Representative Women in Chicago in 1893 the African-American reformer Anna Julia Cooper insisted that 'Women's wrongs are indissolubly linked with all undefended woe' (Anna Julia Cooper quoted in Brown, 1990, p. 210).

Recognition of women's need to work characterized self-help projects in the black communities along with an understanding that gender and race both had to be taken into account in devising alternative economic forms. The low-paid work of black women as domestic servants, homeworkers and laundresses created a pressing need for insurance and credit facilities. By the 1890s an informal financial system had proliferated as a means of mutual defence with names like The Daughters of Bethlehem, The Loving Sisters and The Ladies' Working Club. Maggie Lena Walker, the daughter of a washerwoman who had graduated as a teacher in 1883, was to develop alternative systems of raising finance through these small self-help insurance societies. She formed an insurance company in 1898, the Woman's Union, with the motto 'The Hand that Rocks the Cradle Rules the World' (Brown, 1990, p. 211). A member of a range of organizations, including the Richmond Council of Colored Women, she became Grand Worthy Secretary of the Independent Order of Saint Luke in 1899 and founded the Saint Luke Penny Savings Bank in Richmond, Virginia in 1903. In 1934 she was to see this turn into the Consolidated Bank and Trust Company, the oldest black-owned and black-run bank to have survived.

Elsa Barkley Brown describes how this mutual benefit system in the black community developed into a means of directing economic development by financing large-scale social consumption supported by individual black purchasing power. When Maggie Lena Walker became Secretary of the Independent Order of Saint Luke, she quite deliberately drew a group of women around her to decide what should be done; though she always insisted that the Order's projects helped black men by improving women's standard of living. Among the projects women established was a department store; as well as creating jobs for black women it sought to attract black patronage, to the fury of white retailers.

The values of mutuality were to be consciously passed on to the next generation through social educational projects. The Children's Rosebud Fountain, Grand Fountain United Order of True Reformers was pledged to teach the children to care for one another, emotionally and materially, 'one's distress be the other's distress, one's penny the other's penny' (Brown, 1990, p. 212).

Though she used the language of maternalism, Walker did not confine her concern to the woman's sphere of housekeeping alone, but saw employment and finance as vital in solving women's economic difficulties. She believed that it was important to educate by setting up alternatives, 'First by practice and then by precept' (Brown, 1990, p. 218). Local economic and social initiatives were to be important aspects in later efforts by black nationalists to gain control over consumption and production in the black communities and were to resurface in Black Power in the 1960s and 1970s. Their origins could be traced back into the nineteenth century. Black women continued to set up penny savers clubs when they came from the South as domestic servants. Informal credit arrangements were thus transposed from the rural South in the early twentieth century. Though these self-help financial networks did not become big banks they enabled women to leave domestic service or to support relations. Elizabeth Clark-Lewis observes: 'Although rarely mentioned in the literature, the penny savers clubs served as a vital economic base for the female migrant' (Clark-Lewis, 1987, p. 204).

For black women the need to work affected the forms of action around consumption. Job creation through social purchasing or the accumulation of savings as insurance were not only economic responses but integral to ideas of community and responsibility towards one's kin. Consumer power then could mean the mobilization of ethical consumption in the context of an alliance between women of differing classes, or the creation of forms of social consumption through associative projects as a means of defence within black communities. Association could raise capital among the poor and moral pressure could influence consumption for local economic and social development.

CROWD ACTION

There were also a range of consumer protests by women through crowd action. These were not explicit proposals for cooperatives, but extreme expressions of daily survival strategies. In these communal risings however certain values which would otherwise have remained hidden came to the surface. These are rooted in patterns of mutual obligation within poor immigrant communities, relationships which contained elements of support and of coercion. Communal movements around prices occurred in Providence among the Italians in 1914 but seem to have been most evident in the Jewish neighbourhoods of New York. When the price of kosher meat rose in 1902 the small butchers tried to bring prices down by not selling meat for a week. Women gathered on the streets calling for action. Their rebellion gained legitimacy because they could not do their work as housewives properly and they asserted a pride in women's collective power. Mrs Levy, the wife of a cloakmaker, was heard to say 'Now, if *we women* make a strike, then it will be a strike' (Mrs Levy quoted in Hyman, 1991, p. 93; emphasis as original).

Lower East Side women started the boycott on May 15. The area was soon in uproar as they broke into butchers' shops and flung meat into the streets, fought the police and were arrested. Electing a committee at a mass meeting they went from house to house and synagogue to synagogue to gain support and made contact with labour and benevolent societies. Other committees were formed to plan the creation of cooperative stores. The 'strike' spread to Brooklyn and Harlem. They called their organization the Ladies Anti-Beef Trust Association. Despite internal conflict they gained support from male leaders of the Jewish community and from the Retail Butchers Association. They also considered extending the boycott to Christian women. The food riots had an impact in Boston. The *New York Times* on May 24 called for speedy police repression of this 'dangerous class ... especially the women [who] are very ignorant [and] ... mostly speak a foreign language' (Hyman, 1991, p. 91–2).

The women in Williamsburg were by this time threatening to set fire to shops. The Jewish leaders gave support but urged calm and the English language socialist press explained that the real struggle had to be at the point of production. The women however declared this was 'the great women's war' (Hyman, 1991, p. 99) and that their responsibility was to spend as little as possible of their husbands' hard-earned pay.

The women who started the boycott were from families who had been in the country for several years, their average age was thirty-nine and they had large families still at home. They thought meat should be sold at affordable prices and saw the boycott as a way of reducing demand. By early June, when the strike ended, the wholesale and retail prices were down to 9 cents and 14 cents a pound and the kosher cooperatives survived. But the women did not halt the rise in prices in the long term.

In 1910 Jewish women in South Providence picketed shops to stop people buying meat until prices fell. They demanded 'respectable treatment of the customers' (Smith, 1979, p. 433) and 'polite treatment of employees' (Smith,

1979, p. 433), saying that they wanted 'fresh meat wrapped in clean paper and not in newspaper as has been the custom in some of the shops' (Smith, 1979, p. 433).

In 1917 as war-time inflation hit immigrant working-class families, again a kosher meat boycott started in the Lower East Side. This time Jewish women went from house to house asking people to pledge themselves to boycott. It spread from New York to Boston, Philadelphia, Baltimore, Chicago, St Louis and Cleveland and was successful in bringing prices down temporarily. Food riots also occurred that year on the Lower East Side, in the Bronx and in Williamsburg. The women formed the Mothers' Anti-High Price League and marched to City Hall. Amidst uproar the women appealed to the President – they could not feed their families. They were called German spies; to which Maria Ganz replied,

> What do we women of the East Side know of European politics? We are going hungry. The prices of food have risen beyond our means ... I don't care what happens to the nations silly enough to fight. What we want are the elemental things of life, food to eat, so we can live and do our work. The women are in no mood to endure such lies. (Maria Ganz quoted in Ewen, 1985, p. 181)

The women were hostile to the rich and to the peddlers who sold food. They could not however stop inflation. The only result of their action was that the City authorities reduced the number of peddlers' licences allowed to those who were US citizens. However riots returned between 1917 and 1920 over food prices.

Rent strikes were another means of exerting some control over the cost of living. In the East and West sides of Manhattan and the Williamsburg area of Brooklyn in 1907 six hundred women went from house to house getting two thousand names onto the rent strike rolls. Some landlords reduced rents but others refused. However Elizabeth Ewen comments: 'By 1919 rent strikes had become an ongoing form of consumer resistance' (Ewen, 1985, p. 127).

SOCIAL VISION AND LABOUR ORGANIZING

Some Marxist and syndicalist strands within the socialist movement were uneasy about action around rents and prices and inclined to dismiss ideas of cooperative reorganization of daily life as secondary concerns. Their focus was on the organized working class at the point of production. However there were many currents within Marxism and syndicalism and American socialism included a great variety of perspectives in which a commitment to social entitlement and a utopian vision of transformation survived. These tended to surface during periods of industrial turmoil and ideas of cooperative association persisted in labour unions after World War I.

The communal uprisings among poor women around consumption co-incided with militant trade union organizing in the clothing factories which involved not only men but the daughters of families in the New York Jewish working-class areas. There was, moreover, an awareness of community issues in some trades unions. For example, in Chicago, the Women's Trade Union League, which included middle-class reformers, was involved in the Chicago garment workers strike in 1910. Collette A. Hyman describes how the rent committee tried to persuade landlords to wait until the strike was over for their money, while the relief committee ran a lunchroom where strikers on picket duty could buy sandwiches at cost price. They also fed 500,000 people daily through six stores; an extraordinary feat of communal provisioning. The League explicitly drew the whole family into the struggle and produced leaflets in the languages of the immigrant groups involved (Hyman, 1985, p. 26–8).

In the textile town of Lawrence, Massachusetts, Elizabeth Gurley Flynn and the syndicalist Industrial Workers of the World had the task of uniting over forty different nationalities in the 'Bread and Roses' strike of 1912. Women played a crucial role; Ardis Cameron shows how their networks formed through shopping, through discussing prices, recipes and wages became a basis for resistance. 'My father,' explained an Italian woman, 'never knew our mother had Syrian friends. They would visit each other in the day and eventually my mother would cook like a Syrian' (Cameron, 1985, p. 52).

During the strike women, housewives as well as textile workers, set up informal communal structures. 'Mothers often converted their houses into soup-kitchens for hungry strikers or provided childcare while younger women picketed or paraded' (Cameron, 1985, p. 50). One mother made pizza or bread, others worked in the soup kitchens. Shops, under community pres-sure, provided food.

Ardis Cameron points out that ironically the efforts of reformers had con-tributed to the economic crisis in the strikers' family income. There were new laws restricting the working hours of women and children and restrictions on hunting. Rents were also extremely high in Lawrence. She notes that women justified their militancy sometimes as 'caretakers of the home and family' (Cameron, 1993, p. 10) and sometimes 'struggled against established mean-ings' (Cameron, 1993, p. 10). The young girls for example did not let their parents know they were planning actions in support of the strike. As the strike progressed the women increasingly gained the confidence to challenge soldiers and policemen, scorning them and sometimes stripping and attacking them. Customary activity took on communal forms and the uncustomary experience of the strike led women into uncustomary public acts of violence.

Women in mining communities were mobilized during strikes because the whole community was owned by the mining companies and the owners forced families out of their homes during disputes. In the tent colonies during the bitter and violent Colorado Fuel and Iron Strike in 1913–14, Priscilla Long describes how the organizer Mother Jones, by then in her eighties, kept spirits up (Long, 1985, p. 72–3). In tents and with relief from the union, 'the women played a special and indispensable role in helping to form a cohesive, unified strikers' community – a community of resistance. Within their separate sphere of responsibility, they formed bonds of mutual support and sharing, which extended across barriers of language and nationality' (Long, 1985, p. 72).

This did not spare them when the soldiers charged, shooting women and children as well as the miners. Mary Petrucci lost her three children. She told a reporter after the Ludlow massacre that she did not see how she could 'ever be happy again' (Mary Petrucci quoted in Long, 1985, p. 80). She said the experience of Ludlow showed the need for a union and added: 'I can't have my babies back. But perhaps when everybody knows about them, something will be done to make the world a better place for all babies' (Mary Petrucci quoted in Long, 1985, p. 81). Priscilla Long comments:

> Mary Petrucci was a class-conscious woman, but neither her experience nor her perceptions were those of her husband. Her consciousness was that of a miner's *wife*; her experience of class oppression was a particularly female one; and her class-conscious view of the world took a female form. (Long, 1985, p. 81; emphasis as original)

During World War I the most militant trades unionists were imprisoned; however women did take on jobs which had hitherto been defined as male, and female class consciousness can be seen assuming not one but several forms. In Seattle, white working-class women members of the Women's Card and Label League, formed in 1911 to pledge consumers to buy from stores with the union label, believed both in measures to improve the conditions of housewives and in married women's right to work. Maurine Weiner Greenwald describes how they had worked with middle-class feminist club women before the war reading Olive Schreiner's *Woman and Labour* and Alice Henry's *The Trade Union Woman* and organizing a meeting for Charlotte Perkins Gilman and suffrage leaders (Greenwald, 1989, p. 130–35).

Mary Archibald, a clerk, wrote to the *Seattle Union Record* in 1918 describing herself as

> a square peg in a round hole. I was not domestic by nature. I loved my home, but I hated the everlasting monotony of putting the sugar-bowl on the table and taking it off again three times a day; of wanting something of beauty as well as utility in my surroundings, and never being able to afford it ... And this is my quarrel with marriage ... there are too many square pegs in round holes, and if women enter industry in large numbers, I believe it will force a reorganization, not only of industries, but of the home – to the advantage of both. (Greenwald, 1989, p. 136–7)

Dana Frank shows that the League by 1919–20 was not only concerned with fair shopping policy but demanding an increase in 'the state minimum wage for women' (Frank, 1993, p. 194). This was in the context of the Seattle General Strike when as she says

> trade union activism reached beyond factories and building sites to include weekly mass meetings in the streets, twenty consumer and producer co-operatives, and a dozen organizations of working-class housewives. The unions owned their own savings and loan, their own film production company, and a daily newspaper with a circulation of 100,000. (Frank, 1994, p. 1)

Some Seattle cooperative women saw consumption as their special area of struggle. 'The labor man fights at the point of production, where he is robbed; the labor woman fights at the point of consumption where she is robbed,' (Jean Stovel quoted in Frank, 1994, p. 55) declared Jean Stovel, the organizer of women in the Co-operative Food Products Association (CFPA). It was not completely accurate – all the trustees were men!

In 1919 women set up two city-wide networks of women's cooperative organizations. Lola Lunn formed the Women's Co-operative Guild (inspired by the British organization) and Dora Hayward and Mary Saunders founded a series of Women's Co-operative Clubs which affiliated to the CFPA. They were social and educational. Lola Lunn for example wanted to spread information about the British Rochdale Co-operative system of shop providing their members with dividends.

To be homelike was the ideal; as Dana Frank says, the home became 'the metaphor for co-operation' (Frank, 1994, p. 57) which was to extend into all social existence. It was a personal ethic too; a way of life in the family. Working-class women paid attention to the details of personal solidarity. In January 1921 women cooperators thoughtfully planned to sponsor chaperoned dances for single girls: 'Especially do we desire to reach the lonely ones who dislike to go to the public dance halls and other public places of amusement, and as a result are deprived of the social life which they so much desire' (Frank, 1994, p. 57). What the girls thought about this has not been recorded.

The CFPA women set up the Women's Exchange which sold dry goods, and also recycled jumble clothes for the poor at low prices or free and also created a daycare centre.

Working-class women contributed a distinct political emphasis in the ideal of making social projects homelike but they also participated as producers. The Mutual Laundry was established to assist union militancy by providing alternative employment. Louise Strong recalled how it employed 'agitators who were thrown out of other plants' (Louise Strong quoted in Frank, 1994, p. 72). The waitresses, like other workers, had their 'rest home' (Frank, 1994,

p. 71) which cared for the infirm. Maternalist values thus combined with the needs of labour, acquiring differing meanings in a working-class context.

In 1919 male trades unionists in the American Federation of Labour (AFL) sought women's help. 'Put Women in Second Line of Labor Defense' (Frank, 1994, p. 117) declared the *Union Record* in November 1919. The Women's Card and Label League worked with women in the cooperative groups and members of the Women's Trade Union League and the Seattle Consumers' League to boycott the Bon Marche department stores for using non-union building workers. However the Women's Card and Label League was to lose its radical impulse during the depression of 1922–3 and the AFL shifted to the right from 1921. The Seattle cooperative networks, which, like the AFL, were restricted to whites, were to narrow and gradually to disintegrate during the 1920s.

SURVIVING THE GREAT DEPRESSION

In 1931 Ethel Puffer Howes' institute collapsed; she was however invited to participate in President Hoover's national conference on Home Building and Home Ownership which Dolores Hayden describes as 'dedicated to a campaign to build single-family houses in the private market as a strategy for promoting greater economic growth in the United States and less industrial strife' (Hayden, 1982, p. 275). It seemed that the hope of the Co-operative Commonwealth had grown faint indeed. Dolores Hayden documents her still doggedly advocating childcare centres and cooked food services in housing complexes. But volumes were prepared to refute her case for communal services, showing the advantage of isolated homes with new appliances. The Hoover Report agreed most emphatically with the Muncie, Indiana, Chamber of Commerce which had announced in the mid-1920s: 'The first responsibility of an American to his country is no longer that of a citizen, but of a consumer. Consumption is a necessity' (Muncie Indiana Chamber of Commerce quoted in Hayden, 1982, p. 276).

However if we take a longer view we can see organization around consumption assuming new forms and with these new kinds of gendered class and race consciousness developing among American women. The women's auxiliaries of the union were to play an important part in the Trotskyist-influenced Teamsters' strike in Minneapolis in 1934, and in the Communist-led Popular Front struggles of the mid-1930s. Again women were mobilized to demand union label goods and again a class consciousness based on difference interweaves with demands for equal rights from women workers. The rise of this Congress of Industrial Organization (CIO) unionism in the 1930s led Mary Heaton Vorse in *Labor's New Millions*, in 1938, to hail a new unionism that did 'not stop at the formal lodge meeting' (Mary Heaton Vorse quoted in Faue, 1991, p. 2) but saw 'the union as a way of life which [involved] the entire community' (Mary Heaton Vorse quoted in Faue, 1991, p. 2).

Some of the 'new unionists' were working in the new consumer industries making the domestic appliances which were not only useful to housewives but part of the reshaping of consumer patterns through the market which started in the 1920s and which was to be so powerful after the 1940s.

The Great Depression put the brakes on this expansion for a while and various forms of cooperative activity arose as a means of defence against poverty. The Communist-inspired Unemployed Councils in the early 1930s included many women and one aspect of their work involved distributing clothes and food. In Minneapolis the Hennepin County Farmer-Labor Women's Club formed the Women's League Against the High Cost of Living in 1935, linking a range of church and community groups around prices. Leagues formed in Detroit, New York, Washington DC and Chicago. The Housewives' League of Detroit, started in 1930, was explicitly concerned to direct black consumption towards black businesses as a means of economic development. There was interest too in cooperation in the American black urban communities. Ella Baker helped establish the Young Negroes' Co-operative League which organized co-ops and argued for consumer power in New York. She was hired by President Roosevelt's Workers' Progress Administration to educate on consumption. She also supported cooperative stores.

Cooperative laundries reappeared in rural areas around Wisconsin and cooperatives were encouraged for craft workers in the Appalachians.

Some of these forms of resistance survived into the post-war era. For example women took action around inflation after the war. Moreover collective approaches to organizing daily life were transmitted to the new left of the 1950s and 1960s along with a fierce sense of grass roots democracy. Ella Baker, active in the Civil Rights movements, was distrustful of the charismatic great-leader style of Martin Luther King. She played a crucial role in setting up the Student Non-Violent Co-ordinating Committee.

In an interview with Ellen Cantarow in the 1970s, she said:

> If people begin to place their values in terms of how high they get in the political world, or how much worldly goods they accumulate, or what kind of cars they have, or how much they have in the bank, that's when I lose respect. To me I'm part of the human family. (Ella Baker quoted in Cantarow, 1980)

Though it was to be the America of the Muncie, Indiana, Chamber of Commerce 'Consumption is a necessity' which was to prevail, that other America which had been equally innovative and ingenious in devising social forms for meeting human needs did not entirely disappear.

ACKNOWLEDGEMENTS

The research and writing of this chapter was made possible by the Simon Senior Research Fellowship, Manchester University Sociology Department. I am grateful to Diane Elson, Dana Frank, Temma Kaplan and Hilary Wainwright for their helpful discussions about women's actions as consumers, and to Eileen Boris and Rosalyn Fraad Baxandall for help with some of the source material in this chapter. Thanks to Sonia Lane who typed the manuscript.

BIBLIOGRAPHY

Baxandall, Rosalyn Fraad (1987), *Words on Fire: The Life and Writing of Elizabeth Gurley Flynn*, New Brunswick and London: Rutgers University Press.

Boris, Eileen (1989), 'Craftshop or Sweatshop? The Uses and Abuses of Craftsmanship in Twentieth Century America', *Journal of Design History*, 2 (2 and 3) March, pp.175–92.

Boris, Eileen (1994), *Home to Work: Motherhood and the Politics of Industrial Homework in the United States*, Cambridge and New York, Cambridge University Press.

Brown, Elsa Barkley (1990), 'Womanist Consciousness: Maggie Lena Walker and the Independent Order of Saint Luke' in Ellen Carol DuBois and Vicki L. Ruiz (eds), *Unequal Sisters: A Multi-Cultural Reader in U.S. Women's History*, New York: Routledge, pp.208–23.

Buhle, M.J. (1983), *Women and American Socialism 1870–1920*, Urbana and Chicago: University of Illinois Press.

Cameron, Ardis (1985), 'Bread and Roses Revisited: Women's Culture and Working-Class Activism in the Lawrence Strike of 1912' in Ruth Milkman (ed.), *Women, Work and Protest: A Century of US Women's Labor History*, Boston, London, Melbourne and Henley: Routledge and Kegan Paul, pp.42–61.

Cameron, Ardis (1993), *Radicals of the Worst Sort: Labouring Women in Lawrence, Massachusetts, 1860–1912*, Urbana and Chicago: University of Illinois Press.

Cantarow, Ellen (1980), *Moving the Mountain: Women Working for Social Change*, Old Westbury, New York: The Feminist Press, The McGraw-Hill Book Company.

Clark-Lewis, Elizabeth (1987), '"This Work Had An End": African-American Domestic Workers in Washington DC, 1910–1940' in Carol Groneman and Mary Beth Norton (eds), *To Toil the Livelong Day: American Women at Work, 1780–1980*, Ithaca: Cornell University Press, pp.196–212.

Ewen Elizabeth (1985), *Immigrant Women in the Land of Dollars: Life and Culture on the Lower East Side, 1890–1925*, New York: Monthly Review Press.

Ewen, S. (1988), *All Consuming Images: The Politics of Style in Contemporary Culture*, New York: Basic Books.

Faue, E. (1991), *Community of Suffering and Struggle: Women, Men and the Labor Movement in Minneapolis, 1915–1945*, Chapel Hill and London: The University of North Carolina Press.

Frank, Dana (1993), 'Which "Women" and the Labor Movement? Women's Roles in the Seattle, Washington, AFL, 1917–1929' in Gabriella Hauch (ed.), *Geschlecht-Klasse-Ethnizität*, Vienna and Zurich: Europaverlag, pp.189–97.

Frank, Dana (1994), *Purchasing Power: Consumer Organising, Gender and the Seattle Labor Movement 1919–1929*, Cambridge and New York: Cambridge University Press.

Gordon, Linda (ed.) (1990), *Women, the State and Welfare*, Wisconsin: The University of Wisconsin Press.

Greenwald, Maurine Weiner (1989), 'Working Class Feminism and the Family Wage Ideal: The Seattle Debate on Married Women's Right to Work 1914–1920', *Journal of American History* (1) June 1989, pp.128–42.

Hayden, Dolores (1982), *The Grand Domestic Revolution*, Cambridge, Massachusetts and London: The MIT Press.

Hyman, Collette A. (1985), 'Labor Organising and Institution Building: The Chicago Women's Trade Union League 1904–1924' in Ruth Milkman (ed.), *Women, Work and Protest: A Century of US Women's Labor History*, Boston, London, Melbourne and Henley: Routledge and Kegan Paul, pp.22–41.

Hyman, Paula E. (1991), 'Immigrant Women and Consumer Protest: The New York City Kosher Meat Boycott of 1902' in George E. Pozzetta (ed.), *Ethnicity and Gender: The Immigrant Woman*, New York: Garland, pp.91–105.

Jellison, Katherine (1993), *Entitled to Power: Farm Women and Technology 1919–1963*, Chapel Hill: University of North Carolina Press.

Koven, S. and Michel, S. (eds) (1993), *Mothers of a New World: Maternalist Politics and the Origins of Welfare States*, New York and London: Routledge.

Ladd-Taylor, M. (1994), *Mother-Work: Women, Child Welfare and the State, 1890–1930*, Urbana and Chicago: University of Illinois Press.

Long, Priscilla (1985), 'The Women of the Colorado Fuel and Iron Strike 1913–14' in Ruth Milkman (ed.), *Women, Work and Protest: A Century of US Women's Labor History*, Boston, London, Melbourne and Henley: Routledge and Kegan Paul, pp.62–85.

Seller, Maxine S. (1991), 'Beyond the Stereotype: A New Look at the Immigrant Woman, 1880-1924' in George E. Pozzetta (ed.), *Ethnicity and Gender: The Immigrant Woman*, New York: Garland, pp.59–71.

Shaw, Stephanie J. (1991), 'Black Club Women and the Creation of the National Association of Colored Women', *Journal of Women's History* 3 (2), pp.10–20.

Smith, Judith E. (1979), 'Our Own Kind: Family and Community Networks in Providence' in Nancy F. Cott and Elizabeth H. Pleck (eds), *A Heritage of Their Own: Toward a New Social History of American Women*, New York: Simon and Schuster, pp.417–38.

Strasser, Susan (1982), *Never Done: A History of American Housework*, New York: Pantheon Books.

Tax, Meredith (1980), *The Rising of the Women: Feminist Solidarity and Class Conflict, 1880–1917*, New York: Monthly Review Press.

2. Basket Power and Market Forces: The Women's Co-operative Guild 1883–1920

Gillian Scott

The Women's Co-operative Guild (WCG), an organization of women connected with the English consumers' Co-operative movement, was formed in 1883 and expanded steadily to 10,000 in 1897, and 30,000 by 1914. The national reputation that it gained during these years was based largely on its success in drawing into public life members of the largest but, traditionally, most invisible social group: working-class wives, and taking initiatives to improve the condition of their lives. The WCG, reported one journalist in 1913, constituted a 'microcosm of a woman's democracy, and a mirror of the politics of the millions of disenfranchised working women'.[1]

On the face of it, the WCG during this period presents an unusual example of women using their purchasing power in the market as the basis for an organization which enabled them not only to contribute more decisively to Co-operative trading activity but also to take up national campaigns to advance their rights as women. Yet when one examines the Guild's relationship with the Co-operative movement more closely contradictions enter the frame. On the one hand, Co-operation's exceptional characteristics as a democratic institution of working-class self-help created unusual, perhaps unique, resources for a women's organization intent on improving the condition of their sex; on the other, the movement's respect for the laws of the market place generated socially conservative norms that severely constrained the opportunities available to women.

As the Guild became an increasingly forceful advocate for women's rights, it came into collision with male Co-operative leaders who believed that the Guild's involvement with controversial social questions would be bad for business. This conflict of interests generated a major debate about the nature and purpose of Co-operation, and its status as a movement concerned with social progress. While Co-operative managers and officers complacently claimed that they were social reformers by trade, Guildswomen argued that trade alone, even when modified by the 'moral economy' of Co-operation, would not make a better world for women, and that if they were to contribute to the movement's trading strength as shoppers then they should also be free to pursue their own citizenship campaigns.

This period of the Guild's history suggests that market forces, operating as they do in a gendered social context, tend to reinforce rather than challenge the status quo of relations between men and women. The freedoms and choices available to women have been advanced not by the 'hidden hand of the market' but by social movements that have had as their object political, socioeconomic, legal or cultural reforms, and have in pursuing such objectives moved against the grain of market forces.

WOMEN AND THE CO-OPERATIVE MOVEMENT

It should be emphasized that the Co-operative movement became the home of the strongest and most successful working-class women's organization in Britain at the turn of the century because it did not conform to the norms of economic enterprise in Victorian society. Consumers' Co-operation was the great alternative economic success story of the nineteenth century, a model of working-class self-help which managed to combine sound business sense and viability with an ethos of mutuality and social justice.

Originating in Rochdale in the 1840s, Co-operative societies aimed to overcome the many ways in which private retailing exploited working people. They were democratic institutions which allocated one vote to each member regardless of the number of shares they owned; they distributed their trading surplus as a dividend proportional to purchases not investment; they provided educational facilities; and they supplied wholesome food. From £28 of pooled capital in 1844, the movement grew to be a trading giant, a 'closely knit organization of hundreds of retail shops, grouped into two colossal trading and manufacturing federations' (Webb, 1938, p. 427), viewed by many as 'a new economic system in embryo' (Carr et al., 1938, p. 38). Membership and share capital expanded steadily: in 1880, 600,000 members and share capital of £2,246,000; in 1900, 1,780,000 members and £23,256,000 (Cole and Postgate, 1966, p. 437). By 1920 the Co-operative Societies 'accounted for 18 per cent to 20 per cent of the total national sales of groceries and provisions' (Yeo, 1988, p. 213).

As an exceptional version of the market, Co-operation afforded women opportunities denied them elsewhere in Victorian England. This was for two main reasons, one principled, the other pragmatic. Firstly, the commitment to sexual equality inherited from Co-operation's early nineteenth century Owenite antecedents (Taylor, 1983), meant that women had never been excluded from the terms of its democratic constitution, and, in theory at least, were free to become members on the same terms as men. Secondly, the movement's com- mercial dependence on the trading loyalty of the housewives who shopped at its stores was a strong incentive to sponsor the development of women's work within the movement through the formation of a separate women's organiza- tion. Rather than being excluded because they lacked the wherewithal to be- come shareholders, therefore, women had a role to play in Co-operation pre- cisely because of their role as consumers.

Yet even this comparatively sympathetic market environment took for granted basic inequalities between men and women. The majority of women who joined the Guild were economically dependent, wives of the skilled and semi-skilled working class.[2] Industrialization had created new incom- patibilities between women's productive and reproductive work, and with the exception of the textile industry where it was common for married women to work in the mills, the norm was for women to cease paid employment at marriage unless severe financial hardship dictated otherwise. Women's wages remained at between 40 per cent and 50 per cent of men's, and there was a steady decline in the number of married women in paid work during the second half of the nineteenth century (Lewis, 1984; Rendall, 1990). The assump- tion that women should be in their proper place at home while male workers supported dependent wives and children was as commonplace among Co- operators as it was in the trade union movement where it found expression in the use of the concept of the family wage as a point of leverage in collective bargaining.

Guildswomen, then, belonged to a group that was not so much economic- ally marginal as economically invisible[3]: working women, fully occupied by domestic labour in the home, and without representation of any kind in the public sphere. Their homes

> were the workshops of many trades, where overtime abounds, and where an eight hours' day would be a very welcome reform ... Few men realize how much drudgery and lonely effort there is in the everyday work of a housewife. (Davies, 1904, p. 151)

Previously, this isolation had ensured that the interests, needs and opinions of such women found no expression in public discourse. It was, wrote the Gen- eral Secretary, as though a curtain fell across their lives upon marriage which concealed the suffering that many endured; only when an organization of their own came into being did it become possible for the women themselves to raise that curtain and seek justice (Davies, 1915, p. 8).

As well as signalling the arrival of women as an organized force within Co-operation, however, the Guild's formation also contained the seeds of a point of departure from the received wisdoms of those who were narrowly concerned with the trading side of the movement. For many Co-operators, the justification for a women's organization lay in its potential for building up purchasing loyalty. Yet as well as providing a material base for association in the Co-operative movement, women's shared identity as shoppers reflected their subordinate position in society, and while Guildswomen never sought to contest that role, there was always a strong determination to extend their field of action.

As the founder of the Guild, Mrs Acland,[4] protested in 1883:

> What are men always urged to do when there is a meeting held at any place to encourage or start Co-operative institutions? Come! Help! Vote! Criticize! Act! What are women urged to do? Come and *Buy*! That is the limit of the special work pointed out to us women. We can be independent members of our Store, but we are only asked to come and buy.

Bowing to propriety, Mrs Acland conceded that there should be no thought of 'departing from our own sphere', or of attempting 'work which can be better done by men', yet surely, she urged, 'there is more for us women to do than to spend money. Spend money at our own Store we must, that is a matter of course; but our duty does not end here, nor our duty to our fellow creatures. To come and "buy" is all we can be *asked* to do; but cannot we go further ourselves? Why should not we have our meetings, our readings, our discussions?' (Cole, 1944, p. 216.)

By the 1890s, under the leadership of Margaret Llewelyn Davies, Mrs Acland's modest ambitions had grown into a radical assertion of women's rights which altogether repudiated the notion of separate spheres. 'We are told by some that women are wives and mothers,' wrote the Guild organizer Sarah Reddish,[5] in 1894,

> and that the duties therein involved are enough for them. We reply that men are husbands and fathers, and that they, as such, have duties not to be neglected, but we join in the general opinion that men should also be interested in the science of government, taking a share in the larger family of the store, the municipality and the State.
>
> The Women's Co-operative Guild has done much towards impressing the fact that women as citizens should take their share in this work also.[6]

In addition to its Co-operative activities, the Guild took up Citizenship work to secure 'the reforms needed by wives and mothers'[7] in the public and the private spheres, operating as a self-styled trade union for married women.[8] In addition to support for the suffrage demand, this included campaigns for more egalitarian divorce laws, and for the state to make provision for the care of maternity.

BASKET POWER

The Guild's success in building a 'democracy of working women' stemmed from its ability to mobilize the traditionally feminine activity of shopping for a radical redefinition of women's rights and capacities. 'It has been the aim of the Guild,' wrote Margaret Llewelyn Davies in 1904, 'to arouse women to a sense of the basket power which they specially possessed' (Davies, 1904, p. 65). The shopping basket was emblematic of both the common identity of its members (customers at the Co-op stores), and of the Guild's economic base in Co-operation: the Guild membership card depicted a woman standing on her doorstep holding a basket full of Co-operative goods and looking out at the rising sun. Yet as well as conveying women's traditional role in the movement, 'basket power' also conveyed a means of creating new and liberating opportunities for women.

Most obviously, 'basket power' referred to the Guild as a means by which the women consumers of the movement could influence Co-operative policy. Guild branches enabled the women to participate in the running of Co-operative societies, to press for such changes in store management as the goods stocked, and even the working conditions of the staff. Guild support and training increased the number of women on Co-operative official bodies, and within the movement nationally Guildswomen were able to secure such progressive innovations as a minimum wage for female Co-operative employees,[9] and new trading practices to broaden the social base of the movement to include the poorest section of the community (Davies, 1904, p. 82–95).

'Basket power' also connoted women's contribution to Co-operation as a project of social transformation. The housewife might lack earning power but her responsibilities as wife and mother, and chancellor of the household budget, did furnish her with some spending power. 'By purchasing goods made under Co-operative and trade union conditions,' Guild literature pointed out, a married woman could 'as effectively as her husband in his trade union, be helping forward good conditions of work in the individual factory and building up an International Co-operative Commonwealth'. Thus it was through 'Co-operation that the married woman living at home finds her work and place in the Labour world'.[10]

At a more sophisticated level, however, the concept of 'basket power' signified a means by which working women could gain access to resources that would enable them to set an agenda representative of their specific needs. The commitment to trading loyalty thus implied a point of leverage: by drawing attention to the movement's dependence upon women's purchases, women were able to justify their claim to a share of the wealth that they helped to create for their own activities.

When applying for grants for Guild development, Guild officials emphasized that the movement's commercial health depended upon the role of Co-operative women. From 1890 to 1894 major restructuring increased Guild national expenditure from £19 to £245,[11] and although membership increased from 1,640 to 7,511, subscriptions could not be set high enough to cover these expanding overheads. As the 1894 Annual Report pointed out, the Guild was working to the aims and policies of the Co-operative Union, the movement's federal body, and was convinced that there were 'unutilized forces' that they could reach and put at the disposal of the Union 'but for lack of funds'. Furthermore, while the Guild was struggling with debts, many Society education committees seemed 'to find difficulty in making use of their funds', and others amassed large profits each year. Surely, it was 'a little hard that women should not only give their services, but should have to pay for the privilege of working by subscribing to our funds, while men have money thrust upon them'.[12]

Persistent reminders of the women's value to the movement steadily unlocked the resources which underpinned steady growth. By 1897 the Guild had 223 branches, 10,555 members, and an extremely busy head office.[13] All this created an organizational infrastructure that enabled women of very limited means to come together to study social questions, and develop policy, which broadened the scope of their concerns from the Co-op store to the local and national state, and increasingly encouraged them to make connections between these outside institutions and their own conditions of life. As a 1913 Guild leaflet put it, the Guildswoman's answer to the question 'what is a woman's place?' would be:

My place is in the Co-operative Movement, because I am the wage spender; my place is in my Town and Country, because I am a wife and mother; my place is in my Home because I am the joint maker of family life; and I find I cannot do my work properly in any one of the three places without doing it in all.[14]

FEMINISM AND THE MARKET

In its major Citizenship campaigns – for the vote, for divorce law reform, for state maternity care – the Guild brought a feminist analysis to bear on the situation of working-class women which demonstrated that improvements in their lives would require change and reform that would not come about simply by the buying and selling of Co-operative groceries. Yet here was a problem. As the Guild used 'basket power' to investigate the condition of working women's lives, to reveal the 'hidden suffering'[15] that existed within marriages, and to campaign for social reform and legislative changes that would improve and dignify the conditions of those women's lives, so it began to challenge the commonly accepted verities of Co-operative men whose priority was the smooth running of a commercial trading organization. Co-operative managers and officials were not necessarily opposed to women having the vote, or even to divorce law reform being discussed, but many of them did object to the appearance of such matters under the Co-operative banner.

It was not only that the Guild's efforts on behalf of married women were not specifically designed to improve trade; worse still was the potential for the open discussion of such taboo subjects as childbearing and marital relations to offend customers and actually damage trade. For several years, the democratic, broad church traditions of the movement protected the Guild's freedom of action, and the Co-operative Union Central Board did no more than register mild disapproval of the Guild's suffrage and maternity campaigns.[16] Yet in 1914, when the Guild's position on divorce reform attracted criticism from a Catholic organization claiming to represent large numbers of Catholic Co-operators, the Board took steps to curb the women's freedom of action. This engendered a major debate about the nature of the relationship between trade and social reform which sharply focused the divergence between the Guild's conception of Co-operation as an agent of social transformation, and that of officials who saw the movement as a steadily expanding trading enterprise whose prospects might be damaged by attachment to radical causes.

The Guild's involvement with the question of divorce began in 1910 when the General Secretary was invited to give evidence before the recently appointed Royal Commission on Divorce and Matrimonial Causes, an invitation that was in itself a measure of the Guild's standing as the national representative of working women. To ensure that they were in a position to represent the membership's views with confidence, the Central Committee agreed to conduct an inquiry, the findings of which then formed the substance of its submission to the Commission.[17] The two key questions concerned the legal 'double standard' which, under the terms of legislation passed in 1857, enabled a man to divorce his wife for adultery alone while a wife had to prove some additional grounds; and the high costs which placed divorce proceedings out of reach of all but the rich, with formal separation the only legal provision for working people which necessarily precluded remarriage. A more detailed survey sought opinions on possible extensions of the grounds for divorce.

As Guild leaders well knew, divorce was an extremely sensitive question which aroused vigorous moral and religious opposition. Accordingly, senior Guild officials were deeply impressed to find majority support for reform among the membership. The survey elicited a range of personal and second-hand case histories, graphically describing the many injustices suffered by women within the existing institution of marriage and providing a compelling case for change. As the General Secretary told the Commission: 'I can recall no other subject in the life of the guild which has aroused such immediate response, and elicited such strength and earnestness of feeling'.[18]

The Guild's evidence impressed the Commissioners and the 1912 Majority Report[19] advocated equalization of the grounds for divorce between men and women, and a reduction in costs to bring it within reach of working people. They did not, however, accept the Guild's proposal that a woman should be entitled to end a marriage because she did not want to have sexual relations with her husband. The Guild pressed for reform until the outbreak of war ruled out any possibility of new legislation; change did not come until 1923, and then brought only equalization and a reduction in costs; incompatibility or mutual consent had to wait until 1969.

In October 1913, the Guild Central Committee received a letter from the Salford Diocese Catholic Federation (instigated by one Mr Burn who was employed to look after Catholic interests in political and labour bodies),[20] objecting to the Guild's work for divorce law reform. It claimed that as the Guild received funding from the trading movement, Catholic Co-operators were being 'mulcted of a proportion of their dividends' to propagate a purpose that was alien not only to their beliefs but to those of non-Catholic Co-operators who opposed divorce. Such 'exploitation of legitimate membership for illegitimate purposes,' the letter warned, 'will ultimately disrupt the movement.'[21] The Catholic Federation got short shrift from the Guild Central Committee (they replied that as they considered divorce law reform to be 'one of the most important moral and social reforms which affect Co-operative women' they could not alter their 'action in regard to it'), but found a more sympathetic audience in the executive Board of the Co-operative Union, which then appealed to the Guild to drop the subject.[22]

The General Secretary was privately scathing about the Board's 'feeble' compliance with the Catholic lobby and their readiness to believe that 'at a word from the priests', thousands would leave the movement.[23] Publicly, the Central Committee once again affirmed its commitment to divorce reform, and to the democratic principles of self-government upon which the Guild had grown up. The Central Board, however, swayed by the strength of feeling at the Dublin 1914 Co-operative Congress, and minded that if 'the Board had to pay the piper, they should be able to call the tune,'[24] decided to make the payment of the Guild's £400 annual grant conditional upon it giving up divorce law reform and any other question not approved by the Board.

This ultimatum was unanimously rejected by 864 delegates from 400 branches at the Guild Congress a month later. More than any other aspect of its work, the question of divorce law reform crystallized the Guild's own sense of identity as an autonomous organization of, and for, married working women. 'We reached our highest point at Birmingham', Davies wrote to Leonard Woolf after the critical Congress vote.

> I had no idea that the strength and unity of feeling would be so great, and that the determination to keep our Independence should be connected with Divorce was all the more remarkable ... Someone said that the Guild had found its soul, it has certainly found its feet. I feel the women have now 'arrived' – and they will never go back.[25]

The Guild ensured that the related questions of its support for divorce law reform and its democratic rights as an organization were vigorously debated – in leaflets, articles and correspondence in *Co-operative News*, at meetings and conferences, and again at the Co-operative and Guild Congresses in 1915.

The Guild General Secretary, at an interview with the Co-operative Union Board in 1915, suggested that as well as failing to grasp the importance of this reform to Guildswomen, the Central Board did not understand the seriousness with which the Guild's evidence had been treated by the Royal Commission, nor indeed the Guild's capacity to influence debates at the national level. To give up now, she pointed out, 'simply because a certain sectarian body had come along' would be taken as 'a betrayal of a cause', a lowering of the Guild's reputation in the country, and as an indication that Co-operators were opposed to divorce law reform.

In case the Central Board could not appreciate the value of the Guild's contribution to progressive social reform as worthwhile in itself, or as enhancing the wider reputation of the movement, she rehearsed the more pragmatic reasons for respecting the Guild's autonomy. There was a danger, she warned the Board, that to give up divorce work

> would undermine the faith of the women in the gospel of Co-operation as the hope of the people. Dividends were important matters to the members of the Guild, but they looked to the movement for something more than dividends; they looked upon it as a great social regenerating force. They hoped that out of co-operation a new social birth might come and it was the belief in the spiritual force of co-operation which made their guildswomen such enthusiastic co-operators.[26]

At the heart of the Guild's arguments, then, lay an unshakeable conviction that the movement should be about much more than trade. Guildswomen argued that it was precisely 'the width and variety of subjects' taken up by the organization, 'which keeps it so alive and makes the members value it so much'. [27] As Mrs Wimshurst explained to delegates at the 1915 Co-operative Congress: 'the guild taught its members not only to be co-operators, it taught them to be citizens as well. Social reform consisted of things that merged together; it could not be chopped into sections.'[28]

Of course, the Central Board should not be in any doubt about the Guild's commitment to Co-operative trade. 'We need only point to the remarkable demand at the present moment among our Branches for Co-operative education', a Central Committee leaflet pointed out, 'and to the energy with which our "Push the Sales" campaign has been taken up throughout the Guild, to show that there is no lack of Co-operative enthusiasm and life among the members.' Yet there was a thinly veiled warning at the end of this litany of virtue: 'The knowledge that fruitful ideas and far-reaching reforms may spring out of anything so prosaic as shopkeeping only increases the respect for loyal buying which is the ABC of Guild work'.[29]

Shopkeeping, the Guild maintained, was not and should not be the end goal of Co-operation. To ask the women to 'come and buy' but to deny them the right to improve their own position, would be in the words of one female Co-operative Congress delegate, as though 'the lion and the lamb were asked to lie down together: without discussing which was the lion and which the lamb'. She reminded her audience that a male delegate had spoken of the workers' salvation depending upon them taking their destiny in their own hands: would he 'refuse to the women the same right of salvation?' To do this they needed the freedom to arrive at their own policy and act upon it.[30]

Despite some opposition to divorce law reform as such, the bottom line for the majority of officials was that it went against the grain of political and religious neutrality (Cole, 1944, p. 64). As one Board member, Mr Goodenough, put it, the root cause of the trouble was 'not antagonism to Divorce Law Reform, but objection to its advocacy on co-operative platforms, and in the name of the co-operative movement'.[31] He did not think any subject too sacred to be discussed, 'he was only objecting to it being brought into the co-operative movement. Miss Davies said it was a social problem; another person would say it was a religious question, or a sex question; but he would say it was a boundaries question.'[32]

At the 1915 Co-operative Congress a Central Board resolution sought to confirm the Board's authority to withhold funding from 'any organisation which, in its opinion, is pursuing a policy detrimental to the best interests of the co-operative movement'. As Mr G. Hayhurst argued

> they should keep the movement clear of all politics and religion. They were working for co-operation; and surely in the name of reason there were a thousand and one economic subjects in civil life which could be taken hold of without introducing politics or religion into the movement.[33]

In a similar vein, Mr F. Maddison claimed that divorce was 'an outside question. He, personally, would probably agree with the attitude of the guild on the subject of divorce; but it was an outside question.' For the Catholics it was a religious question, and he

> begged the Congress, for heaven's sake, to let the movement be one that did not make men or women, worshipping at their own altars, feel that their consciences were being outraged by an alien question being introduced into the movement. This was a business question, too. It had to do with the selling of tea and sugar and treacle and the rest of it. Co-operators were social reformers by trade, and they must be aware that in their great communities in Lancashire they had a great number of loyal co-operators to whom this was an offence.[34]

The Guild's formal position, a reiteration of its right to self-government taken as an amendment to the Central Board's resolution, had significant support from delegates, many of whom had already been alerted to the issue by Guild work in the local Co-operative Societies.[35] Mr Johnston, for example, stated that it would be 'a great misfortune to the co-operative movement if the work of the Women's Guild was curtailed'; all they were after was a change in the law to make it 'equitable for the bulk of the people'.[36] Mr J. Penny insisted that the 'co-operative movement did not stand merely for selling sugar and treacle; it was to uphold democratic principles, and divorce law reform was simply to establish equality between man and woman. That was a fundamental co-operative principle'.[37]

While the Guild was not strong enough to carry a majority against the weight of the Central Board, the vote of 796 to 1,430 demonstrated that it was nonetheless a significant force in the movement. As a Guild Central Committee leaflet pointed out:

> to have stirred Congress in the way that it was stirred, and to have concentrated the interest of delegates on a subject involving matters of principle is a tribute to the force of the Guild, and a reward to all those who have worked so well for our resolution in their local societies.[38]

CONCLUSION

True to its principles the Guild struggled on without the grant, raising extra money through a Self Government Fund, and receiving discreet assistance from the General Secretary.[39] At the end of the war, however, its position dramatically improved. In 1917 the Co-operative Congress voted to seek direct parliamentary representation through the formation of a Co-operative Party, and a year later women over 30 won the vote. The Guild had supported the suffrage campaign since the 1890s, and was now well placed to start building female support for the Co-operative Party. 'Guildswomen', wrote Davies in 1918, 'will find that they have suddenly become much more important, and that their views and actions will receive far greater consideration'.[40]

Anxious to have the Guild's full co-operation in the new political initiative, the Co-operative Union came up with a mutually acceptable basis for a settlement, and in 1918 the grant was restored. Celebrating 'the happy termination of the four "lean" years', and affirming its readiness to assist every part of the movement, the Guild Annual Report that year nonetheless restated the firmness of its attitude 'as regards both self-determination and greater equality'.[41]

Post-war reconstruction opened a new chapter in the Guild's history. Changes in both the political landscape and in the priorities of its own leadership following Davies's retirement in 1921, combined to moderate its policy. Its former independent and radical approach to the politics of working women evaporated as it was tugged into the orbit of the Labour Party and the Labour women's sections. In these circumstances, the commitment to an autonomous working women's movement evaporated and the social policies it upheld, alongside the Co-operative projects with which it became involved, signified a more traditional, home-bound version of womanhood.

Yet the Guild between 1890 and 1920 stands out as perhaps the only example in British history of a pioneering organization based in a successful commercial institution, which fostered a forceful and democratic movement of working-class women. The conditions which gave rise to the Guild's achievement during these years were highly specific however. Arguably, consumers' Co-operation constituted the only available material base for such an enterprise but without the injection of dynamic leadership, and the appropriate political agenda, women's purchasing role in the movement would have remained a necessary but not sufficient condition for the emergence of an effective organization. 'Basket power' played a significant role at the turn of the century in advancing women's social and political rights: it was powerful precisely because the Guild did not remain locked within the role assigned to it by the narrow trading concerns of the movement but used the slogan as a springboard for a bolder and more ambitious project of intervention in Co-operative and national affairs.

NOTES

1   *The New Statesman*, 21 June 1913, Gertrude Tuckwell Collection. This journalist, like the Guild itself, used 'working women' as short hand for 'women of the working class'.
2   This was not exclusively the case: the Guild benefited from the contribution of a number of middle-class women most notably Margaret Llewelyn Davies (1861–1944), General Secretary 1889 to 1921, daughter of the Christian Socialist John Llewelyn Davies, and niece of Emily Davies, founder of Girton College, Cambridge (Bellamy and Saville, 1972).
3   From 1881 the census returns began to classify women not in paid employment as 'unoccupied', an innovation which sharply reduced the apparent economic activity rates for women (Lewis, 1984, p. 146).
4   Alice Acland (1849–1935), founder and first secretary of the WCG, wife of Sir Arthur Acland, Liberal MP, Oxford don, and an active Co-operator (Bellamy and Saville, 1972).

5   Sarah Reddish (1850–1928) daughter of a prominent Bolton Co-operator, textile worker from the age of 11, President of Bolton Guild, 1886–1901, full-time paid organizer of the Guild 1893–5, and subsequently for the Women's Trade Union League; she was also an active suffragist (*CN*, 3.3.28, p. 13; Liddington and Norris, 1978, p. 93 and 291).

6   Organizer's Report, 'Annual Report of WCG', *Co-operative Congress Report (CCR)*, 1894, p. 58.

7   M.L. Davies, 'Co-operation at the Fountainhead', typed MS article for *Life and Labour*, Chicago, Vol. K, No. 7, (September 1920), p. 199–202, 'Material Illustrating the work of the Guild and kindred interests', (1890–?1944), 11 Vols, Vol. 1, Item 25, British Library of Political & Economic Science.

8   R. Nash (1907), *The Position of Married Women*, Manchester: CWS, p. 9.

9   *WCG Annual Reports*.

10   M.L. Davies, 'Co-operation at the Fountainhead', 'Material Illustrating the work of the Guild ...', Vol. 1, item 25.

11   Sarah Reddish speaking at a joint meeting of the Co-operative Union Educational Committee and the WCG at the 1894 Co-operative Congress, *CCR*, 1894, p. 139.

12   'Annual Report of WCG', *CCR*, 1894, p. 56.

13   *Annual Reports of WCG*.

14   WCG (1913), *The Education of Guildswomen*, p. 2.

15   WCG (1916), *The Women's Co-operative Guild 1895 to 1916, A Review of Twenty One Years' Work*, Annual Congress Handbook, London , p. 11.

16   M.L. Davies to Leonard Woolf, Friday, n.d. (?1914), Monks House Papers.

17   WCG Central Committee Minutes, 5 & 6 May 1910.

18   'Evidence of Miss Margaret Llewelyn Davies', *Minutes of Evidence taken before the Royal Commission on Divorce and Matrimonial Causes* (1912), Vol. 3, Cd. 6481, PP 1912–13, XX, p. 149.

19   *Report of the Royal Commission on Divorce and Matrimonial Causes (1912)*, Cd 6478, PP 1912–13, XVIII.

20   M.L. Davies to Leonard Woolf, Sunday, n.d., Monks House Papers.

21   General Secretary, Catholic Federation Diocese of Salford, to General Secretary, Women's Co-operative Guild, 22 October 1913.

22   *Annual Report of the WCG*, May 1913–194, p. 27.

23   M.L.Davies to Leonard Woolf, Sunday, n.d., Monks House Papers.

24   Meeting of the Central Board, *Co-operative Union Annual Report (CUAR)* 1914, p. 15.

25   M.L. Davies to Leonard Woolf, Friday, n.d., Monks House Papers.

26   Miss Llewelyn Davies, Guild Deputation to the Central Board, *CUAR*, 1915, p. 23.

27   WCG Central Committee letter to Central Board (published in *CN*, 18.4.14), *Annual Report of the WCG*, May 1914–15, p. 28.

28   *CUAR*, 1915, p. 522–3.

29   WCG Central Committee letter to Central Board, *Annual Report of the WCG*, May 1914–15, p. 28.

30   *CUAR*, 1915, p. 523.

31   C. Goodenough (1914), *The Central Board and the Grant to the Women's Co-operative Guild*, Manchester, p. 4.

32   *CUAR*, 1915, p. 25.

33   Ibid., p. 527.

34   Ibid., p. 522.

35   WCG, Annual Congress 1915, *The Self Government of the Guild*, London, 1915, p. 1.

36   *CUAR*, 1915, p. 522.

37   Ibid., p. 524.

38   WCG, *Self Government*, p. 2.

39   References to a loan from the General Secretary and agreement that she should take over a debt on literature, Central Committee Minutes, October 19 & 20, 1914.

40   M.L. Davies (1918), *The Vote at Last! More Power to Co-operation*, Co-op Union Limited, Political Pamphlet No. 2, London, p. 1.

41   *Annual Report of WCG*, 1918–1919, p. 2.

BIBLIOGRAPHY

Bellamy, John and Saville, John (1972), *Dictionary of Labour Biography*, Vol. 1.

Carr, A.M., Sargant Florence, P. and Peers, R. (1938), *Consumers' Co-operation in Great Britain: An Examination of the British Co-operative Movement*, London: George Allen & Unwin.

Cole, G.D.H. (1944), *A Century of Co-operation*, George Allen & Unwin for the Co-operative Union.

Cole, G.D.H. and Postgate, R. (1966 edition), *The Common People 1746–1946*, London: Methuen.

Davies, Margaret Llewelyn (1904), *The Women's Co-operative Guild*, Kirkby Lonsdale: Women's Co-operative Guild.

Davies, Margaret Llewelyn (ed.) (1915), *Maternity: Letters from Working Women*, London: Virago 1978 reprint.

Killingback, Neil (1988) 'Limits to Mutuality: Economic and Political Attacks on Co-operation during the 1920s and 1930s' in Stephen Yeo (ed.), *New Views of Co-operation*, London: Routledge.

Lewis, Jane (1984), *Women in England 1870–1950: Sexual Divisions and Social Change*, Brighton: Wheatsheaf.

Liddington, Jill and Norris, Jill (1978), *One Hand Tied Behind Us: The Rise of the Women's Suffrage Movement*, London: Virago.

Rendall, Jane (1990), *Women in an Industrializing Society: England 1750–1880*, Oxford: Blackwell.

Taylor, Barbara (1983), *Eve and the New Jerusalem*, London: Virago.

Webb, Beatrice (1938), *My Apprenticeship*, Vol. 2, Pelican.

Woolf, Leonard (1972), *Beginning Again: An Autobiography of the Years 1911–18*, London: The Hogarth Press.

Yeo, Stephen (ed.) (1988), *New Views of Co-operation*, London: Routledge.

PART TWO

Modernizing Domestic Spaces:
Liberating Women?

3. False Promises? Modernization of the Kitchen in France 1920–1960

Claire Duchen

INTRODUCTION

This chapter represents part of a broader investigation into the tangled and complex nature of women's relation to domestic space, in particular into the relationship between domestic technology and women's domestic labour, and into the ways in which definitions of femininity are embedded within a discourse of domesticity (Duchen, 1994). The aim here is to begin to explore the relationship between modernity, modernization and domesticity – as discourse and as experience – to see how, and with what success, the post-war image of the housewife, happy and fulfilled in her kitchen, was sold to women. The ideology of the housewife was developing in visible and concrete ways in Britain and the United States during the 1930s, but in France it was more discernible in the 1950s; the emphasis in this chapter is therefore on those years, although brief reference will be made to the inter-war decades and to the 1960s as well.

In writing about post-war periods, emphasis has tended to be placed on changes to women's participation in public life, such as accession to citizenship in France after World War II, or women's entry into the labour market or indeed their exclusion from it as the war-time need for women's labour power was replaced by the priority given to jobs for men returning to civilian life after both world wars. Less attention has been paid to the impact of the end of war on the home, and in particular to women's relationship to the home in these periods. This is subject to its own stresses and anxieties in times of transition, which may take a number of forms, ranging from an emphasis on a hoped-for return to 'normality', to a leap forward, away from war and into the modern era.

The kitchen has been selected as the focus for symbolizing women's relation to the home, as it seems to be portrayed as the woman's space rather than simply another room in the home. The images accompanying texts extolling the role of the *femme au foyer* or housewife, are more likely to show the woman in her kitchen than anywhere else. The kitchen is represented mostly as a place of work for women, but it is also the hub of the household, the heart of the home; the kitchen has become a metaphor for family life (Craik, 1989, p. 48).

A woman in the kitchen (*her* kitchen) is in her rightful place. However, the kitchen is the rightful place for a particular kind of woman, although this pre-selection is unstated. The woman in her kitchen is unremarkable: not too young nor too old, neither beautiful nor ugly, she is assumed to be married and probably a mother, seemingly classless, generally white. Women who do not conform to this image do not seem to have a kitchen; or at least, they are of no interest to policy makers and producers of domestic appliances and simply do not appear in the imagery of domesticity.

INTER-WAR FRANCE

French political structures did not change in the years immediately following World War I: unlike their British sisters, Frenchwomen did not gain their political rights as a result of the war. Employment structures did not change significantly either. In the early part of the twentieth century, women's rate of participation in the labour market in France was higher than in many other European countries, constituting 36.6 per cent of the labour force in 1911 (Sohn, 1992, p. 95), mainly because of the pre-eminence of agriculture in the economy and the large number of women who worked on the family farm. Approximately 46 per cent of working women were still involved in agriculture in 1921 (Sohn, ibid.). The period following the war was a period of conservatism in French politics (at least until the election of the Left-wing Popular Front coalition in 1936), and of the slow evolution in the labour market towards a more urban, industrial and service-oriented society, with 'progress' hindered by the Depression.[1]

The 'modern', in France, although in fashion after the war, was treated with suspicion; the modern woman in particular was viewed with horror, and the figure of Monique Lerbier in *La Garçonne*, Victor Margueritte's bestselling 1922 novel, became an icon of modernism, with her short hair connoting loose morals and denial of womanhood. Indeed, a woman with short hair was the symbol of more than dubious morality; according to Mary Louise Roberts, she came to represent the more generalized cultural anxiety associated with the immediate post-war years (Roberts, 1994). Modernity, then, was not sought and praised in inter-war France.

In concrete terms, modernization – of industry, of agriculture and of the home – was not a phenomenon that could be readily observed. Cultural historian Gary Cross attributes this to several specific factors, such as low wages for French workers, which meant that 'food continued to absorb over half of French workers' income' (Cross, 1993, p. 165). He goes on to argue that 'the French placed higher priority on ephemeral pleasures like dining and quality clothing rather than on domestic improvements' (Cross, ibid.). In spite of this, as Robert L. Frost has suggested, a consumer mentality was developing (Frost, 1993). In 1923, the first *Salon des Appareils Ménagers* (Domestic Appliance Exhibition) was held, becoming an annual event and renamed the *Salon des Arts Ménagers* (Domestic Arts Exhibition – or Ideal Home Exhibition) in 1926 (Werner, 1984, p. 72–3). Alongside the Exhibition, there appeared a new journal, *L'Art Ménager*, whose main objectives were to bring new ideas and inventions for the home to those Frenchwomen who had the time, the space and the budget to accommodate them. The influence of Christine Frederick, doyenne of domestic science and the Taylorized home in the USA, was imported into France by Paulette Bernège, whose bestselling book *De la méthode ménagère* was first published in 1928. Bernège makes no overt allusion to the class status of the women she hoped to address, but domestic science as she envisaged it was clearly a middle-class affair. Domestic appliances were still for the privileged few: while the cost of the electricity needed in order to operate large domestic appliances dropped sufficiently for 12 million – mainly urban – households to be equipped by 1939 (Fourastié in Sauvy, 1972, p. 443), the era of the washing machine and the refrigerator had not yet arrived.

This absence of a domestic market for consumer goods constituted a major problem for producers of these goods. Frost explains the lack of market by suggesting that the implementation of rationalization and automation in the workplace was acceptable because its consequences were economic: it was considered at that time that machines would replace workers and that machines would make workers more time- and cost-efficient. The relationship between time and money was clear on the factory floor, but an argument of this kind was difficult to apply to the home in the 1920s and 1930s (Frost, 1993, p. 128).

It was only when material conditions improved to the extent that it could convincingly be argued that the home too was a place of work with a specific technology appropriate to its needs, that the domestic consumer market began to develop. When this situation coincided with higher salaries and increased disposable income (particularly of men whose earnings would permit their wife's purchases), a powerful family lobby in parliament and a system of family allowances that favoured large families (Duchen, 1994), modernity seemed to become an appropriate marketing strategy for domestic consumer goods, sending a clear message and specifically targeting women. This did not happen until the 1950s.

POST-WAR FRANCE

France was traumatized by World War II. Six weeks after the invasion of France in May 1940, the army was defeated and an armistice signed. This was followed by four years of Occupation, marked by collaboration with the Nazis, deportation of Jews, resisters and others to concentration camps, the growth of a Resistance movement in France itself and also in conjunction with the allied forces outside France. There was no war effort comparable to that of the United States and Britain; such industry as remained contributed to Germany's strength and workers of both sexes were first encouraged, and after 1943 obliged, to work in Germany itself.[2] The arch-conservative government of Marshall Pétain promoted a vision of a hierarchical nuclear family, with the wife preferably at home with her children. Legislation was introduced to keep married women out of the public sector, albeit with limited success.[3]

Women were given the vote in 1944 and hoped for recognition – finally – as full partners with men in public life. They were to be disappointed, but in the years immediately following the war, their hopes were high (Duchen, 1995). On the political agenda was reconstruction. Agriculture, industry – the entire economic infrastructure demanded attention. Housing was not a top priority in spite of the very poor conditions endured by the majority of the population. By August 1946, a social security system was set up, following Britain's example, together with a separate system of family allowances, begun pre-war by employers, and taken over comprehensively by the state afterwards (Ambler, 1991; Prost, 1984). As far as women were concerned, the importance placed on the birth rate by de Gaulle and his provisional government, supported by the Christian Democratic party, the *Mouvement Républicain Populaire* (MRP), meant that they were seen as actual or as potential mothers rather than as partners with men in the labour force. Family policy was given high priority and inducements to procreate were offered: these included family allowances, ante-natal and maternity benefit, housing allowance, transport allowance and the single wage benefit, paid to families with only one wage coming in (Laroque, 1986).

The post-war years are commonly represented as a time when women were urged (or kicked) out of the labour market; when women embraced the home as stability, normality after the upheaval of war and when the return of the male members of the household meant that women were dispensed from the responsibilities they had shouldered during the Occupation. These, then, were the years when the state, in the interests of raising the birth rate, promoted the vision of the happy housewife mother of three, a version of womanhood that was also dominant in popular imagery. In France, statistics from the 1950s seem to back up this stereotype: rates of female participation in the labour force fell, the birth rate rose. Women constituted 32 per cent of the labour force in 1946, 29.8 per cent in 1954 and 27.6 per cent in 1962, the lowest point of the century (*Données Sociales*, 1984).[4] The birth rate rose to a figure consistently over 800,000 live births annually, maintained until the mid-1960s (Dyer, 1978, p. 134); furthermore, women were having more children – two or three became the norm, replacing the frequent *enfant unique* (only child) of the inter-war years.

A close study of post-war policy, however, shows that women were not in fact 'kicked out' of the labour market after the war because they had not occupied it in great numbers during the war years.[5] Nor were they encouraged into it in order to contribute to reconstruction. At the end of the war, there was no clear policy at all concerning women and paid employment. Policy makers believed that the drop in women's labour force participation resulted from the inducements provided by family policy, but even the well-known demographer and pronatalist Alfred Sauvy acknowledged that the relationship was impossible to prove (Duchen, 1994, Chapter 5).

MODERNITY AT HOME IN THE 1950s

The reality of the housing situation in France after the war did not make the ideal of the happy housewife easy to fulfil: living conditions in urban slums and rural households changed little. In 1954, 41.6 per cent of all dwellings were still without running water and 22 per cent were considered formally to be overcrowded - six people or more living in three rooms (Duclaud-Williams, 1978, p. 125). The rural exodus aggravated the housing crisis and the provision of new housing stock never reached the top of the government's agenda for investment. In 1953, 33 per cent of the French population claimed that they were 'dissatisfied' with their housing (Duclaud-Williams, ibid.).

France in the 1950s is frequently described as embarking on a period of growth, prosperity, social and professional mobility and modernization.[6] The modern was treated far more positively than had been the case after World War I. Anything that put a distance between the war and its memories of hardship and deprivation, and post-war modern life, was welcomed and the newly-developing consumer culture looked to America as its model of modernity.

Other post-war trends that influenced attitudes towards the home, although possibly less obviously, included the blurring of some previously rigid class boundaries and more working-class families aspiring to middle-class status, with modernization of the home representing upward mobility; the shifting of employment structures towards the tertiary sector and the associated rural exodus; young women who would previously have worked as domestic servants finding other sources of employment; and middle-class women having to manage without servants, many for the first time. The coincidence of these factors seems to have meant that Frenchwomen were expected to be more receptive to messages of domestic consumption.

In 1928, when Paulette Bernège first published her famous manual *De la méthode ménagère*, she specifically noted that her emphasis on routine, regularity and method in performing domestic tasks was intended to allow the mistress of the house to change her servants without interrupting the smooth flow of the household. After the war, the specialist magazines tended to address women who were now newly involved in the day-to-day running of the home because they no longer had domestic staff. They had to be taught how to be the accomplished mistress of the house imagined by policy makers, producers of domestic consumer goods and advertisers alike. Domestic science instruction in one form or another permeated women's magazines: treating housework as science and as something to be learned at the feet of experts was possibly accepted more easily when it formed a seamless part of instruction in the art of being a woman. Learning how to do household tasks in a scientific and rational way both taught a woman how to manage without servants, and claimed to elevate her role to the status of a profession, with its own practices and rewards – rewards which could not be quantified in financial terms as they were rooted in nobler sentiments, but which nonetheless made her work in the home a fair exchange for the husband's wages. In targeting the housewife, arguments of industrial rationalization were newly transformed into arguments about saving – not necessarily money – but time and effort.

Housework was presented as scientific, the kitchen as a laboratory, the tasks to accomplish as essential to the well-being of the family, if somewhat monotonous in themselves: women were encouraged to look beyond the immediate tasks and appreciate the overall picture. Housework was explicitly recognized as tedious, but a woman was supposed to understand the broader context, that of the happy, harmonious household which it was her responsibility both to create and to maintain. The home was to be presented to them in glowing terms:

> What is a house? A company to run, a business that is exciting to set up and to take forward... each little task, however uninteresting it appears to be in itself, has a greater meaning: it is only one cog in the marvellous machine that it is your job to oversee. (*La Maison Française*, No. 2, 1946)

Domestic appliances, it was said, helped a housewife control her work time and relieve the drudgery and were advertised as being the only way forward to a woman's emancipation (*Le Monde*, 4 April 1953). Appliances were sold via the notion of freedom and leisure for women – one advertisement for a washing machine shows a woman sitting doing her embroidery while the machine takes care of the laundry – or on the more scientific or technical grounds of technical superiority or efficiency. Equally important was the question of the rational organization of a housewife's working day; together these would free her for some leisure time or time for her children. Timetables of the ideal well-organized day (or week or month or season) appeared in domestic science manuals and in magazines. Paulette Bernège was the least flexible in her approach, with every 15 minutes accounted for and free afternoons timetabled for Thursday (between three and seven) and Sunday (between two and seven). By the time the model timetables reached a wider female public, in *Elle* or *Marie-France* for instance, the tasks were the same but the presentation offered women some choice over when to do what. Monday, however, was always washday.

Indeed, the time and effort that women resented most was the laundry, hardly surprising given the state of housing in the post-war decades (Chombart de Lauwe, 1956, p. 44). One of the slowest changes in the provision of appliances was the advent of the washing machine, and when it occurred, the provision was uneven, revealing vast disparities of standard of living between different socioeconomic groups. Those working-class women who no doubt most needed a machine (living in poor housing, in overcrowded conditions and with no space for a washing machine, possibly still without running water, having large numbers of children and low wages) were more than likely to be those who did not have one. The semi-automatic washing machine and even the fully automatic washing machine were praised in women's magazines as an essential item for the home by the mid-1950s, but the price was still prohibitively high. In 1954, 8.5 per cent of the households of industrial workers owned a washing machine, compared with 23.4 per cent of senior managers and members of the liberal professions. By 1960, this had risen to 27.2 per cent for industrial workers' households, a higher rise but still low in total when compared with the 49.4 per cent of senior managers and members of the liberal professions, who had bought a washing machine and yet were also those more likely to have domestic help in the house and/or to send their heavy washing out to a laundress (*Données statistiques*, 1969).[7]

FALSE PROMISES?

Women were promised modernity, exemplified by organization of time and space and technological innovation. Modernity promised women freedom. The imagery of freedom in advertising showed women turning their backs on household chores, flinging off their aprons or sitting down at leisure whilst the machinery worked in their place. Freedom, however, came with strings attached. A woman with leisure on her hands caused great anxiety: what would she do with her time? Newspapers nervously referred to the archetypal bored housewife, Madame Bovary, whose adultery was obviously caused by the fact that she had nothing else to do. While the advertising appeal to women was made in terms of saving time and effort, a frequent sub-text told women that their time and effort was being used quite properly by doing things in the correct way. Buy a washing machine (but be careful, because your bedlinen will wear out more quickly); buy a refrigerator (but your family needs fresh food); buy a vacuum cleaner (but it uses a lot of electricity and misses those awkward corners). The type of freedom imagined by advertisers and created through better organization and mechanical aids maybe allowed women simply to be better housewives, that is do more around the house.

However many appliances a woman had in her home, domestic machinery still did not do the work without her, and nobody actually wanted or expected women to abandon housework altogether. Time-budget studies showed that, throughout the 1950s, women's time was just as absorbed by work, paid and domestic, as before. The authors of one French study of married women's work in urban France concluded: 'at the end of the war, the number of households equipped with domestic appliances was far from what it is today. In spite of this, the length of the married woman's working day does not seem to be any shorter' (Girard, 1958, p. 618). The only sure way to cut down on time spent on housework was paradoxically to be in full-time paid work; and then the overall time spent in combining paid employment and housework was higher than ever. The time that was sacrificed was any leisure time that a woman might have had, that is, her free time.

The same study revealed that between 1947 and 1958, a full-time housewife's time spent on housework dropped by 1.7 per cent to 54.3 hours a week if she had no children and by 0.2 per cent to 77.5 hours a week if she had three (Girard, ibid., p. 616). As the author noted, 'Domestic appliances may have lightened the work and improved the conditions in which women are living, but have not reduced the time it takes to accomplish their different household tasks' (Girard, ibid., p. 617).

This, of course, was at least partly due to the way that the modernization of the kitchen in no way seemed to affect the gendered division of household labour. It may have been less onerous to service a washing machine than to wash by hand; but the person who serviced the washing machine was still the woman. The husband's task was to pay for the washing machine, the vacuum cleaner, the refrigerator. Advertisements show the husband delighting his wife by paying for the equipment, confusing a gift for his wife with a piece of equipment for the home ('The most useful of all useful gifts: Tornado makes your house shining and your wife happy'; 'she has just used her Laden washing machine for the first time. She is thrilled! She is so grateful to her husband for giving it to her ... she understands that her life will be transformed!') (advertisements in *Nouveau Fémina*, in *Elle* and in *Marie-France* throughout 1955); but his involvement with domestic technology seems to stop there. Confidence that technology would banish domestic drudgery seemed to mean that no thought was given to reassessing the social relations of its use. This is the generous interpretation: a more cynical view might be that men knew full well that it was not in their interest to take on any responsibility for the running of the home; and while women demanded an equal share in the world outside, men did not reciprocate in the home. But then again, this particular promise had never been made.

How can the success of the rhetoric of modern domesticity be evaluated? When comparing the presence of a rhetoric of modernity and consumption with the actual provision of domestic consumer goods to French households, a definite disparity is clear. While the mid-1950s marked the high point of the happy housewife message, French women were not well provided with vacuum cleaners, washing machines and the like until the mid- or even late-1960s. The success and spread of domestic technology through French households cannot therefore reliably be attributed to any particular marketing message or to the imposition of a particular ideology. By the time that ownership of the larger domestic appliances had reached over 50 per cent of households, the number of married women (that is, likely housewives) in the labour force had risen quite significantly (up by 28 per cent between 1954 and 1962) (*Etudes et conjonctures*, 1964), a trend that was to accelerate throughout the 1960s.

The chronological mismatch between the discourse and experience of domestic modernization makes it impossible to establish a causal relationship between the two. It could be argued that new needs and aspirations for the home were created in the 1950s and only fulfilled later. It could also be argued that far from responding to a message of contented feminine domesticity, women's own agenda was quite different, perceiving domestic appliances and organization of their domestic time and space precisely in terms of their double workday: hence the increase in ownership of appliances when women were going out to paid employment in the 1960s. Saving time and effort was still important but for different reasons: there was less time available, and the double workday increased their levels of fatigue. I would suggest that far from being the passive recipients of consumer messages, women domestic consumers selected their purchases according to criteria that had resonances in their own lives. By the time that the 'average' French kitchen corresponded to some kind of modern ideal, the vision of the happy housewife, totally absorbed in her domestic environment, was nowhere to be seen.

ACKNOWLEDGEMENTS

I would like to thank Christine Zmroczek, without whom this would not have been written.

NOTES

1   The Depression hit France slightly later than Britain, and was felt more acutely after 1931. France was also slow to pull itself out of the Depression (Jackson, 1985; Sauvy, 1965–1975).·
2   Married women or women who were substitute heads of household were exempt, and the age of women workers who were required to participate in this *Service du Travail Obligatoire* was limited to 18–35 year olds.
3   On World War II in France generally, see Robert Paxton (1972), *Vichy France: Old Guard and New Order*, New York: Norton; on women's experience of war, see Miranda Pollard, 'Femme, Famille, France: Vichy and the Politics of Gender 1940–1944', Unpublished PhD thesis, Trinity College, Dublin, 1990; Hanna Diamond, 'Women's Experience during and after World War II in the Toulouse Area 1939–1948: Choices and Constraints', Unpublished DPhil thesis, University of Sussex, 1992. On women in the immediate post-war period, see Claire Duchen (1994, Chapter 1).
4   It must however be remembered that the percentage of women in the labour force may have dropped, but that there were positive reasons as well as negative ones to explain the drop, such as younger women remaining in full-time education. In percentage terms too the relative participation of women was reduced in part because of immigrant labour increasing the overall size of the labour force. The drop in actual figures is not very dramatic – from 6.7 million in 1946 to 6.646 million in 1954, mostly due to women leaving agriculture and to the new availability of pensions for older women, who could now stop working whereas previously they did not have this option (Guelaud-Leridon, 1964).
5   No research specifically on the experience of women in paid employment during the Occupation has yet been completed to my knowledge. For oral evidence from the Toulouse area, see Diamond, 1992.
6   See for instance, Jean Fourastié *Les trente glorieuses ou la révolution invisible de 1946 à 1975*, Paris: Fayard, 1979; J-J Carré, P. Dubois and E. Malinvaud, *La Croissance française* Paris: Le Seuil, 1972.
7   Other factors that influenced the purchase of domestic appliances were the age of the head of household and the number of members of the household. A household with over six people in it was 11 times more likely to have a washing machine than a household of one (*Données statistiques*, 1969, p. 66).

REFERENCES

Ambler, John (ed.) (1991), *The French Welfare State: Surviving Social and Ideological Change*, New York: New York University Press
Attfield, Judy and Kirkham, Patricia (eds) (1989), *A View from the Interior. Feminism: Women and Design*, London: Virago.
Bernège, Paulette (1928), *De la méthode ménagère*, No publisher.
Chombart de Lauwe, Paul-Henry (1956), *La vie quotidienne des familles ouvrières*, Paris: CNRS.

Craik, Jennifer (1989), 'The Making of Mother: the Role of the Kitchen in the Home' in Graham Allen and Graham Crow (eds), *Home and Family: Creating the Domestic Space*, Basingstoke: Macmillan.

Cross, Gary (1993), *Time and Money: The Making of Consumer Culture*, London: Routledge.

Donnée statistiques sur l'évolution de l'équipement des ménages jusqu'à la fin de l'année 1968 (1969), Paris: Documentation Française.

Données sociales (1984), Paris: Documentation Française.

Duchen, Claire (1994), *Women's Rights and Women's Lives in France 1944–1968*, London: Routledge.

Duchen, Claire (1995), 'Une femme nouvelle pour une France nouvelle?', *Clio* No. 1.

Duclaud-Williams, Roger (1978), *The Politics of Housing in Britain and France*, London: Heinemann.

Dyer, Colin (1978), *Population and Society in Twentieth Century France*, London: Hodder and Stoughton.

Etudes et Conjonctures (1964), December.

Frost, Robert L. (1993), 'Machine Liberation: Inventing Housewives and Home Appliances in Interwar France', *French Historical Studies*, Vol. 18, No. 1, Spring.

Giles, Judy (1993), 'A Home of One's Own: Women and Domesticity in England, 1918–1950', *Women's Studies International Forum*, Vol. 16, No. 3.

Girard, Alain (1958), 'Le budget-temps de la femme marreé dans les agglomérations urbaines', *Population*, No. 4.

Guelaud-Leridon, Françoise (1964), *Le travail des femmes*, Paris: PUF.

Higonnet, Margaret et al. (eds) (1987), *Behind the Lines: Gender and the Two World Wars*, Newhaven: Yale University Press.

Laroque, Pierre (1986), *La Politique Familiale en France depuis 1945*, Paris: Documentation Française.

Jackson, Julian (1985), *The Politics of Depression in France 1932–1936*, Cambridge: Cambridge University Press.

Martin, Martine (1984), *Femmes et société: le travail ménager 1919–1939*, Unpublished thesis, University of Paris 7.

Prost, Antoine (1984), 'La politique familiale en France de 1938 à 1981', *Le Mouvement Social*, No. 129.

Reynolds, Siân (1986), 'Marianne's Citizens? Women, the Republic and Universal Suffrage in France' in Siân Reynolds (ed.), *Women, the State and Revolution*, Brighton: Wheatsheaf.

Roberts, Mary Louise (1994), *Civilization Without Sexes: Reconstructing Gender in Postwar France 1917–1927*, Chicago: University of Chicago Press.

Sauvy, Alfred (1965–75), *Histoire économique de la France entre les deux guerres*, Paris: Fayard, 4 Volumes.

Sohn, Anne-Marie (1992), 'Entre deux guerres; les rôles féminins en France et en Angleterre' in Françoise Thébaud (ed), *Histoire des femmes en Occident*, Vol. 5, *Le XXe siècle*, Paris: Plon.

Thébaud, Françoise (1986), 'Maternité et famille entre les deux guerres: Idéologies et politique familiale' in Rita Thalmann (ed.), *Femmes et fascismes*, Paris: Tierce.

Werner, Françoise (1984), ' Du ménage à l'art ménager: l'évolution du travail ménager et son écho dans la presse féminine française de 1919 à 1939', *Le Mouvement Social*, No. 129.

4. Chinese Women and the Kitchen: Views from Four Generations

Xu Min

The interviewees of this article:

Generations	Name	Age	Status	Education
Great-Grandmother	Mrs Li	87	housewife	finished primary school
Grandmother	Mrs Zhang	63	retired doctor	graduated from special medical school
Mother	Mrs Wang	35	university lecturer	BA
Daughter	Lianlian	5	at infant school	N/A

It is a truth universally acknowledged that the kitchen is after all a world of women. During the last 15 years, many radical changes have taken place in this particular world, including the modernization of kitchen facilities and the transition of women's values. In the process of these changes, however, some aspects of this world still remain unchanged or difficult to change. This article focuses on the examination of these changes in China, providing an empirical analysis – based on interviews with women from four generations of one Chinese family – of Chinese women's relationship to the kitchen and the transformation of that relationship.

THE MODERNIZATION OF KITCHEN FACILITIES

Lianlian received a number of nice presents on her fifth birthday, but her absolute favourite was the plastic toy kitchen from her father, which cost about US$25. It was the equivalent of two weeks of his salary. The toy kitchen was small but complete, with almost everything required in a modern kitchen, such as a refrigerator, electrical cooking facilities, a microwave oven, sink, cupboard, colourful dishes and pans, waste bin, and even a telephone.

Watching her daughter play with such a beautiful toy kitchen, all sorts of feelings welled up in Mrs Wang's mind. When she was a child, she remembered, she had also had a toy kitchen, but it was made of iron. With those little iron coal cookers, iron pots and spoons, Wang and her childhood friends had 'cooked' innumerable dishes for themselves. She had been so proud of her toy kitchen, insisting that it was better than the clay kitchen facilities her mother had used.

It was only ten years ago that Lianlian's grandmother, Mrs Zhang, first had her own kitchen. Although it was very small, a mere two metres square, Mrs Zhang was very pleased to have it. To her, it was quite simply a gift from heaven. When newly married, Mrs Zhang and her husband lived in a dilapidated residential building where there was no kitchen in any of the flats. So, Mrs Zhang and the other ten households on the same floor had to use their two-metre-wide corridor as the cooking area. A dozen small 'kitchens' were then lined up along the corridor, and coal stoves with briquettes were the typical facilities.[1] The building had no water supply either, and the residents normally carried water (with a shoulder pole and buckets) from a public water station 500 metres away, paying one *fen* each time for two buckets of water. There was a well nearer to the building. The housewives preferred to carry water from the one further away, because that could save money.

A few years later, Mrs Zhang moved into a new building, where each floor had a communal kitchen with shared tap water. It was about ten square metres in size, and was shared by seven households. Egg-shaped briquettes were the most common fuel for Chinese families in those days, and logs were also used to make a fire. Although honeycomb briquettes later became quite popular in cities as an improved form of fuel to reduce pollution, firewood and logs remained in demand as firelighters. Almost every day, the communal kitchen was filled with smoke and steam, and weekends could be even worse. Apart from one small window, there was no other form of ventilation in the kitchen. Thus, the kitchen walls soon became dark and greasy. At that time, Mrs Wang often helped her mother to light the fire, and she had always dreamed of discovering some kind of smokeless firewood when she grew up. She had also hoped that, by the time she herself became a mother, there would be clean and advanced kitchen facilities as beautiful as her toys.

In fact, rapid change in the kitchen has far exceeded Mrs Wang's expectations. Six years ago, as soon as she got married, Mrs Wang had her own kitchen in the flat, and it was twice as large as the one her mother was using then. Initially, she had a gas stove running off a gas cylinder. In 1993, gas pipes were installed in the building by the government company, and she then decided to spend some money on refurbishing the kitchen. In no time at all, a modernized kitchen emerged: a white cupboard was fixed on the wall, pleasantly inlaid with jade green ceramic tiles, a shining gas stove of stainless steel replaced the original iron one, and a brand new ventilator was installed above the window. Mrs Wang tried to persuade her mother to acquire some modern facilities for her own kitchen, but Mrs Zhang preferred to keep it unchanged. She was happy enough using her old-fashioned sink and cooker in her two-square-metre kitchen, since she believed that a kitchen was basically the place to cook, and that there was no need to have it as luxurious as the sitting room or bedrooms. Mrs Wang criticized her mother for her traditional ideas about family life, but Mrs Zhang argued that it was simply a waste to 'throw money' on the floor, or at the wall of the kitchen.

Lianlian did not seem to like her mother's newly decorated kitchen either. She told Mrs Wang that, when she grew up, she would like to have a kitchen of 20 square metres. It must have enough room to include a dining table and a huge refrigerator with several freezer compartments. She also wanted to have a dishwasher, a microwave oven, and an electric cooker in her future kitchen. She described how her kitchen would be clean and pleasurable, full of the smell of fresh air and flowers but not greasy smoke. There should be hot water round the clock, and of course, a telephone and television in her kitchen, she added. Lianlian even considered putting a computer in her future kitchen to allow her to shop without leaving the house.

Such demands for the modernization of the kitchen have been growing fast during the second half of this century. During the first 30 years of the century, demands for change had been relatively modest due to limitations in the development of the kitchen industry. Since the 1980s, Chinese women's desire to improve their kitchens has become more and more ardent. Getting a private kitchen has been the first important condition for people to move house. During the late 1980s and early 1990s, intense popular interest in fitted kitchens engulfed almost all the cities in the country. Even the peasants in developed rural areas had learned to invest in and refurbish their kitchens. This movement to modernize kitchens is by no means over. Many families have had their kitchens redecorated twice or three times by now, and their kitchen facilities have been constantly renewed. This tendency has promoted a rapid boom in the commercial market for kitchen facilities in China.

WOMEN'S CHANGING ATTITUDES TO HOUSEWORK

Lianlian's great-grandmother, Mrs Li, has been a housewife throughout her life. The kitchen, therefore, is the only place where she can prove her worth. Women of her generation used to demonstrate their virtue and importance by two means: one was to bear a son to ensure the continuation of the husband's family, and the other was to be noted for housework. Mrs Li has five daughters but no son, so naturally, doing housework has been her only chance to establish her talents and her value.

Since the first day of her marriage, the kitchen has always been her main working area. Every day before dawn, she would get up and go to the kitchen to prepare swill for her pigs. She would have to cook two big pots of food for them, and the diameter of the pot she used was about 80 centimetres. She would not leave the kitchen until after ten o'clock in the evening every day. Her husband left home soon after she had given birth to their fifth daughter, and she has not heard from him since. Mrs Li is now 87 years old, and lives with her five daughters in turn, helping them with the housework. She has a serious problem with cataracts, and quite often she cannot see things clearly at all. Using her other senses and her experience, however, she insists on working in the kitchen every day. Worried about her safety and health, her daughters and grandchildren are always trying to stop her doing the housework and the cooking. She sometimes gets very angry with them, saying: 'You think I'm useless now, do you? So you all want to get rid of me. I am not going to wait for death'.

To Mrs Li, housework appears to be quite an ambiguous concept. On the one hand, the work she has engaged in throughout her long life seems to have just proved to her that women are of no importance or worth. She explains: 'Women of my time are useless, because we couldn't make money and always relied on our men. Useless women have then nowhere to go but to stay in the kitchen'.[2] On the other hand, only by doing housework could Mrs Li express the value of her existence, and if she had not been able to do certain housework, she would have no confidence at all.

Unlike her mother, Mrs Zhang happened to live in an age when equality of the sexes was stressed, and women were encouraged to participate in social labour as men do. Most women of Mrs Zhang's generation are proud of being professional women. To them, 'housewife' is a title for those who are incompetent, and therefore have no social position. Furthermore, such a small field as the kitchen was thought to be absolutely the wrong place for them to attain personal value. In their times, a woman who devoted herself too much to housework was likely to be regarded as a 'backward element' by society, and most women would thus strive to be an advanced worker in their social roles. For this the reason, Mrs Zhang has spent very little time on cooking and housework in her life, not even as much as her husband has done. While her mother, Mrs Li, is around, she is in charge of most of the housework for her daughter, and when she goes to stay with her other daughters, Mrs Zhang and the family would normally have their dinners in the canteen of her work unit. Because of this, Mrs Zhang's cooking skills cannot compare with those of her mother, nor with those of her daughter Mrs Wang.

Mrs Wang is a university lecturer. Like her mother, she is also a woman who takes her career seriously. However, she has very different views than her mother about housework and the role of a woman in the family. Mrs Wang feels that a woman with good qualities should not merely seek for success in her career, but should also aspire to being a good wife and mother at home. How she handles family life (including housework) then becomes an important measure to judge whether she is competent to be a wife and mother. Mrs Wang's opinion simply reflects social expectations about the role of women of her generation. Since the beginning of the 1980s, people have started to question Mao's idea that 'men and women are equal'. Chinese men and Chinese women have all felt that there was an overemphasis on the equality of the sexes in the past, and that it was not necessarily correct to ask women to be equal with men in performing heavy labour such as carrying weighty sacks and sledge hammering. So, both Chinese men and women have called for a return of femininity. For the men, they would like to see women become active again in the kitchen, and for most women, they are happy to play the feminine role in their families. Like Mrs Wang, professional women then have to bear a double burden of work and family. Quite often they feel exhausted and complain about their lives under such pressure; nevertheless, they do not feel that housework is worthless. On the contrary, Mrs Wang has a better understanding than Mrs Zhang of her grandmother's idea that only the kitchen reflects women's personal worth. To Mrs Wang, the kitchen may at least reflect some aspects of the value that women have.

What will be the future for Lianlian is still unclear, but 100 per cent of Lianlian's school girl friends have got toy kitchens. It is also true that 100 per cent of Lianlian's school boy friends have no such toy as a 'kitchen'. Lianlian likes to play with one of the boys in her class, and she once told her mother that 'If I get married to him in future, I would be a very lucky girl, because his father is a *chef*, and I may not have to cook much then'.

The kitchen is now facing great changes: more and more modernized kitchen facilities are coming onto the market, and more and more pre-processed and semi-prepared foods are available. All these changes have meant a constant shift in ways of working in the kitchen. At the same time, men are starting to enter into the kitchen, and their role of being master in the family is also changing. However, the fact that women still play the leading role in the kitchen has remained unchanged, and they may never ever be replaced by men.

Translated by Chen Jie.

NOTES

1   This arrangement, albeit with gas cylinders rather than coal stoves, is still common in China [Editor's note].
2   This seems a typical housewife's self-deprecation, since Mrs Li obviously could not depend on her husband, but was forced to fend for her large family herself [Editor's note].

PART THREE

Cultural Representations and Resistances

5. Domestic Space in Italian Cinema: *Ossessione, Ladri di biciclette* and *Ladri di saponette*

Maggie Günsberg

Domestic space can be seen represented in varying degrees across a wide range of film genres: melodrama, realism, *film noir*, sci-fi, horror, and even the Western, the archetypal genre of the outside, of public/male space.[1] The portrayal of domestic space in a Western like *The Man Who Shot Liberty Valance* (1962), or in a *film noir*/melodrama like *Mildred Pierce* (1945), is crucial to the films' investigation and definition of femininity and masculinity. However, one might argue that the most 'natural' cinematic home of domestic space is the realist genre.

In its aim to depict 'reality', rather than provide escapism in the manner of conventional Hollywood cinema, the realist genre focused on the rigours of working-class life by concentrating on mundane, everyday necessities. The frequent centrality of the domestic zone to this invariably bleak scenario is attested to by the telling label 'kitchen sink' which was applied pejoratively to British 'New Wave' realism of the late 1950s and early 1960s, when audience support for this version of cinematic realism began to dwindle. Italian Neo-realism, which began in the early 1940s, had in certain cases been similarly criticized for painting too depressing a picture of Italian life.[2] Neo-realism too showed mostly lower-class, regional characters in its attempt to redirect the course of Italian cinema away from the escapist tendencies of the 'peplum' epics set in Roman times, the costume dramas and above all the bourgeois *'telefono bianco'* films.

Several major issues arise here. The first concerns the problematic nature of realism in its claim to mirror social reality, while providing a representation which is in fact partial, tendentious and highly selective, yet given as immutable. Realism in this way works to naturalize the social and exclude the possibility of change. Another issue centres on the two paths taken by patriarchal capitalist ideology and mirrored by realism. One is the devaluation of the domestic sphere which realism, while appearing merely to describe it as part and parcel of downmarket, working-class dreariness, in effect often reinforces. The second route is the idealization of domestic space as a haven from the outside world. The realist mode of representation also reiterates the insidious process whereby not only is domestic space devalued or idealized because it is the woman's sphere, but also, conversely, any work categorized as 'women's work', whether inside or outside the home, is automatically accorded a low status in relation to the public sector. 'Domestic work' usually refers to housework (cooking, cleaning and childcare) performed in the context of a marriage; however, in this study its use includes cooking and cleaning carried out as part of a money-making business, but still regarded as 'domestic' or 'women's' work.

The idealization of domestic space took on a new dimension during the post-war economic and technological boom of the 1950s as advertising sang of the sheer ecstasy of housework with the advent of new cleaning fluids and innovatory gadgets. However, this idealization not only belies, but actually helps to sell, the reality of a very unideal low status, and is merely the other face of realism's fixing of the status quo of power relations. Domestic space, and the work of childcare, cooking and cleaning which goes on within it, has been recognized as occupying a hidden and separate but crucial position in terms of both reproduction and production-for-use in relation to capitalist modes of production for exchange. As such it is, as Ellen Malos argues, 'economically important as well as ideologically functional' (Malos, 1980, p. 23). Devalorization and, we might add, false idealization keep it hidden and ensure greater surplus value, the value on which capitalism thrives.

Fatalistic devalorization and false idealization of the domestic sphere in patriarchal capitalism work to perpetuate the association of domestic space with femininity, which in turn remains locked into a position of inferiority in respect of masculinity and its public space. When internalized, this fatalism manifests itself in the assumption that nothing can change and that there are no choices. Rather than operate in both domestic and public space, femininity is constructed as a compulsion for the former. Any aspiration to move beyond this space represents a punishable transgression, a threat both to capitalism as a mode of production and to patriarchy as its ideological underpinning. In *Ossessione* (1942), the first of two very different moments in Italian Neo-realism on which this study will focus, this aspiration finds a voice which is duly silenced with the closure of the narrative. However, in terms of spectatorship it is a voice which continues to resound after the end of the film. The film is essentially driven by the choice made by the central female character to move from her position in domestic labour to one of ownership of the means of production. Economic and sexual desire provide a doubly-transgressive combination, more characteristic of *film noir* than of realism, which is lethal for all concerned: husband, lover, and of course the female character herself.

De Sica's *Ladri di biciclette* (1948) fixes its female character firmly within the domestic sphere. Her virtual exclusion from the major action of the film, namely the search by her husband and son for the stolen bicycle, serves to devalorize domestic space, which recedes into the background as the film progresses, in a manner illustrative of its hidden and taken-for-granted role in patriarchal capitalism. I shall look at this Neo-realist classic through the lens of its latter-day spoof, Nichetti's *Ladri di saponette* (1989), translated as *Icicle Thieves* but meaning, literally, *Thieves of Bars of Soap*. In Nichetti's film the female character is transformed into an aspiring theatrical singer and dancer who refuses to be contained by the domestic sphere. *Ladri di saponette* is a complex film of great interest not only in its reworking of the representation of domestic space in *Ladri di biciclette*, but also in the effects of its parallel portrayal of 1980s domesticity. The spoof of *Ladri di biciclette* constitutes an 'inner' film which, together with the commercials that interrupt it, are watched on a television by a pregnant, middle-class wife in her sitting room. While the inner film satirizes the fixing of the female character in domestic space in *Ladri di biciclette*, its viewing in the 'outer' film serves to reinforce, and update, the original, Neo-realist situation. Domestic spaces from different historical periods intersect, and comedy meets realism.

EVERYTHING BUT THE KITCHEN SINK

Our first encounter with Giovanna in *Ossessione* (1942) is with her voice. Together with Gino, a vagabond who appears at her husband's roadside cafe, we follow her siren-like singing into the kitchen. As Gino stands in the doorway, all we see of her is her gently swinging legs. With the subsequent shot-reverse shot sequence during which Giovanna and Gino look at each other, the sexual attraction between the two is established. They will become lovers and together murder her husband; the film ends with the pregnant Giovanna's death in a car accident and Gino's arrest.

Ossessione is regarded as Italy's first Neo-realist film, and indeed has many realist features. It is set in the bleak marshland of the Ferrara delta, and the narrative unfolds in real time. There are no flash-backs and the absence of a voice-over denies any one character a controlling viewpoint with which the audience may identify.[3] However, the manner in which the main female character is introduced is more characteristic of a type of film banned in Italy at the time, namely *film noir* (the sexually-alluring, disembodied voice, the fetishistic fragmentation of the female body, the repeated focus on her body as she paints her nails, all listened to and observed voyeuristically by Gino/the audience until the moment when she looks up). This particular blend of *film noir* with realism is a major determinant in the depiction of domestic space in the film, a domestic space to which Giovanna is linked from the outset and from which she will attempt to escape.[4] While the drudgery and isolation of domestic labour *are* depicted, what drives the film is Giovanna's desire to reposition herself in relation to it, a desire which in turn adds another dimension to scenes in which it is 'realistically' depicted.

Her eventual death is in effect not simply the culmination of events precipitated by a crime of passion. Her desire to own the cafe, in whose kitchen she has been slaving, is also problematized. In other words, while a female character may occupy the domestic space of the cafe kitchen, she cannot be permitted to own the means of production. Property considerations are a major feature of this film, and in an overriding patriarchal context Giovanna is seen to be breaking the rules, a subversiveness for which she must be punished. Other examples of *film noir* similarly figure economically dependent female characters who use their sexuality as a means to achieving independence and financial security by enlisting the help of a lover, behaviour which often proves fatal for the woman.[5]

With Giovanna's first appearance in *Ossessione* crucial signals are given about her relation to the domestic space in which she is situated. Like Cora in *The Postman Always Rings Twice* (1946), Giovanna's overt sexuality intrudes into and transgresses the domestic scenario.[6] The emphasis on Cora's lipstick and Giovanna's nail varnish works to reaffirm the cultural construction of femininity as located in the body, as image, a construction which is doubly enforced by the screen image. Although duly clad in her apron, Giovanna is neither cooking nor cleaning, but, sitting on the table on which she should presumably be working, she paints her nails and sings a love song to herself. A few scenes later her husband screws the top on her nail varnish, an act symbolic of the repression of her sexuality, complaining that while she lounges around, *his* place is in a mess.

It is precisely the fact that the cafe/business belongs to Bragana which places his wife inside the domestic space within which she cooks and cleans. Importantly, the private, domestic sphere here overlaps with the public world of business; there is a coincidence of domestic production for use (cooking for consumption by husband and wife) and profit-making production for exchange (cooking for consumption by cafe customers). This overlap is particularly insidious in that it serves to mask the fact that Giovanna's labour is unpaid; she works not just within domestic, but also within business space, in exchange for the security of a home, in other words, marriage. Giovanna performs this work reluctantly not simply because she finds Bragana distasteful, as the overt storyline would have us believe; as the narrative progresses we learn that she is quite happy to work once she is the owner of the cafe. For her these tasks are not devalorized 'women's work'; it is the effect of her marriage in concealing the exploitation of her labour power, which has made them obnoxious to her. Moreover, in his role of property/ business owner and husband, Bragana is in control both of her productive and reproductive labour power.

However, he cannot contain Giovanna's sexuality, just as he is unable to maintain his position of mastery over her labour power. The arrival of Gino acts as a catalyst and activates Giovanna's sexual, and later economic, desires, which the film then proceeds to explore in true *film noir* style. Giovanna is a *femme fatale* who invokes anxiety on both patriarchal and capitalist levels. Rather than suppressing her sexual desire, she acts on it, manipulating Bragana into retaining Gino as a worker so that she can have access to him. Female desire includes pleasure and recreation in its concerns, in opposition to the duty and procreation prescribed by patriarchy, a reductive circumscription with particular resonance in Roman Catholic Italy. The autonomy of a female desire which exceeds the patriarchal bounds of its male-centred definition poses a threat to the patriarchal order. In terms of capitalist relations of production, Giovanna is not content to remain dependent and oppressed in a hidden and exploitative pre-market position. She wishes not merely to be directly involved with the process of production for exchange, but aspires to the actual ownership of the means of production. What is more, there is evidence that she is highly competent in this field; her idea of hiring a band, for instance, brings in more business to the cafe. Particularly problematic for traditional power relations is the combination of autonomous female sexual desire and economic aspiration. Using the former to achieve the latter spells danger for the male position, expressed in *film noir* terms through the imprisonment and/or death of the male character.

In the world of the film, the only possible life for women outside the domestic sphere of marriage is that of prostitution, as we see in the case of the other, minor female character, a dancer/prostitute who lives on her own and with whom Gino has a brief encounter. Entry into the public sphere of production for exchange, particularly as owner of the means of production to whom the profits accrue, provides economic independence and is the way out of the madonna-whore trap. However, the narrative works in such a manner as to deny this as a viable process: it is notable, for instance, that Gino's desire for Giovanna fades when she takes over the cafe (in the overt story-line, this occurs simply because of Bragana's death). When he learns of the insurance policy which she can now cash in, he becomes positively hostile, despite the fact that there is no real reason to disbelieve Giovanna's claim that she was unaware of its existence until after her husband's murder. It is also notable that his desire for her rekindles when he realizes that she is pregnant with his child. His remark: 'Don't worry, from now on I'll take care of things' reveals his approval of her to be contingent on her dependency on him. As owner of the cafe, her autonomy presents too much of a threat. Her pregnancy ensures both that he will be in charge of the cafe and, moreover, that his child will inherit the business.

At this point it is worth examining Gino's position in relation to the modes of production exemplified by the film. With his mechanical skills, he has both skilled and unskilled labour power to sell for wages, and, in the case of his work at the cafe, for subsistence. His previous jobs include quarrying and unloading, carried out in various parts of Italy. He is therefore directly involved in the process of production for exchange, and can sell his labour power whenever he finds work, enjoying the life of a vagabond at the same time. This is in direct contrast with the woman's experience. For Giovanna, denied direct access to production for exchange, life outside marriage and on the open road means life 'on the streets', as she tells Gino at the beginning of their affair. In desperation she later agrees to leave with him, and they set off down the long country road away from the cafe to start afresh together.

However, she soon turns back: the problem is an economic one, and it is not enough merely to exchange an undesirable male partner for one who is desirable. In other words, this is not simply a love story. This scene offers a dramatic depiction of the gendered private vs public dichotomy which informs their lives. While a carefree Gino strides on ahead playing his harmonica, Giovanna stumbles awkwardly along behind him in high-heeled shoes that prevent her from walking properly. The outside world is not for her. Her attempt to insert herself into the public sphere of production is also problematized, most notably in its criminalized alignment with murder.

Giovanna's high heels, together with the wide-brimmed hat she sometimes wears, have connotations of glamour. In effect, her desire for financial independence and the concomitant choices this offers her in her personal life also involve issues of class. Bragana complains that she behaves like a '*signora baronessa*' (a lady baroness), rather than getting on with domestic chores. Giovanna herself tells Gino almost immediately 'I'm no cook', and later she says 'Do I look like a cook to you?', to which he replies 'You're no cook, you deserve to be a lady'. These remarks betray Giovanna's class ambitions, as well as bearing out the lower-class associations of tasks defined as domestic work. In the words of Ann Oakley, '[D]iscontent with the traditional role of housewife is seen as a middle-class prerogative' (Oakley, 1974, p. 61). Lindsay Anderson's comment on the unenthusiastic reception of his 'New Wave' realist film *This Sporting Life* in 1963 makes a similar implication: 'to label writers and films as "kitchen sink" is a very middle-class attitude'.[7] The leisured wife, argues Roberta Hamilton, became a middle-class status symbol during early capitalism as an indicator of the husband's worldly achievements, which meant that he was able to support a wife who did not work (Hamilton, 1980). These class associations are extended to 'domestic' tasks performed unrewarded as production for exchange in *Ossessione*.

In addition to connotations of class and gender, the traditional commonplace linking food and sex appears throughout *Ossessione* (a feature which is not as clearly developed either in Cain's *The Postman Always Rings Twice* or in the film of the same name). The problematized interplay of domestic space with sexual desire surfaces here. The association is set up at the beginning of the film with Gino's first words to Giovanna, 'Can one eat here?' She stops singing, looks up from her nails and cannot believe her eyes. Later in the film, when they have made love for the first time, he answers her question 'When did you realize I liked you?' with the words 'Straightaway, when I asked you for food'. Instead of waiting for his food at a table in the cafe, he dips his fingers into her pot to taste its contents, and then strips down to the waist before her admiring eyes. When he learns that Giovanna is married to 'that fat man', the reference to her cooking in his response is full of sexual innuendo: 'He's lucky to have a wife like you who cooks so well'. He will later express his loss of desire for her by refusing the food she offers him.

Food recurs in a sexual context when the implicitly homosexual Lo Spagnolo, with whom Gino has joined forces after leaving Giovanna, asks if he is hungry. Gino declines his offer to buy him food with the reply 'I'm not usually hungry when I travel, and besides, in the last few days I've had a lot to eat'. The sexual subtext here is Gino's rejection of Lo Spagnolo's advances – he has had plenty of sex, and, as the presence of a woman's stocking in his suitcase confirms, much to Lo Spagnolo's disgust, he is heterosexual. The association of food with heterosexual sex is reinforced at another stage when Gino eats food out of the hand of Anita, a prostitute. Giovanna herself uses food as a euphemism for prostitution when she explains to Gino that running away with him would mean 'going back to getting myself invited to dinner by men'.

With the introduction of Lo Spagnolo, domestic space itself is aligned with heterosexuality, and in particular made to correspond with a claustrophobic and dangerous association with women. Homosexuality, on the other hand, is idealized as an outward-looking, non-materialistic life of freedom on the open road. While Gino's heterosexual affair is seen to lose him his freedom (he is taken away by the police at the end of the film), the husband is portrayed as paying an even higher price. Bragana observes that 'Gino's always game for free food and drink'. It is Bragana who foots the bill, not just for Gino's food and drink, but for his affair with Giovanna for which he is also 'always game', and for which he has been induced to commit murder.

The homosexual relationship which Lo Spagnolo offers Gino is, moreover, in direct contrast with the Oedipal dynamic which is played out to its conclusion by the love triangle, and for which domestic space provides both context and goal. The relationship between the older Bragana and the younger Gino is that of father and son: Bragana refers to him with the terms 'son' and 'boy', treats him with some affection and provides him with a home, and Gino is dependent on him. Gino is thereby positioned as son in relation to the mother/wife, Giovanna, whom he desires. Like Oedipus, Gino both makes Giovanna/Jocasta pregnant and kills Bragana/Laius. In this Oedipal triangle, however, it is not the sexual/property desire of the male/'son', Gino, which is problematized, but that of the female/'mother', Giovanna. While the film as a whole carries out this problematization, it is underlined through reiteration in the idealized homosexual alternative which associates domestic space with a fatal, spiderwoman-type of femininity.

Although Gino's failing desire for Giovanna is rekindled at the end by her pregnancy, the avenging forces of patriarchy and capitalism are drawing near. With her death in a car accident, Giovanna forfeits not merely her life, but is also punished in her maternity as her unborn child dies inside her.[8] In this way the film can be seen to set up a matrilineal dynamic (Giovanna owns property and chooses the father of her future child) only to dismantle it.

MAKING ENDS MEET

In contrast to the lower middle-class couple in *Ossessione*, and the socio-sexual aspirations of its central female character, *Ladri di biciclette* (1948) shows a destitute working-class family whose young mother, Maria, is simply concerned with staying above the breadline. We first see her out of doors amongst a group of women collecting water in buckets which she then struggles to carry home. Her husband arrives to tell her that he has at last been offered a job sticking up posters for the council, steady work with over-time which will ensure the family's survival. However, his bicycle is still at the pawnshop, and must be redeemed by pawning the sheets if he is to be able to accept the job. The bicycle is stolen on his first day while he is up a ladder sticking up a Rita Hayworth poster (possibly a dig at the glamour and unreality of Hollywood escapism), and the remainder of the film sees Antonio and his young son out on the streets looking for it.

While much of the narrative of the love triangle in *Ossessione* is played out in the countryside, in a roadside cafe miles from anywhere and seemingly beyond any meaningful historical specificity, the family tragedy in *Ladri di biciclette* is set in Rome against the background of post-war unemployment and civil unrest. Furthermore, the dynamics of the family, made up of father, mother and two children, remain undisturbed by any intrusions of a personal nature, unlike those of the couple in the earlier film; and the relationship of the parents soon takes second place as the father-son pair moves to centre stage. With its portrayal of working-class suffering, its use of non-professional actors and its focus, not on a romantic love story, but on the unsuccessful search by father and son for the missing bicycle as the key to the family's economic survival, the film is considered as the apotheosis of Italian Neo-realism. Despite the fact that various non-realistic elements work to introduce melodrama into the film (the musical soundtrack, the pathos of the father-son relationship, devices creating suspense), its subject matter still serves to place it within the realist genre.

In this context the depiction of domestic space is made to seem an integral part of the miserable working-class scenario. While Maria does the house-work (cooking, cleaning and looking after a small child) in extremely basic conditions, the two male members of the household, Antonio and the young Bruno, go out to work. Bruno, who is only about eight years old, already has a job at a petrol station, and his identity as the 'little man' is expressed throughout the film in various ways. On Antonio's first, and only, day of work, father and son even look and behave the same; they wear the same overalls, and Bruno imitates his father by also putting his lunch in his top pocket. At one point during their fruitless search for the bicycle, Antonio confides all his hopes and fears to Bruno over a meagre snack in a cafe, and even gives him some wine to drink, rather than go home to Maria. Although Bruno is very young, this is still men's talk. Similarly, looking for the bicycle is a task for men, as Antonio enlists the help of a team of male friends who scour the market hoping to find parts of the bicycle for sale.

It is assumed throughout this 'realistic' portrayal that the only problem is the loss of the bicycle which prevents the family from earning its living, and to all intents and purposes this is true. Life at subsistence level rarely allows for the luxury of questioning traditional power relations, and there is no doubt that the family's life would have progressed happily had the main bread-winner not had the means to work taken from him. Nevertheless, the fixing of Maria within domestic space, and indeed the absence of any critique of the wider context of class, and especially gender, inequalities, appear fatalistic and thus supportive of the status quo. Even highlighting the exist-ence of unemployment merely seems to add to the fatalism in that the entire situation appears as an inevitable offshoot of that particular historical moment.

Maria's housework follows a traditional pattern of tasks, and the film does not allow for any development of her as a character beyond that of a stereo-typical housewife. Devaluation of the domestic sphere is apparent when one considers the relatively extensive and detailed attention which the activities of Antonio and Bruno outside the home receive. Theirs is the important story, not Maria's; her domestic work, and indeed character as a whole, remain in the background after the first few scenes, while the 'real' work of the menfolk, or their search for the means to perform it, together with each innuendo of feeling at every step of the way, takes filmic precedence. Even reading domestic space here as an idealized haven from which the male characters are reluctantly excluded does not obviate the fact that Maria plays a secondary role in the plot. Apart from two brief scenes when she visits a fortune-teller, from which we learn that she is superstitious, and when she appears at the club in tears after the theft has occurred, we are not allowed into her world, in which, it is implied, nothing of interest takes place. On the latter occasion she is promptly infantilized by Baiocco, the male friend who organizes the search for the bicycle; he calls her a child for crying, and sends her back home.

Maria's support act to the men's starring role involves servicing her two male wage earners. She fetches water, washes sheets, prepares their packed lunches, tightens Antonio's cap which he has been given as part of his uniform, looks after the baby, and generally provides a nurturing home environment. Another stereotypical instance of this type of domestic work occurs in the glimpse we get into the home of the male thief, whose mother furiously stirs the spaghetti as accompaniment to a vociferous defence of her son, while Antonio and a policeman search the flat for the stolen bicycle.

With Maria's visit to the fortune-teller, the Santona, one of the film's actual working female characters is introduced. However, although she seems to be making a fortune, her work, carried out in her own home, is decidedly low in status, as is indicated by Antonio's jocular disbelief when he realizes that this is where Maria has gone. The emasculating nature of his later spiral down into despair is underlined when he takes recourse to the Santona's professional talents. With his pursuit of the thief into a brothel, another low-status female profession is added. In other words, whether women work within domestic space as housewives, or whether they work indoors at socially ridiculed or stigmatized professions, the major features they have in common are those of marginalization and devalorization.

Ladri di saponette, made forty years later, picks up on the material concerns of *Ladri di biciclette*. While the historical setting of the inner film's reworking of the Neo-realist classic remains the same, the new Maria is no longer concerned merely with a life of subsistence and utility goods, but desires luxury items (a chandelier, no less). From existence on the breadline, the accent has shifted to consumption, and in particular to the spending power which the husband's work can generate for his non-working wife, whose domestic responsibility it is to take charge of the household shopping. It is significant that Maria in the 1989 film is lured back into the domestic space from which she strays, in the first instance by the promise of a steady income when Antonio starts a new job, and finally by trolley-loads of consumables which she can take home with her.

Representations of domestic space in *Ladri di saponette* are governed by the complex structure of the film, whose different levels not only intersect but also begin to invade each other. The title refers both to the film, in colour and set in the late 1980s, which we watch in its entirety, and to the inner black and white film, the spoof of *Ladri di biciclette* set in the early 1940s, which is being broadcast from a television studio in the presence of its director, Nichetti himself. Nichetti the director-as-character anxiously monitors the ill-timed interruption of his film by adverts, while the end-product is being watched by a family on the television screen in their living room. We, as the omniscient audience, are thus privy to this scene of family viewing, while at the same time we watch the inner film with them whenever it fills our screen. Unlike the family of viewers, however, we also have access to the events taking place in the broadcasting studio, and to the attempts of Nichetti-the-character to gain control of his film, which include him leaving the studio to enter the world of the film and of the adverts.

His problem is not simply that the adverts appear abruptly, when the characters are mid-sentence, but that some of the characters themselves begin to become aware of the interruptions, and, in the case of Nichetti and Bruno, even of what is going on in the sitting room of the family watching them on television.[9] After a power cut during an advert, affecting both the studio and the viewing family's home, the colour world of modern advertising intrudes into the black and white scenario of the 1940s film as a semi-nude model finds herself drowning in the river which Antonio is cycling past on his way home from work. Shortly afterwards Maria walks into the river, to emerge, grey and dripping, into the middle of an advert for washing powder. With the appearance of Heidi, the model, in the 1940s narrative, and Maria's subsequent disappearance from it, the plot deviates from its course. Before its screening on television, the storyline of the inner film involved Antonio's paralysis after a car crash, Maria's prostitution and the departure of the children to an orphanage. This tragic storyline is transformed into a comedy with a happy ending by, significantly, the intrusion of 1980s consumer culture.

This complex structure, together with the satirical approach, articulate the representation of domestic space in interesting ways. In particular, the stereotypical and limited way in which *Ladri di biciclette* deals with this area is thrown into relief by the fuller portrayal of Maria in Nichetti's parody of the Neo-realist classic. Unlike Maria I, who carries out her domestic work as a matter of course, Maria II sings and dances in the theatre, using the famous bicycle, rather significantly, to get to rehearsals. She is even seen practising her song routine in church while the rest of the congregation sings hymns and Antonio kneels in the first pew, weeping. Her subversiveness extends beyond leaving domestic space for the public world of the stage, to carry out what were, for the time in Italy, still rather risqué activities, and then proceeding to rehearse these in church during mass.

The way in which she deals with her housework (cooking, cleaning and childcare) is also portrayed as contrary to the norm in that she is extremely negligent, not least in the area of childcare. While she is on stage rehearsing, her baby crawls around the floor unsupervised, putting his fingers into electric sockets to the sound of sizzling. On one occasion his mother leaves without him, returning when she realizes she has left him behind. At home he plays under the table with a huge carving knife, sucks on a gas pipe and puts the end of an electric lead into his mouth. This child neglect, however comically portrayed, would seem to signal the mother's rejection of her role of domestic, self-sacrificing womanhood in favour of a more glamorous femininity on the stage. As far as cooking and cleaning are concerned, Maria II fares little better, leaving Bruno, the young boy, to cook the cabbage, while the flat remains uncleaned and she slams doors in Antonio's face when he complains. However, all this subversiveness is contingent on her husband's unemployment. Once Antonio starts work in the glass factory, she becomes a model housewife, leaving her singing and dancing behind her once and for all to come home and wash the children, clean the flat and prepare a meal for him to come home to at the end of his first day at work. In the last resort, then, her subversiveness is defused and she is successfully recuperated for domestic space.

With Maria's entry into the 1980s world of colour television commercials, and the concomitant intersection of different historical periods, another dimension is added to the Neo-realist expression of domestic space. The impoverished 1940s housewife is now shown experiencing another way of life, a life of using her talents as singer and dancer outside the domestic sphere, but this time in the lucrative field of advertising. Her modern existence allows her a life of colourful consumption which she does not wish to leave. Most importantly, the fact that she can now sell her labour power empowers her as an active participant in the market. Meanwhile Heidi, the glamorous, self-possessed model who is ensconced in Maria's black and white home, is only too happy to return to the modern world. The juxtaposition of a 1940s housewife with a 1980s working model, and other working female characters such as Clara, the television producer, serves to highlight the development of possibilities for women as the century progressed. However, pleasure in consumerism unites Heidi and Maria as the latter returns to the Neo-realist world of scarcity with numerous supermarket trolleys laden with consumables, which Heidi unpacks. For the second time spending power has brought Maria back into the domestic sphere, but on this occasion it is likely that she herself has earned the money working in television commercials (although it is possible that Nichetti, who accompanies her back into the black and white film, may have paid for the mountains of food and drink in order to persuade her to return).

The depiction of the viewing family's sitting room offers a further comparison in terms of both historical period and class in relation to domestic space. In this modern middle-class family only the husband goes out to work, while his pregnant wife looks after their two children and generally does the housework. The major difference between her world and that of the 1940s *Ladri di saponette* and the original *Ladri di biciclette* is that of levels of spending power. The actual role of the married woman within domestic space has not changed. While the modern husband sits reading his newspaper after a day's work, the wife and mother busies herself round the house and keeps an eye on the children. In other words, the prosperity of the 1980s has not perceptibly changed the domestic–public space divide. If anything, it has reinforced it (although we do not see the home lives of Heidi and Clara, and the other women working outside the domestic sphere).

VIEWING DOMESTIC SPACE

The extra dimension provided by the depiction of the viewing family in *Ladri di saponette* raises issues of spectatorship which it is useful to address as regards the three films we have discussed. Of particular interest is the relation of the female spectator both to the representation of domestic space and to the female characters who inhabit it. Questions which could be asked are: 'How might the viewing practices relevant to each of these films affect the female spectator's perception of the way in which domestic space is portrayed?', 'Is the female spectator offered a choice as far as her interpretation of the portrayal of domestic space is concerned?', 'Can she identify with the female characters in any way, and if so, does identification only take place with those characters which approximate to the category of Hollywood stars?' and 'Does the opposite process, that of pleasurable non-identification and distancing take place in the case of female characters whose lives correspond to the dreary, unglamorous model of realist representation?'

Without embarking on a survey of actual female spectators, such as that carried out by Jackie Stacey in *Star Gazing* (1994), any attempt to answer these questions must necessarily remain production- rather than consumption-oriented. In other words, a theoretical speculation as to the various types of spectator position which might be generated by the text must supersede an empirical approach which would analyse the ways in which spectators have in reality decoded these filmic representations of domestic space.

As *Ladri di saponette* shows, viewing at home can be a fragmented process. These viewers are of course themselves also characters in the film, and Nichetti here offers an insight into a director's perception of the consumption of his film. The female spectator in the film is not alone, and, moreover, does not remain seated because she is performing domestic tasks at the same time. This spectator also continues to talk in monologues to her taciturn husband, her unresponsive children, and, on the phone, to her mother, especially during the commercial breaks which also fragment the film. She appears to become fully involved with the film only at its end, with the romantic reunion between Maria and Antonio, which reduces her to tears, much to her husband's scorn. Maria's domestic chores, which are sharply satirized in the film, hold little interest for her, presumably because they are too familiar, while romance with her husband is not. Her emotional reaction to Maria's return to her original domestic space, however, would seem to affirm Maria's choice of family and home over a career in commercials. The gendered contrast in viewing pleasures comes to the fore here. Whereas she weeps, her husband is uninterested in the film, only taking note when the semi-naked model appears on screen. At this point he actually gets up from the sofa and speaks, referring transparently to her nudity with the remark 'Doesn't she act well?' This contrasts sharply with the bustling, pregnant female spectator's overt disinterest in (or perhaps denial of) glamorous femininity. Her emotional response to the final kiss between the Italian Maria and Antonio is not matched by any sense of identification, or projected desire, in relation to the semi-nude, Northern European Heidi, or to Maria in her errant phases.

This brings us to the question of how female spectators might respond to the female characters in each of the films, and, specifically, to the portrayal of these characters in terms of domestic space. The visuality of female characters on screen is particularly significant for the female, rather than male, spectator, in the cultural context of femininity itself as image. She may also select or reject specific images. The spectator/wife in *Ladri di saponette* accepts images of domestic femininity, particularly when laced with romance (a lethal patriarchal mix), and she dismisses the images of glamorous blonde femininity which draw her husband out of his seat to the screen. The implication here for the consumption of images relating to domestic space in the film is that choices are made by the fictional spectators and by Maria. Maria opts initially for the glamour of performance rather than for domestic routine, but reverts to the latter, while the spectator/wife condones her reversion/ recuperation. As far as the female spectator outside the film is concerned, the thread of satire running through both the inner and outer films of *Ladri di saponette*, in conjunction with the film's complex structure, means that she is made more aware of choices than would otherwise be the case.

Ladri di biciclette, on the other hand, offers no such overt choices, its classic realist style in complete contrast with its 1989 spoof. We see little of Maria I, and in order even to register her subsequent absence the female spectator would need to inform her viewing of the film with a conscious awareness of the issues concerning domestic space, notably the hidden nature of unpaid labour power discussed earlier. The character of Giovanna in *Ossessione*, with her subversive sexual and economic desires, raises different questions of spectator identification. The portrayal of Giovanna illustrates that a female character, or indeed any character, is not necessarily mono-lithic. In other words, it is incorrect to talk in terms of 'character' as a seamless identity, since the same character may be represented differently, and even in conflicting ways, on separate occasions. As a consequence, the processes of identification may change throughout the film. Giovanna can be seen to move between positions of power (on the *film noir* side) and of pathos (her realist side).

As *femme fatale*, or spiderwoman (particularly in the garage scene when she draws Gino to her immediately prior to Bragana's murder), she may invite the positive identification which will be accorded to many of the power-ful female characters who will follow her when *film noir* takes off as a genre. On the other hand, in the classic realist scene when, at the end of a hard day's work at the cafe, she is rejected by Gino, who refuses to eat with her, we watch her sit alone surrounded by dirty dishes, eating out of a saucepan and reading a newspaper until she nods off. The poignancy of this scene, which contrasts sharply with her previous power positions, stimulates a different type of identification.

On the occasion of the first showing of the film which Visconti himself attended, he recalls 'I was standing at the back of the projection room, and I could see the scandalized reaction of all those fur-coated ladies: "How disgusting", they were saying' (Tonetti, 1987, p. 30). The choice of a main-stream Italian cinema star, Clara Calamai (the leading female star of the Italian studio, Cinecittà), for the part of Giovanna, was dictated by the hope that 'she would give us a veneer of respectability in the eyes of the Fascist authorities' (De Santis in Servadio, 1982, p. 77). However, this does not seem to have had the desired effect on these particular female spectators; or rather, to have offended bourgeois sensibilities can perhaps be regarded as a positive outcome, as Visconti himself in fact believed.

Stardom and female spectatorship are inextricably linked, and particular stars attract a faithful following. It is tempting to speculate that in the period of the film's release, Clara Calamai's star identity would in some way have helped to validate her portrayal of subversive desires to go beyond the traditional female relation to the domestic sphere, not least in the light of her own lower-class origins. As Stacey puts it, '[Hollywood] stars function as role models encouraging desire for female attractiveness, attachment to a man and *possession of property'* (Stacey, 1994, p. 154, emphasis added). For the feminist spectator of the 1990s, *Ossessione's* classic *film noir* problematization of female desire for economic independence, and for a radically different relation to domestic space, as desire fulfillable only through murder, cannot fail to appear as a transparent patriarchal ruse.

This study of domestic space in films from pre- and post-boom Italy has attempted to show how the differing relation of female characters to that space is contingent on the historical and socioeconomic context of the film's production, a context which can also be seen to interface with varying cinematic practices. In the desolate, rural, early 1940s Italy of *Ossessione*, female economic and sexual desire combine to briefly empower the female character in the market through ownership of the means of production and reproduction, a subversion of the traditional female relation to domestic space which is punished. In the contrasting, urban *Ladri di biciclette*, we see an impoverished but not disaffected housewife in the historical context of the immediate post-war years of unemployment in Italy. In market terms, she has no consumer power, which, together with her restriction to the domestic sphere, translates into a lack of narrative presence and power, as the film follows the attempt of the male wage earners of the family to regain the means to employment in the public sector. Nichetti's satire of *Ladri di biciclette* in the inner film of *Ladri di saponette* transforms Maria's relation to domestic space in ways which all relate to the market in terms of consumption and active participation. However, it is significant that, alongside the 1980s Maria and her autonomous position in the market, the traditional relation of women to domestic space continues to exist, namely in the form of the female spectator of the outer film.

NOTES

1   I should like to thank Zygmunt Barański and Barbara Einhorn for their constructive comments on an earlier draft of this chapter.
2   Mussolini walked out of the première of *Ossessione*, saying 'This is not Italy', and the film was banned in some towns. It was also severely criticized by the *Centro Cattolico Cinematografo* and the press (Buss, 1989, p. 150).
3   In the American version, *The Postman Always Rings Twice* of 1946, Frank, the vagabond, is given a voice-over, and most of the narrative is in the form of a flash-back seen from his point of view as he is about to be taken to the electric chair. The use of voice-over and flash-back is characteristic of *film noir*, even if, in a film like *Double Indemnity*, being in possession of the voice-over is no guarantee of an omniscient power position.

4 The strong element of *film noir* is due to the fact that the film is based on James M. Cain's *The Postman Always Rings Twice* (1934), one of a trio of crime thriller novels to be made into American *film noir* classics (*Double Indemnity* (1944), *Mildred Pierce* (1945) and *The Postman Always Rings Twice* (1946)). In his depiction of crime, Cain's work has been characterized as stark realism. However, once on screen a darker side emerged, particularly regarding the central female characters, and also in the visual play of shadow which gave the genre its name.

5 One example is Phyllis in *Double Indemnity*. Alternatively, as in the case of *Mildred Pierce*, the female character is recuperated for patriarchy and re-consigned to domestic space at the film's closure. Mildred has moved from being a kitchen-bound housewife with the beginnings of a cottage industry (she bakes cakes at home for sale) to owning a restaurant chain, a transition which cannot be portrayed as viable.

6 Cora's introduction, skimpily-dressed, into the domestic space of the film also takes place fetishistically; she is preceded into shot by her lipstick rolling across the floor to Frank's feet at their first encounter, and the lipstick is also the last we see of her as it rolls out of her dead hand.

7 *Hollywood U.K.: British Cinema in the 1960's*, part 1 'Northern Lights', BBC Documentary.

8 In a similar way, and for the same reasons, in *Mildred Pierce* Mildred's young daughter falls fatally ill with pneumonia just as she is setting up her restaurant business, and while she is away with Monty, her business associate/lover.

9 This effect was heightened when the entire film was shown on Channel 4 television in Britain, which interspersed its own advertising.

BIBLIOGRAPHY

Buss, Robin (1989), *Italian Films*, London: Batsford.

Hamilton, Roberta (1980), *The Liberation of Women: A Study of Patriarchy and Capitalism*, London: Allen & Unwin.

Malos, Ellen (1980), *The Politics of Housework*, London: Allison & Busby.

Oakley, Ann (1974), *The Sociology of Housework*, London: Martin Robertson.

Servadio, Gaia (1982), *Luchino Visconti: A Biography*, London: Weidenfeld & Nicolson.

Stacey, Jackie (1994), *Star Gazing: Hollywood Cinema and Female Spectatorship*, London: Routledge.

Tonetti, Claretta (1987), *Luchino Visconti*, London: Columbus Books.

FILMOGRAPHY

Anderson, Lindsay (1963), *This Sporting Life*.

Curtiz, Michael (1945), *Mildred Pierce*.

De Sica, Vittorio (1948), *Ladri di biciclette / Bicycle Thieves*.

Ford, John (1962), *The Man Who Shot Liberty Valance*.

Garnett, Tay (1946), *The Postman Always Rings Twice*.

Nichetti, Maurizio (1989), *Ladri di saponette / Icicle Thieves*.

Visconti, Luchino (1942), *Ossessione / Obsession*.

Wilder, Billy (1944), *Double Indemnity*.

6. Chinese Women and Chinese Film: Problems with History and Feminism

Stephanie Donald

In this chapter I address the question of representation in recent Chinese film. I focus on women: women as directors and women as filmed characters. My argument is, briefly, that the post-Mao – arguably post-ideological – period in Chinese history has seen the emergence of a complex aesthetic relationship between film-makers and their immediate historical experience. Filmed representations of that experience reveal tensions and ironies which are characteristic of the conflicts arising from the recent traumatic shift from revolutionary romanticism through *tansuo* (experimental film-making) to market-led internationalism on the big screen.

I look closely at two films from the mid-1980s, *Yellow Earth* and *Sacrifice of Youth*. For those readers who have not seen these films I will provide plot synopses, but of course I cannot do justice to the visual brilliance of either film. I am working within the discipline of film studies, and so I approach my investigation armed with certain theoretical mores. For the purposes of this collection, an interdisciplinary project aimed at a varied readership, I have tried to keep theoretical underpinning to a minimum. This may sometimes leave my arguments a little unguarded and unfinished. I would ask the reader then to take the next few pages as a *relaxed* foray into film analysis and as a spur to seek out and view the films themselves.

FILMS AND CRITICS

Yellow Earth was made in 1984 by Chen Kaige, and *Sacrifice of Youth* in 1985 by Zhang Nuanxin. Chen is a highly successful male director whose work is internationally acclaimed. He belongs to the group of film-makers known collectively as the Fifth Generation. Zhang Nuanxin is a Fourth Generation woman director who has been working since the early 1960s. She has also been a director of the Beijing Film Academy. Her critical success in the

1980s and 1990s is due to her facility in meshing her experience with the new skills and styles of a younger generation of film-makers. The labels-by-generation are not uncontested categories but they are a useful marker of change and development in the Chinese film industry. The Fourth Generation are extremely interesting as their training and careers have spanned a period of thirty years. They were brought up in a time when revolutionary realism was sacrosanct in film aesthetics, their work was interrupted by the 'life-over-art' fervour of the Cultural Revolution, and during the 1980s their experience, combined with a willingness to learn from the inspiration of younger colleagues, contributed in no small measure to the revival of the Chinese film industry.

The Fifth Generation consists of a small group of film-makers who graduated from the reopened Beijing Film Academy in 1982. They had been selected in the late 1970s to attend courses in acting, directing, cinematography and screen-writing. Most of these new film-makers were urblings – educated youth who had participated in the early years of the Cultural Revolution and then in 1967–8 were sent to the agricultural hinterlands to do manual labour. Many of them had missed much of their secondary schooling and tertiary education, in the form of film training, came late. Given the extraordinary emotional and artistic maturity of their early films (*One and Eight, The Big Parade, Yellow Earth, Bloody Morning, Red Sorghum*), this unorthodox progression seems to have done more good than harm.

In order to discuss the two films in a disciplinary context I have turned to the work of two of the most exciting cultural critics dealing with Chinese film, Rey Chow and Esther Yau. Both are of Chinese origin, Hong Kong and Han Chinese respectively. This is relevant as both writers, now working in America, are keen to state their subjectivities within their writing. The issue of subjectivity is also central to the way in which discourses of feminism will be addressed in this discussion. I have isolated two main theoretical themes that are common to the writings of both Chow and Yau, authenticity and narcissism. Chow tends to address these concepts directly, whereas Yau is more concerned with some of their implications. My principal observation is that the two are closely related, to the extent that the representation of the Other woman/women may be (perhaps always) a coded address to the Self.

The twin themes are applied in a cross-cultural context. Narcissism is the tendency for one to seek characteristics in the Other, the foreign, the different, which either complement oneself or which represent an ideal of something we want but will not admit into our own experience. For instance Chow has cited Julia Kristeva's *On Chinese Women* as an example of an internal argument being projected onto an international metaphor – here China, the feminine, the Oriental:

Even though Kristeva sees China in an interesting and, indeed, 'sympathetic' way, there is nothing in her arguments as such that cannot be said without 'China'. What she proposes is not so much learning a lesson from a different culture as a different method of reading from within the West. (Chow, 1991, p. 7)

This relationship, which is close to that between colonizer and colonized, may also be observed *within* a particular national experience. Yau suggests that the Han Chinese culture has just this narcissism in its aesthetic interactions with non-Han minority peoples within its political borders.

Authenticity operates as a twin concept in this process of projection and appropriation. The other culture is squeezed into a discourse of authenticity. Thus it becomes observable from the outside in the terms of the observer. Its reality is unchanging, its meanings are bound into the epistemological prejudices of the outsider, and it can only speak in a voice recognizable within the imposed identity. Furthermore, none of this may be questioned as the 'authentic' is given a moral overtone which legitimizes the narcissism of the observer.

Yau reads China from without whilst engaging with a kind of 'colonial discourse' within. In her work on Chinese film she notes that unacknowledged narcissism is here at the point of production and reception. When a film concerns the non-Han peoples the authorial voice is unmistakably Chinese, as in Han/dominant culture, and the narrative turns on representations of minority peoples which accommodate the desires and absences in the lives of the Han audience. Unsurprisingly perhaps it is the feminine attributes of these peoples that are elaborated, exaggerated and exploited. This hardly disguised voyeurism works through a discourse of nature and authenticity to complete the narcissistic self-image of dominant Chinese-ness. It is the relationship between narcissism and authenticity which emerges in the films and their reception, by critics and by domestic and international audiences, which I suggest confuses and complicates the imagined relationship between women in different places and occupying different roles in the production and consumption of contemporary film.

THE NEW CONTEMPORARIES

On 16 April 1994 the *South China Morning Post* reported that

all films made on the mainland, including Hong Kong co-productions, will now have to be censored and processed in China by the central authorities before being allowed out of the country or distributed inside. ... The seven directors (include) Tian Zhuangzhuang [maker of *The Blue Kite*]. The ban covers features, short films, music videos and even advertisements. A directive was sent from the ministry

[Ministry of Radio, Film and Television] to China's 16 official film studios, plus film-processing laboratories, equipment hire companies and other film-related concerns, forbidding any contact with the seven.[1]

This kind of action demonstrates on the part of the current Chinese Government a will to achieve total control over the symbolic order. Certain individual imaginations are stifled and the supposed benefit of a market economy – diversity – is sacrificed to political considerations. However, banned films and politically suspect directors tend to assume a moral authority, an authenticity, in the eyes of a select international spectatorship. When discussing recent Chinese film from an international perspective it is therefore safer to avoid questions of effect and to look at the structure of the film itself. We cannot prove, and maybe we cannot even guess, the extent of a particular film's effect across the Chinese audience. Some films enjoy only *samizdat* distribution and others are under-distributed and under-marketed. Furthermore, where a film represents immediate national memories as a way of engaging with the present, one audience might mistake irony for authenticity whilst another will avoid a film that undermines the very roots of revolutionary narcissism. I believe that *Sacrifice of Youth* falls into the first category, and *Yellow Earth* into the second.

PROBLEMS WITH HISTORY

The historical status of the films under discussion lies mainly in the fact that they were produced post-Mao. They emerged from the memory of the Cultural Revolution and as an alternative to, or more precisely a progression from, the 'wound' films of the late 1970s when the melodramatic certainties of Socialist Realism[2] were simply re-employed with new villains and villainesses to provide a catharsis for the people.

In view of the political and historical scepticism apparent in much recent Chinese film it is perhaps ironic that the symbolic power of cinema carried much weight in the cultural policy of post-Liberation China. The nexus of historical fact, national memory and cultural practice underlined the Maoist emphasis on a close, one-directional association between life and art, theory and practice – first outlined by Mao at the Yenan talks of 1942. This interaction has now been taken up as a point of contestation, and in *Yellow Earth* it is used to devastating ironic effect. This aesthetic unstitching was taking place in a wider period of disintegration. Previously the Government had been at pains to present the aims of economic policy as dependent on ideological objectives. This certainty was stretched to breaking point in the early years of reform as economic efficiency began to take precedence over philosophical purity in the maintenance of Communist Party power. As Gordon White has said:

> the project of market-orientated reform, while clearly a response to glaring deficiencies in the previous economic system, was given particularly powerful impetus as a response to problems caused by China's previous *political* experience. In essence, the economic reforms were an attempt to re-establish the hegemonic authority of the Communist Party on a different basis: by abandoning the Maoist notion of development as a political struggle and attempting to accelerate economic development and increase the material welfare of the population more rapidly. Success in the latter, it was hoped, would provide a new form of legitimacy for the regime. (White, 1993, p. 11)

The link between economic improvements and political legitimacy has been undermined by popular unrest. Some of the causes of this unrest can be seen in films of the early 1980s when the aesthetic of Socialist Realism no longer represented Chinese experience. Instead, the traumatic discovery of economic and aesthetic modernity replaced the Revolution in the nation's imagination.

IRONIZING THE PAST

Yellow Earth is set in 1938. An Eighth Route Army soldier, Gu Qing, has been sent from the Communist headquarters in Yenan to collect authentic peasant tunes. These are to be taken and used for new songs, the songs of liberation and revolution. He arrives in a poor farming village and is billeted with a local family. The family is small, a father, his thirteen year old daughter Cuiqiao and her younger brother Hanhan. They live in a cave, and the domestic scenes are unsurprisingly dark and oppressive. By contrast the external shots are breathtakingly wide and open. A harsh landscape of mountains and rocky fields is framed by the dictates of its own extent and by the enormity of a cold sky. The anthropocentric framing of most earlier Chinese films is abandoned and the result is magnificent and terrifyingly cruel. In *Yellow Earth* the landscape is an unyielding contributor to the suffering of the people.

The soldier lives and works with the family and tries to make them sing. However, their songs are *ku*, bitter, and they will only sing them at moments of appropriate misery. The soldier is persistent and his example and enthusiasm for change begin to inspire the children. When Cuiqiao discovers that she is to be married off to an older man, she decides to run away and join the army. Gu Qing refuses to take her with him but promises to return for her once he has obtained the necessary permission. He does come back but he is too late. Following her marriage and nuptial rape Cuiqiao has tried to escape by boat down the Yellow River. She is swept away and drowns, cut off in mid-phrase as she sings one of Gu Qing's new songs to an old tune.

In the film *Yellow Earth* the conflict between tradition, revolution and modernity, underlaid by the memory of resistance to external negativity and internal oppression, is made clear. In one scene the girl peasant Cuiqiao is asking the Communist soldier, Gu Qing, to take her with him to join the army at Yenan. The soldier refuses. Cuiqiao sighs, knowing that she is to be married off in April and that the soldier is unlikely to return in time to save her from her traditional fate as a woman. The scene ends with the soldier looking into the heroic Communist future, signalling to the audience that this moment, 1938, is the cusp of history.

If we look to him as the personification of the ideal future we will collaborate in this Socialist Realist gaze and our identities will merge with the ungendered revolutionary present. All will be well. Cuiqiao looks down and then up into his face – but as she moves away (the clearest and most effective version only remains in an early cut, removed from the approved version for distribution) she sings a song bewailing her destiny in which she sees nothing but nostalgia for a future that never came to pass. The soldier is the Revolution, Cuiqiao is the victim of tradition – both that which dictates village mores and that which constrains the soldier to go back and ask permission for her to join before her pressing need to escape can be answered.

It is also perhaps tradition that confines her to articulating the misery of her condition through bitter songs rather than through a direct heart to heart with the soldier himself. And the modern gaze inserts yet more conflict into this exemplary moment of history. For Chen Kaige knows that the audience of 1984 will not collude with the soldier's gaze into the horizon.[3] They have already lived through his horizon and are on their way to another: 'Socialist Capitalism with Chinese characteristics'[4] as President Jiang Zemin has termed it. Moreover Cuiqiao, the archetypal poor peasant, is traditionally the backbone of the Chinese Communist Party's success, but here she is torn between faith and fatalism. Modernity – through the eye of Chen Kaige's direction – is casting a look of ironic disbelief on the soldier, a contemporary shrug in which the audience share as they fail to follow his gaze off screen as though it were their own. The soldier has come too early for Cuiqiao and too late for 1984.

Yet Cuiqiao is not written into the present either. She is aware of her fate as a female in patriarchy, but ready for her revolutionary role in defence of her class and her country – she is also operating in the film as the authentic anchor of Chinese suffering. When she finally drowns in the Yellow River, singing the Communist song that she has learnt from the soldier, her death is in one way an heroic, revolutionary exit, in another a traditional end for the unconventional woman. Director, soldier and audience have abandoned her to her fate. Or perhaps we could say that the authenticity of her suffering in life and death is represented in the film partly to expose the narcissistic relationship between the Chinese Communist Party and the peasantry. But of course that leaves open the question of the director's own interaction with Cuiqiao, the figment of that history, and finally of our own position as members of the international audience.

Yau has argued that *Yellow Earth's* aesthetic success is partly due to the use of Taoist discontinuity to disrupt the narrative flow, and presumably to thus allow the insertion of readership and modern reflexivity into the text (Yau, 1987, p. 22–33). In this reading Taoist silences are responsible for the subversive possibilities of the film. Chow has made the counter-argument that Taoism has always been complicit in the patriarchy of Confucian traditions – acting as a spiritual excuse for female passivity – and that the Taoist silences in *Yellow Earth* actually preserve the patriarchal narration of the film in moments of inarticulacy and make it seem natural (Chow, 1990, p. 82–109). I would add that these perspectives are not contradictory, that the subversion in the film's silence is aimed not at patriarchy but at the smaller target of Socialist Realism. The film ironizes the collective gaze into an ideal future but sets up a new collective narcissism where history – and women as objects of fantasy within that history – is targeted for appropriation by the contemporary modern Chinese male. It is an inescapable sadness that Cuiqiao is the first in a string of suicidal women in Fifth Generation films.

PROBLEMS OF FEMINISM

Rey Chow's work is always aware of the dichotomies of post-colonial existence. Resisting a hostile symbolic order does not simply mean that a single oppositional structure will form as a result. She points out that the tendency for women in the Third World to be either spoken for through the liberatory voices of the indigenous male culture or to be tied into a kind of *national* feminism prevents women, and groups of women, from challenging the very particular and very familiar source of their disadvantage – patriarchy thinly disguised as tradition and authenticity.

> The attempts to champion a 'Chinese Feminism' on the part of some feminist Chinese scholars do not really create avenues for modern Chinese women to come forth on their own terms, but rather compound deep-rooted patriarchal thinking to which 'woman' is now added as the latest proof of, once again, the continuity and persistence of a pure, indigenous 'tradition'. For Chinese women who go through the most mundane parts of their lives with the knowledge that it is precisely this

notion of an 'originary' Chinese tradition to which they cannot cling, the advocacy of a 'Chinese Feminism' in a nativist sense is exclusionary in nature. What it excludes are their lived relations to Westernization and the role played by these relations, however contradictory, in their subject positions. (Chow, 1991, p. 97)

Esther Yau extends this problematic of feminism into a painful understanding of racism within the Chinese territories. She argues that when China represents itself as the Other of the West it does so to fuel a narcissistic drive for competitive power and economic influence. In this pursuit, or rather this construction of the motivations of recent and present history, China refuses to acknowledge any internal differences that might challenge the integrity of its oppositional subjectivity.

This newly proffered *authenticity* is acute in the Chinese context of post-ideology. As China reinvents its Revolution and its certainties become subject to the wavering needs of the economy, a hankering after authenticity appears – which utilizes revolutionary and pre-revolutionary myth for its raw material.

SACRIFICE AND MINORITY

Sacrifice of Youth tries to tackle the problems of cross-cultural representation. A Han director, Zhang Nuanxin, who based her script on the semi-autobiographical novel of another Han woman, Zhang Manling, has produced a sympathetic and very beautiful portrait of the Dai people.

The story of *Sacrifice of Youth* concerns an urbling, Li Chun. Whilst a teenage girl she is sent to the countryside, to a Dai village. The Dai are one of the minority peoples living on the peripheries of Chinese territory. Li Chun is a Han, the dominant group in China, and the film traces her experience of living within a different culture that is yet Chinese – in terms of geographical and political influence. Although she is assimilated on one level – she assumes Dai clothes and is wooed by a Dai man – her difference is inescapable. In fact her departure is precipitated by the sexual interest of the Dai 'brother', and she returns only to say farewell to Ya, the old lady who has cared for her during her time in the village.

As Esther Yau has recorded, some of the representational practices in the film are a direct attempt to undercut the ethnographic films of the years of Mao and Socialist Realism when Han, and especially Party, hegemony meant that the minority voice was always shown on a teleological journey towards Han-led liberation.[5] Non-Han characters were played by Han actors and actresses, there was very little, if any, dialogue in the regional language, and the characters were valorized according to how completely they assimilated themselves into the Communist Party project of a homogeneous national identity.

The films tended, as have most Chinese films since the 1920s, towards melo-drama and spectacle.[6]

Zhang Nuanxin tried to subvert the genre and thus align her work to that of contemporary 1980s film-makers. Her attempt is marked with ambiguity as she struggles to divorce sexuality from its accepted signs in a puritanical Han culture. Dru Gladney has described the importance of minority women's bodies in Han culture as a visual displacement of sexual desire. He argues that they also provide a 'national style' and 'metaphorical resource' for cultural production that would otherwise struggle to represent the Han to themselves. One of the most common settings for this national resource is the nude bathing scene which has been repeated across China in many unlikely settings (includ-ing murals at the Beijing International Airport – which were removed after outraged complaints from minority representatives). 'The image of Dai (Thai) and other minority women bathing in the river has become a *leit-motiv* for ethnic sensuality and often appears in stylized images throughout China, particularly on large murals in restaurants and public spaces' (Gladney 1994, p. 103).

Zhang's own bathing scene, of Dai girls slipping their dresses off and gliding out into the river, is transgressive in so far as a Han girl spectates on screen, and regrets that she cannot participate in the swimming. Moreover, by the end of the scene her voice-over has informed us that she will soon learn to swim naked herself. The gaze of the Han spectator cannot indulge its de-sire without acknowledging the sexual potential of the Han girl. Yet once again sexual potential is firmly located in the minority spectacle. Here a kind of mimicry in reverse is at work. The Han girl imitates the dress and habits of the Dai, but can finally only seek recuperation into her former social identity. She leaves her on-screen sexual potential back in the river.

Zhang's cinematography also veers away from established practices of Socialist Realism. Yau observes that 'She makes a number of experiments new for Chinese film practices, including shooting in sync sound, setting up elaborate long takes, filming in extremely low light situations, and handling in an unusually sensitive way what can be a monotonous green colour in that subtropical environment' (Yau, 1989, p. 129).

The story from which the script is taken is called *Such a Beautiful Place* and the film slips rather easily into voyeuristic meditations on the endearing beauty of the Other within, the Dai – who are apparently all kind and gentle (except her adoptive Dai brother and admirer who is seen to get violent when drunk and rejected – and who – her (Han) voice-over informs us – was more like a Min) and who work hard, sing and dance and never offer an opinion on their contemporary situation. Any commentary is always given by Li Chun, the Han visitor, or by Ren Ju, her Han boyfriend who is posted in a neighbouring village.

Authenticity is achieved in stylistically contrasting but effectively compatible ways. The visual style is painterly, pandering to the narcissistic projection of the minority living picturesquely in colourful simplicity. However, there is a narrational emphasis on the ordinary and the everyday – no-one looks into a Socialist Realist horizon – and the acting is persuasively unmelodramatic. The Dai are played by Dai (but by local found amateurs rather than by professionals). Although, as have been most Chinese films, it is an adaptation of a written text, the spoken text does not dominate the visual narration. (Although I would claim that the voice-over operates as a hegemonic interpretative device which serves Han perceptions to the detriment of the power of the visual narrative.)

Zhang's reforms of the minority film genre, however, are problematic. Her respect for an authentic minority tradition does challenge the earlier constructions of minority people as those who need to learn from the Han. Yet it also leads her to present a closed representation of the Dai people, which denies that they have any reality beyond an outsider's perception of their traditions. In *Sacrifice of Youth*, the authenticity of the Dai is insisted upon – their purity, political transparency, natural decency, collective consciousness inspired not by an external ideal but grounded in an eternal materiality of daily life.

Yau has quoted Zhang saying that the Dai civilization is 'that which is primitive, sincere, befitting to human nature' whilst the Han is 'that modern, partly hypocritical, and distorting to human nature' and she claims that this tension is what turns Li Chun's life into tragedy (Yau, 1989, p. 129). Zhang does not acknowledge that her Han reading of both Han and Dai essential characteristics is also responsible for Li Chun's reading of her own situation, which is what enables the narration of the story of the Han girl to achieve its self-reflexive poignancy. She is from the dominant culture but she has no home. Her relationships with the other Han in the area are informed by political awareness and by the drive to return to the public arena of political life which lies in the urban heartlands. Any desire to remain in the seeming paradise of *Such a Beautiful Place* is tempered by their understanding of the difference between the present and the future – and of course the determinations of the past.

Li Chun is telling her story in flash-back and it is at the end of the film that we realize how much the film-maker has privileged the Han perspective on this story. Once Li Chun leaves to become a teacher we do not see the village again after the burial of Ya, her adoptive Dai grandmother, several scenes earlier. It is as though the emphasis on Dai continuity can only be seen through the mediation of a Han viewpoint and in this case the unhappiness of Li Chun's own experience is too painful to exist beside the continued paradise of that beautiful place. Moreover, without her there the Dai might start speaking their own stories and the paradise could well peel away into just another contemporary tale of post-Cultural Revolution confusion and discontent.

CONCLUSION

The new wave in Chinese cinema moved away from Socialist Realism and un-reflexive melodrama in order to confront the traumatic memories of the Cultural Revolution and of earlier struggles since Liberation in 1949. This problematization of the accepted norm of Chinese Communist self-representation produced new conflicts around questions of racism and sexism within China. The push for economic reform in the 1980s happened during a period of ideological breakdown. This has made it hard for Han film-makers to address the present or past except through a very particular urban Han perspective.

The youngest generation of film-makers – the independents – are perhaps the closest we can come to authenticity in this context. These are known as the Sixth Generation and their work has been little seen in Europe and North America except at film festivals. They are urban, more or less dismissive of the past, which touches their experience only as a grotesque obsession of an earlier generation, inappropriate to their work and irrelevant to their aesthetic concerns. Their cinema is reactive, rough and reflects the random madness of urban development. It is hardly surprising that a Government intent on urban modernization should disagree with the vision of many of the new talents in its film industry.

NOTES

[1] For further reports see Marie Cambon's piece on the withdrawal of Chinese archive material from the Hong Kong Film Festival 1994 as a Beijing protest at the screening of unapproved independent films, 'China, Cultural Imperialist', *The Asian Wall Street Journal*, 25–6 March 1994.

2   For further information on the history of Chinese cinema see: Bergeron, R (1983/84), *Le Cinéma Chinois 1949–1983*, Paris: L'Harmatton, and Clark, Paul (1988), *Chinese Cinema, Culture and Politics since 1949*, London: Cambridge University Press.

3   See Zheng Dongtian, 'Starting from the Loess Plateau', *China Screen*, Vol. 1, 1985, p. 12–13. The review, which was only published after the film had received acclaim at the Hong Kong Film Festival in October 1984, ignores any possibly subversive textual ironies, and markets the film as a paeon to the national character and the Chinese sense of the Earth as its mentor.

4   For an account of the move into a new economic philosophy see: Wen Wei-Chang, David
     (1988), *China Under Deng Xiao Ping: Political and Economic Reform*, London,
     Basingstoke: Macmillan Books. Jiang's inspiration may have come from Deng Xiao
     Ping's speech to a Japanese delegation on 30 June 1984: 'Build Socialism with Chinese
     Characteristics', *Speeches and Writings of Deng Xiao Ping*, Oxford: Pergamon, 1987,
     p. 95–8.
5   Yau, Esther C.M., 'Is China the End of Hermeneutics? Or, Political and Cultural Usage of
     Non-Han Women in Mainland Chinese Films'. See also her article, 'Cultural and Economic
     Dislocations: Filmic Phantasies of Chinese Women in the 1980s', *Wide Angle*, Vol. 11,
     No. 2, 1989, p. 6–21.
6   See Clark, Paul op. cit. for an overview of Chinese film. See also Pickowicz, Paul, 'Melodra-
     matic Representation and the "May 4th" Tradition of Chinese Cinema' in David Der-wei Wang
     and Ellen Widmer (eds) (1993), *From May Fourth to June Fourth: Fiction and Film in
     Twentieth Century Literature*, Cambridge Massachusetts: Harvard University Press,
     p. 295–326; and Kaplan, Ann E. (1991), 'Melodrama, Subjectivity, Ideology: The Relevance
     of Western Melodrama Theories to Recent Chinese Cinema', *East-West Journal*, Vol. 5,
     No. 1, 1991, p. 6–27.

BIBLIOGRAPHY

Barme and Minford (eds) (1989), *Seeds of Fire: Chinese Voices of Conscience*,
    Newcastle-upon-Tyne: Bloodaxe Books.
Chow, Rey (1991), 'Seeing Modern China' in Rey Chow, *Women and Chinese
    Modernity – the Politics of Reading between East and West*, Minnesota, Oxford:
    University of Minnesota Press.
Chow, Rey (1990), 'Silent is the Ancient Plain: Music, Film-making and the
    Conception of Reform in China's New Cinema', *Discourse*, Vol. 12, No. 2,
    pp.82–109.
Gladney, Dru C. (1994), 'Representing Nationality in China: Refiguring Majority/
    Minority Identities', *Journal of Asian Studies*, Vol. 53, No. 1, pp.92–123.
Kristeva, Julia (1977), *On Chinese Women*, London, New York: Monica Boyars.
Li Tuo and Zhang Nuanxin (1973), 'The Modernization of Film Language', *Beijing
    Film Art*, No. 3.
White, Gordon (1993), *Riding the Tiger*, London, Basingstoke: Macmillan Books.
Yau, Esther (1987), 'Yellow Earth; Western Analysis and a Non-Western Text' in
    Chris Berry (ed.) (1992), *Perspectives on Chinese Cinema*, London: BFI.
Yau, Esther (1989), 'Is China the End of Hermeneutics? Or, Political and Cultural
    Usage of Non-Han Women in Mainland Chinese Films', *Discourse*, Vol. 11, No. 2,
    pp.115–36.

7. Fashioning (Western) Sexuality for Sale: The Case of Sex and Fashion Articles in *Cosmopolitan Hong Kong*[1]

Lisa Leung

INTRODUCTION

> Lurking within *Cosmo[politan]*'s verbosity about sex is the sexual liberation notion that 'true' individuality is found and fulfilled in the sexual quest: sex is a means of discovering yourself; sex is the centre of a relationship; sex is a step to other things; sex is always something that can be bettered or varied ... sex is something you-never-can-forget. (Winship, 1987, p. 112)

Theories of sexuality and consumption are increasingly entwined in the critical discourse of women's magazines. This reflects the growing importance of sexuality in the shifting representation of femininity. Women's magazines are seen as pivotal, not only in charting women's lives, but also in asserting the importance of consumption in constructing femininity. Contemporary women's magazines in Western societies feature the dominance of sexual images, from sexy models to the discussion of sex. Underpinning this trend is the notion that sexuality sells. Sexuality thus becomes a dominant phenomenon in the commodification of Western femininity.

In this paper, I want to question the universality of this phenomenon in the context of franchised magazines. The result of internationalization has precipitated the flow of images across overseas editions. Imported into the local editions, do these images of sexuality and sex necessarily sell in the same way as they do in the parent titles? Existing research around women's magazines concentrates on the sale of sexuality in the Western culture, without questioning its relevance to overseas editions. As a result, it neglects the importance of social and cultural specificities which affect the reading of women's magazines. Using *Cosmopolitan Hong Kong* as an example, I will redress this monolithic view by examining how a non-Western culture responds to the inflow of Western elements. Positing sexuality as a site for cultural debate, I will investigate the extent to which sexy images and sex articles pose a problem for the local edition, and how the edition has to repackage these images to cater for local readership. The analysis of images in the Hong Kong edition seems particularly urgent, as it is situated in a society which is undergoing rapid political and economic changes. In so doing, I will also demonstrate the dynamism of women's magazines as a form of business as well as a cultural commodity.

SEXUALITY AS AN IMAGE AND AS A CULTURAL VALUE IN WESTERN WOMEN'S MAGAZINES

Women's magazines have a long history of existence in Western cultures, as the first issue of such magazines appeared around the seventeenth century.[2] Addressing their readers in a personal tone, they appeal to readers as friends, counsellors and even teachers, establishing with them a strong bond of loyalty, trust, and habit (White, 1970, p. 299).[3] As Ferguson coins it, women's magazines set themselves up as high priestesses of femininity (Ferguson, 1983, p. 110). Since the beginning of this century, women's roles have been much diversified, and as a result the ideal images of femininity these women's magazines depict have changed as well . Women's magazines used to stress women's role as domestic producers (wives and mothers), which are referential social roles. Contemporary magazines, on the other hand, emphasize women as consumers. The reason why they target readers within the age range of 20–35 is because of this age group's purchasing power. This also explains why there is an increasing volume of advertisements in the magazines, rendering the latter 'advertorials' (McCracken, 1993, p. 47).

Contemporary women's magazines also see a rise in the representation of sex (Craik, 1994, p. 48). Sexy models are often found on the front cover of the magazines, as well as cosmetics and fashion advertisements, which dominate the magazine content. They are often dressed in seductive designer labels which articulate their standard measurements (36–24–36 inches). But the sexy image is mainly expressed in the 'look' these models display. Heavy make-up, thick supple lips, and reclining postures, features described as the *'femme fatale* image', are often found in these models.

As if to provide a textual-visual link in the magazine messages, these glossy magazines also include sex articles alongside the sexy images. The titles of these articles often appear as trailers on the front covers. Trailers such as 'The Plague of Routine Sex', 'The Sexually Aggressive Woman' provide a glimpse of the sexually explicit articles in the magazines. The articles often discuss sex acts, different sex positions, and exotic cases such as sex mania, and the sexual practices of other cultures.[4] There seems to be competition between magazines in both the number and the sensational quality of the sex articles. The more sexual the text, the more sales it will hope to attract. These recent changes demonstrate the rising importance of sexuality, not only as an image, but also as content in contemporary women's magazines. Indeed, sexuality has become the centrepiece of the rhetoric and visual representation of women's magazines in Western cultures (Craik, 1994, p. 51–2).

SEXUALIZING CONSUMERISM: WHY ARE SEXUAL IMAGES SO IMPORTANT IN WOMEN'S MAGAZINES?

Feminist theories of representation have likened erotic representation found in women's magazines to pornography (Frow, 1984, p. 35). Unlike hard core pornography, which services male sexual desire, soft porn images enable women readers to derive pleasure. The soft porn images inject subtlety into the sexual representation of women, so that they become romanticized. This unique form of soft pornography is said to mediate between hard porn and romance (Frow, 1984, p. 37). Enclosed in a safe arena such as women's magazines, women are allowed to derive pleasure (even sexual desire) gazing at these sexy images. Women's magazines therefore, act as the venue which legitimizes/ filters erotic images for the satisfaction of women's sexual desires.

Other critiques about women's magazines, however, use economic arguments to explain why magazine photography is often presented in an erotic manner (Myers, 1989, p. 201). Women's magazines do not simply exist to diversify women's pleasure of the gaze. The underlying objective is that these desirable images lure consumption. Described as the 'sexual sell', sexuality is essentially being used as the means to consumption, and women's magazines are the channels which foster the marriage of sexuality and consumption. Sexy images allow body parts to be sexualized into commodities (Craik, 1994, p. 112). As a result, they multiply the parts of the body accessible to marketability (Coward, 1984, p. 54).

The explicit sex articles, on the other hand, provide an exotic quality that is related to the idea of consumption itself. Theories around consumption emphasize the 'shock of the new' as an underlying principle of consumption. Consumers are often lured into consumption with the advent of 'new' products. Within the notion of newness, the desire for novelty and exoticness can be enclosed (Campbell, 1992, p. 57). By discussing sex blatantly and in a sensational tone, contemporary women's magazines distinguish themselves by an outrageous outlook, and an 'affront to morality' (Campbell, 1991, p. 58). In this sense the sex articles perform a function similar to the fashion system, which also provokes the desire for the new with its exotic designs (Campbell,

1992, p. 65). The exoticness of the sex articles is thus seen as an essential quality which arouses sexual desire and transforms it into the desire for consumption. Like sexy images, they act as selling points in women's magazines. This explains the reciprocal relationship between consumption and sexuality: they reflect and reinforce each other in women's magazines (Ballaster, 1991, p. 110).

Such perspectives explain the importance of sexuality in consumption, but leave new questions unanswered. Why do sexy images and sex articles dominate only in contemporary women's magazines? Why is the discussion of sex necessarily deemed as 'outrageous and immoral' but then seen as an allure to consumption? To decipher further the role of sexuality in women's magazines, one has to look beyond the parameters of consumption, to detect the social significance of sexuality in Western societies. Not only is sexuality an essential language in women's magazines, sexuality as a social value is very much entwined with notions of beauty and fashion in the shaping of modern femininity. This, in turn, reflects at large the society's changing attitude towards sex. In the following section, I will trace the shifting social and cultural configurations of sexuality in shaping Western notions of fashion and beauty, which themselves also directly affect the portrayal of women in glossy magazines.

CONSTRUCTING REALITY: SEXUALITY IN WESTERN SOCIETY

The rising importance of sexuality as a form of representation in women's magazines, especially in fashion pages, is said to reflect the equal significance of sexuality in the Western fashion system. Because fashion ascribes social identity, gender (especially femininity) is said to be worn through clothes. Fashion represents feminine beauty, and charts the changing ideals of beauty through time (Finkelstein, 1991, p. 89). Psychoanalytic theories, on the other hand, articulate the sexual function fashion performs. Linking fashion with the human biological drive, psychoanalysts assert that the main function of fashion is to heighten sexual arousal (Bergler, 1985, p. 94). Flugel, using feminist perspectives, asserts that because the fashion designing industry is mostly dominated by men, the designs reflect their sexual desire for women (Flugel, 1930, p. 80). The Victorian corset is a prominent example illustrating an extreme emphasis of women's physique in Western fashion. Contemporary analysts (including feminist critics) have argued against the notion that this pleasure is gender specific, but assert that women also dress to please other women (Wilson, 1985, p. 34). Arguments about sexuality in fashion are thus even more complex, but they all confirm the importance of sexuality in the representation of femininity.

Extensive literature has shown how this preoccupation with sex in the language of women's magazines, and the reason for its appeal, essentially reflects the changing notion of beauty in Western society (Craik, 1994, p. 13). Sexuality has become pivotal to the notion of femininity, as the need to look sexy predominates in the modern sense of beauty (Coward, 1984, p. 94). Modern women have to conform to 'the look' and 'the figure', demonstrated and reinforced by models shown in the media. Psychoanalytic approaches stress that the underlying motive of this 'look' is to emphasize the sexual attractiveness of the body (Coward, 1984, p. 18). For Elizabeth Wilson the race among modern women for slimness reflects very much the persistent bondage of women to existing social codes of beauty (Wilson, 1985, p. 99). The obsession with getting thin to the point of anorexia shows its extremity. These debates, nevertheless, reveal that to be sexy in one's appearance has become the prime element in the homogeneous image of modern femininity.

The increasing significance of sexuality in fashion (designs) and beauty, however, mirrors in turn the changing mores of Western sexuality. Sexuality in Western cultures is said to be shaped by Judeo-Christian morality, which was enforced by general social oppression in Victorian times (Foucault, 1979, p. 87). Socioeconomic changes in Western societies, however, have meant a constant challenge to repressed Western sexual mores. Charting the development of sexuality in Britain, Jeffrey Weeks asserts that the women's movement not only strives for women's economic independence and individualism on a social level, but also to reclaim sexual freedom for women.[5] One of the aims of the sexual revolution was a subversion of the traditional repressive attitude towards sex (Ash and Wilson, 1992, p. 41). The result of this revolution, however, is that as the walls of taboo were dismantled, there was always a drive to further liberate sex attitudes. Sex and sexuality are thus regarded as crucial aspects in the ideological construct of the modern woman, and a means of expressing women's liberation.

The changing social and cultural background of sexuality in Western cultures offers a site to explain why sexuality has been so visibly represented in women's magazines. The image of sexuality is tied in with Western notions of beauty, femininity and sex attitudes. These different parameters are further knitted together with consumption in the representation of women's magazines. Is this a similar phenomenon in the franchised editions within different social cultural settings? Will sexuality be as firmly grounded in franchised editions as in their parent in the Western cultures?

MEDIA INTERNATIONALIZATION: TRANSPORTING CULTURES?

The world is witnessing the flow of different forms of media products, including women's magazines, across cultures,[6] and current analyses confirm internationalization as the prevailing trend in media ownership (Driver and Gillespie, 1993, p. 191–201). Cross-cultural movement of information and ideas has resulted in extensive discussions on the features and effects of media globalization. Media analysts have labelled media globalization as an agent of cultural imperialism (Hamelink, 1988, p. 73). Mattelart, for example, condemns this hegemony, criticizing it for obstructing the development of the local culture (Mattelart, 1979, p. 96–101). Contemporary discussions about the global/local nexus, however, focus on the many features involved in the global flow of media. Appadurai offers a new critique of such movements in the current global cultural economy (Appadurai, 1990, p. 295). Rather than a centre-periphery model, she proposes that they should be analysed under five dimensions of global cultural flow. They can be termed: ethnoscapes, technoscapes, mediascapes, finanscapes, and ideoscapes. The suffix 'scape', in relation to the term 'landscape', is used to denote the complex global flow situation, which involves many actors, from villages to nationstates (Appadurai, 1990, p. 296). These different scapes outline the different 'imaginary worlds' involved in international movements, from people to ideas. Media internationalization, for example, incorporates the mapping of technoscapes, mediascapes and ideoscapes. Because of multinational enterprises, not only capital and technologies are involved (which denote technoscapes and finanscapes), but also images and ideas (in mediascapes and ideoscapes).[7]

Women's magazines in Western cultures have also been through the process of internationalization. Titles such as *Cosmopolitan, Marie Claire, Elle, Harper's Bazaar* have launched their editions in overseas markets, from as early as 1965.[8] But while media internationalization has been much analysed, little research on women's magazines has examined the features and effects of its globalization in overseas markets. Employing Appadurai's 'scape' theories, how is the interaction of these different scapes realized in the production of overseas editions? How are the ideas and images from the parent edition interpreted in the overseas titles? Sexuality is very much entwined in the portrayal of women's magazines with consumption; will it pose a problem in the interaction of the different scapes in the global flow of culture? Using *Cosmopolitan Hong Kong* as a case study, I will investigate how the overseas edition adopts and adapts the incoming flow of Western elements (especially sexuality), and the problematic involved.

THE SELL OF SEXUALITY AND SEX: THE CASE OF *COSMOPOLITAN*

One successful magazine in Western societies which draws considerable academic attention is *Cosmopolitan*. The chief editor of US *Cosmopolitan*, Helen Gurley Brown, had created the 'Sex and the Single Girl' column in 1965. Her book, which justified her *Cosmopolitan* philosophy, became a best-seller, at a time when Betty Friedan's *Feminine Mystique* emerged as the bible for the 'new feminism'. Since then the sexy *'Cosmo* girl' has become the overall image and look of the magazine.

Cosmopolitan was at the forefront in the explicit discussion of sex. Like other women's magazines, the magazine takes fully on board sexy photographs, selling to readers the sexual fantasies derived from these images. '*Cosmopolitan* shows you the way to bring out the ravishing you ... the real and loveable sexy you ... to help you find and keep love in your life ... and to win the man of your dreams' is the message printed on the subscription order card of the magazine (McCracken, 1993, p. 159). On the other hand, the magazine acquired its identity by being the first magazine to include open and frank sex discussions. The sex articles in *Cosmopolitan* are known for their blatant use of terminology about sex, which raised a few eyebrows in the 1970s (Winship, 1987a, p. 111).

Taking advantage of changing social attitudes towards sex, *Cosmopolitan* appeals to readers as the forerunner in the sexual revolution. Riding against the dominant repressive attitude towards sex, *Cosmopolitan* proclaimed (and reclaimed) that it is a woman's right to enjoy and express sex. Faust implied that the reason for the magazine's success was that it was able to stray from the hardline feminist approach (of the time) by preaching success through 'running through the cracks of the system' (Faust, 1980, p. 148). *Cosmopolitan* provides a motto for the modern woman, glorifying sexual liberation as the modern clue to success in the male-dominated world. It also proves that sex is indispensable as a consumption language, as it is very much embedded in Western societies (Winship, 1987, p. 115). If sexuality has been the trademark of *Cosmopolitan US*, how is it dealt with in the Hong Kong edition?

TRANSPORTING SEXUALITY IN *COSMOPOLITAN HONG KONG*: PREACHING (WESTERN) FEMININITY?

Launched in December 1984 by the giant Hearst Corporation (which owns the parent US *Cosmopolitan*), *Cosmopolitan Hong Kong* was the first franchised title in Hong Kong. It is one of the 21 overseas editions of *Cosmopolitan US*.

Besides *Cosmopolitan, Elle, Marie Claire, Eve* and *Moda* have found their way into the local market, most around 1990. They charge the local equivalent of £3.00 (HK$36), three times more than other local downmarket women and entertainment magazines. They have common features of glossy front covers, larger size, better paper quality and more visuals.

The emergence of these foreign titles in the Hong Kong market reveals the advent of magazine internationalization. *Cosmopolitan Hong Kong* was launched by the local media mogul TVEI Limited, and the parent Hearst Corporation. Both the parent and local corporations are bound by a contractual agreement for the launching of the title. Besides agreeing on the share of financial risk (and gains) incurred in the local production, the local party has to render royalties for the use of the foreign title. In return, local editions of *Cosmopolitan* gain access to materials and articles in the foreign editions. This is one of the major benefits for local editions in an international franchising magazine agreement.

Taking advantage of this benefit, *Cosmopolitan Hong Kong* is found to be borrowing heavily in terms of content from the parent US edition. The average 120 pages (the magazine with the highest number of pages) contain 40 per cent imported articles and photos. The local edition is required by the parent title to include sex articles. Because of the lack of local contributions, the local edition has to import such articles from the US *Cosmo*.

The front cover of *Cosmopolitan Hong Kong* often originates from the US edition. Like other franchised magazines such as *Marie Claire, Elle* and *Moda, Cosmopolitan* includes Western models on its front covers. Heavy make-up, sexy clothes and reclined postures are common features of these front cover models in the local edition. Front covers are considered the most important marketing element, the signboard appealing to readers to consume the magazine. They also represent the genre of the magazine, providing identification to the target readers (McCracken, 1993, p. 19). On the other hand, they also embed the identity, the image of the title. As such, the model is the personification of the magazine's ideal image of femininity. These front covers become the trademark for local titles, a visual guarantee for their foreign origin. The Western model performs the function of the title, helping local readers recognize the issue as a *Cosmopolitan*. She is thus part of the icon besides the cover layout constituting the *Cosmo* look. Retaining the Western model, the corporate *Cosmo* identity is thus enhanced in the local edition.

Added to these front covers, the illustrations for articles in *Cosmopolitan Hong Kong* are also imported. These illustrations, either in the form of photography or drawings, often appear in translated articles on subjects such as relationships, career and sex life. Though the texts are all in Chinese, the illustrations often comprise (seductive) Western models. These models are seen as visual aids to the article, enhancing the contextual meaning of the texts.

Western models are also extensively portrayed in a sexy fashion in imported fashion series. In the twelve issues of *Cosmopolitan Hong Kong* in 1993, five series were directly cropped from the US *Cosmo*. Rich in visual language, these fashion series are also consistent in the formula of appeal, by portraying the models as sexy. Even in the depiction of casual wear, the same sexy formula applies. In 'Delicious Derrière' (July 1993) lighting is emphasized at the rear of the models, who showed their back in a reclining position, attracting the gaze from men. In the depiction of lingerie ('Lacy Looks' May 1993), the erotic language is fully expressed. Using different lighting and contrast, the model's breasts and cleavage are necessarily enhanced to highlight her seductiveness.

Besides the front cover, Western images also dominate in the overt advertisements (distinct from the implicit advertising function of front covers) in *Cosmopolitan Hong Kong*. They are often foreign productions contracted between advertising companies and the parent corporation to be published in the local edition. Fashion, cosmetics, and accessories advertisements often depict 'glamorous' women with supple lips, the *'femme fatale* look'. In one perfume advertisement, the model's sexy body occupies two-thirds of the page, so much so that she overshadows the appeal of the perfume. Using semiotics in analysing the codes of these overt advertisements, McCracken criticizes the fact that women's bodies are sexed to enhance male voyeurism (McCracken, 1993, p. 124). For the women readers, McCracken continues, the model's body is also deliberately fragmentized to justify the need for consumption. The sexy body arouses pleasure and desire for the women readers; but necessary parts, which correspond with the marketed products, are isolated, so that 'they can buy back this lost part through consumption' (ibid., p. 122).

This domination of Western images on front covers, in advertisements and even illustrations reveals the fact that the local edition relies heavily on the parent US title. The reason behind this, according to publisher Angie Wong, is the need for the local edition 'to conform to the parent image'.[9] By directly adopting visuals and texts from the US edition, the local title will retain the *Cosmo* look. The presence of Western images and texts implies a guarantee of authenticity, being originated from the parent edition. An underlying reason for retaining this US look, however, is for the local edition to create an aura of foreignness. In analysing recent trends in Western fashion, Craik asserts that Western fashion is able to cannibalize elements from other cultures into its designs; as a result exotic themes have become the leitmotif of the latest Western fashion trends (Craik, 1994, p. 37). An extension to this argument is that there is often an exotic quality in one's conception of other cultures.[10] As in theories of consumption, there is a sense of novelty in exotic themes. Images of the 'Sahara' or 'India' are often found in the fashion pages of the parent *Cosmo*.[11] By employing these foreign images, which often originate from ex-colonies, the parent edition reinforces a 'distinct look' in their fashion pages. By the same token, the adoption of Western images and texts creates an image of the exotic 'Other' in the local edition. Western models thus act as an icon of the 'exotic foreign' to the local readers. Because the Western models are often sexy-looking, the exotic 'Other' is also made erotic.

The image of sexy-looking Western models, on the other hand, is not novel in Hong Kong, and certainly not created by women's magazines. The area has been subject to the influx of American films and television programmes to Hong Kong from as early as the 1960s.[12] This confirms Wong's statement about why she considers the local edition more affiliated to the parent US edition. The influx of Hollywood movies and television soap operas into Hong Kong implies that readers are used to adopting/appropriating foreign images. American women have long been an icon of Western femininity in Hong Kong.

This imagery of Westernness/foreignness, however, does not confine itself only to the media. The history of Hong Kong reveals that the area has been politically and economically exposed to Western cultures. Hong Kong has been a British colony since 1842, and British officials filled the colonial bureaucracy of the territory.[13] Colonialism did not only bring about a different government; it imported British culture in terms of way of life, which was distinctly disparate from that of local Chinese people. More importantly, it instilled a sense of hierarchy between the two cultures, where the colonialists were considered superior. This was a common feature among colonized cultures.[14] Although both cultures basically led their own lives (because of the British policy of segregation), the local subjects were provided a glimpse of 'Westernness'.

The exclusivity of British culture as 'Westernness' was soon undermined because of Hong Kong's rapid economic development. Since its rapid economic take-off in the 1960s, Hong Kong has been exposed to different international (Western) cultures. Hong Kong was designed as a 'haven for trade', and the development of industry and trade led to business interactions between Hong Kong and the rest of the world. As foreign investments poured in, Western cultures in the form of commodities and services converged in Hong Kong. It was in this fashion that Western (mostly US) media were brought in to satisfy the booming Hong Kong market.

Because of the political and economic settings of Hong Kong, Western images have a special appeal in the Hong Kong edition of *Cosmo*. Although they are associated with the area's colonial history, economic development results in the proliferation of these images. The colonial overtones these images (used to) convey are overshadowed by a commercial one. Western images as the 'colonial Other' are thus complicated with the notion of the 'exotic Other' in the franchised edition.

Given this background of multicultural interaction, there should be no problem in the influx of Western images and texts into local women's magazine editions. As Hong Kong is used to appropriating diverse cultural elements, then what has been the selling point in the parent edition will also sell in the Hong Kong edition. One might assume that the latter will have equally explicit sexy images and texts as its US parent. However, despite the dominance of Western models in *Cosmopolitan Hong Kong*, sex articles are deficient compared to its parent edition. The publication of sex articles in fact poses a problem in the local edition. While *Cosmopolitan* prizes its success in selling the sex formula, is the local edition prepared to appropriate this culturally added phenomenon? The following section examines how the portrayal of sex may not be an appeal in the local edition, and how sexuality is a problem in the flow of culture between the parent and local editions.

SEX ARTICLES: A SOURCE OF CULTURAL CONFLICT

The depiction of sex has been a source of editorial conflict between the parent and local editions of *Cosmopolitan*. One of the general criticisms from the US parent editor to the Hong Kong *Cosmopolitan* concerns the lack of sex articles, so that the discussion of sex is 'too conservative and not explicit enough'.[15]

The Hong Kong editorial team, however, retorted that too open a discussion of sex, and the explicitness of sex depiction is 'beyond the tolerance of local readers'. Wong comments that local readers are 'not particularly interested in the sex articles'. She recalled having refused articles which elaborated on orgasms, changing sex positions and sex eroticism. She found them 'too obscene for readers' tolerance'. The US articles are also too blatant in their language, using terms describing sexual intercourse and oral sex. She asserted that they do not suit the image of *Cosmopolitan Hong Kong*, which aspires to a more upmarket feminine look, rather than the sexy image that the American edition depicts. The inclusion of such topics might also 'tarnish the image of the magazine as being vulgar'. Compared to other editions, the Hong Kong *Cosmopolitan* has only one column on sex, named 'sex life'. Where there are both imported and locally written articles in other sections in the edition, such as fashion or beauty, only one sex article is translated. This could also explain why there is a lack of contributions on the issue, as magazine columnists are reluctant to be labelled as 'sex experts'.[16]

The lack of sex articles, the failure to keep up with the sexy look of *Cosmopolitan*, reveals a deep-seated disparity in sexual attitudes between the parent and the local culture. Sexuality in any society has always been a socially constructed phenomenon (Comfort, 1963, p. 60). It is necessary then to look into the sexual attitudes of Hong Kong, to trace the difference.

Hong Kong has been fast developing since its economic take-off in the 1960s. This process of modernization has not, however, entailed a more liberal attitude towards sex as in Western cultures. Although Hong Kong has been a hinterland of different cultures, the roots of conservative Chinese values still retain a stronghold there. The scarce literature written by a Hong Kong sexologist, Dr Ng Mun Lun, associates the sex attitudes of Hong Kong with those of traditional Chinese values.[17] There are still traits of double standards on sex, especially between sex attitudes and the expression of sex in Hong Kong. Within the family, sex is seldom brought up for discussion. Children tend to know about sex from their peer groups. Sex education was only adopted in secondary school curricula in 1988. While the Family Planning Association of Hong Kong is dedicated to providing social services on issues around pregnancy, birth control, and even to educating the public about sex, sex still remains a myth in Hong Kong.

Given such ambivalent sex attitudes, the local edition has to exercise caution in the treatment of sex. Besides the policy of including only one article, imported sex articles are also screened. The criteria for selection, according to the chief editor, Winnie Lee, is that the topics 'are not too blatantly vulgar'.[18]

This process is, however, seen as more one involving elimination than selection of articles 'that are too explicitly sexed'. Articles which were axed include: 'Sexual Secrets of the East' (June 1993), 'Physiology of Sex from A–Z' (September 1993), 'Date Rape' (January 1994), 'Not Only is the Man Sexy – He is a Sex Addict' (March 1994). Other articles that were left out include: 'A Prude's Guide to Erotica' (May 1993), 'Sex Tips from the Experts' (July 1993), 'Sexual Violence' (September 1993), 'I Am a High-Class Call Girl' (October 1993), and 'Married to One Man, Having Sex with Another' (May 1994). Extrapolating from the above, articles that are eliminated usually fall under the following type of content: i) explicit sex terms are mentioned; ii) sex eroticism or addiction; iii) extra-marital and casual sex; and iv) violence related to sex.

The screened articles are further filtered during the translation process. During my interview with one of the regular translators, Jeany Leung, I learnt that the chosen articles are often translated such that the sexual overtones are downplayed. Although the article contents are directly translated, colloquial expressions are added 'to make the article read more locally'. In the translated article entitled 'Virginity – a Rare Species' (May 1993), it could be seen that particular terminology was left out. On the other hand, culture-specific terms are found in the Hong Kong edition, deeming some promiscuous men 'prince-charmings' practising 'universal love'. 'Tasting the forbidden fruit' is a dramatic euphemism for 'having sex for the first time'. Colloquial metaphors such as these are found to be a unique feature of these sex articles, compared to the other articles. The more they are employed, the more they reveal the extent of sexual conventions at work, and the more they show the cultural norms of an area.

SEXY IMAGES AND SEX ARTICLES: A SIGN OF CULTURAL DISJUNCTURE?

Cosmopolitan Hong Kong differentiates in its treatment of Western sexy images and sex articles. On the one hand, Western images (in terms of fashion pages and advertisements) are extensively portrayed in the local edition. On the other hand, extra care is exercised in screening imported articles. In Appadurai's terms, there is a disjunctive image of sexuality in the Hong Kong edition. Explicit sex articles are considered not acceptable to the (conventional) sex attitudes in Hong Kong. On the other hand, the local editions allow a more extensive coverage of Western sexy images, because they create an appeal of the exotic foreign.

The varying attitude towards Western sexy imagery and texts reveals a larger cultural disjuncture in Hong Kong. Although Hong Kong readers have been used to sexy Western images, mostly originated from the American media, they uphold an attitude towards sex which is more conservative than Western cultures. Hence, there is a clash of the mediascape and ethnoscape within Hong Kong's own cultural milieu. While sexiness as a form of imagery is tolerated, sexual liberatedness as a cultural value is regarded as foreign.

This ambiguous cultural situation in Hong Kong may aggravate/complicate the reading of Western sexy images in *Cosmopolitan Hong Kong*. As Western imagery dominates the representation in the local edition, it not only confirms the fact that sexuality is a universal marketing (selling) phenomenon; readers are further reminded of the foreignness of these translated articles. As Western women are often portrayed as sexy, they become icons of sexuality and beauty in the local edition. And as the presence of sexy images and sex articles in the edition makes 'to be sexy' a condition for 'getting a man to bed', Western models are altogether stigmatized as sexually liberated.

The presence of these Western models also puts in question the role of these front covers as a form of identification for the readers. Western readers can mirror themselves with the Western models, who provide for them a source of aspiration. This reader-model rapport, however, is deficient in the local edition. Western models obstruct readers from identifying with the front cover, as a result of their cultural difference. Local readers have constantly to appropriate Western ideals of beauty as their own image of modern femininity. The cultural difference in between, however, means that there is always a distance when they try to adopt the image. Women's magazines seem to offer consumption (of cosmetics, fashion, or even indulging in fitness training to acquire the Western standard measurements) as a shortcut to achieving this goal. The result is that despite the endless acquisition of beauty products, local women could at best aspire to a hybrid 'same but different' image. This reveals one of the contradictions and ambivalences in the consumerist web: women are lured into an endless craving for 'the look' or 'the figure'. In the case of Hong Kong women, the cultural difference further distances them from this ideal sense of beauty.

LOCALIZATION OF MAGAZINE IMAGES: DE-SEXUALIZATION AND DE-WESTERNIZATION OF MAGAZINE IMAGES?

Recent changes in the images of the local edition reflect an attempt to redress this balance. Since early 1993, the front covers of *Cosmopolitan Hong Kong* have been employing local celebrities instead of Western models, who have a different image. Rather than the sexy look and reclined posture, these celebrities are depicted with an eye-level gaze, and broad open smile. Though heavily made up and dressed up, they are not under-dressed as in the sexy-looking models. They are seen rather as an icon of beauty than of seductiveness. The change, according to Wong, is not to redress the over-sexy image on the front cover. Rather, this is seen as the result of marketing strategy. A recent survey shows that local readers find local celebrities more appealing than Western models. Wong asserts that the policy of portraying local celebrities on the front covers also boosts sales. An underlying reason for this change, however, is the change of direction of the target market. The local edition is extending its readership to the mainland Chinese market. With the recent adoption of the open-door policy, China is swinging quickly to market capitalism. The marketization of the Chinese economy leads to an influx of foreign investments. *Cosmopolitan Hong Kong*, being a form of cultural commodity, will be part of this inflow of Western elements into Chinese culture, as the Chinese economy becomes increasingly marketized. According to Wong, the local edition will be targeted both at the Hong Kong and the mainland Chinese market. For the local edition, the 1997 question is seen above all as the tapping of an even larger readership/market, rather than as an end to colonialism.

A combination of images, sometimes contradictory, has become a unique feature of the recent Hong Kong editions. While Chinese celebrities dominate the front covers and in part the fashion series, Western models still occupy illustrations and advertisements. On the other hand, the sex article still appears in every issue, with the number of imported articles remaining unchanged. This could reveal a confusing state where the local edition feels a greater need to cater for the specific tastes of local (Chinese) readers, while still trying to abide by the parent image. The result is a multiple, but ambivalent set of images: the juxtaposition of Chinese and Western images, the presentations of which are essentially different. The continued presence of sexy-looking Western models, especially in imported articles, will aggravate the image of sexuality as foreign. On the other hand, the increased coverage of local celebrities and models not only enhances the readers-magazine rapport, it also alters the outlook of modern women. The image of modern woman does not have to be seductive, nor Western. The sexy *Cosmo* girl is replaced by a famous, glamorous Chinese celebrity. The mixture of images in *Cosmopolitan Hong Kong* thus reflects the multiple yet fragmented discourse of women's magazines, as well as the contradictory images of modern femininity.

The case of *Cosmopolitan Hong Kong* demonstrates what Appadurai (1990) asserts as a collision of scapes: modern capitalist cultures clashing with ethnicity. It also throws light on the question of modern images of femininity in the global flow of culture. Cultural theorists have warned of the increasing homogenization of images in the international movement of images. Sreberny-Mohammadi, on the other hand, doubts the adequacy of the notion of cultural imperialism in explaining the ambivalent and disorganized global flow of images (Sreberny-Mohammadi, 1991, p. 121). Echoing Appadurai's theory of the disjunctive global cultural economy, Mohammadi further questions the ability of the local culture to resist and cannibalize the imported foreign images. She alerts contemporary discussions to the need to further decipher the problematic involved in the global flow of culture.

The production of the local edition of *Cosmopolitan* depends on the capacity to manage cultural differences: responding to parent control on the one hand, and catering to local social reality on the other. Because of the unique cultural situation in Hong Kong, there is a need for the local edition to maintain the proportion of sex portrayed in the magazine to the sexual standard of the local society. While sexuality still sells in the Hong Kong media, the local edition has to repackage/fashion sex in such a way that it does not exceed the level of tolerance in the society. The local edition as the 'moral barometer' which tests this level of tolerance may be even further contested when the local edition is sold to the wider Chinese market. On the other hand, it also has to retain sexual elements to instil the image of modern woman: sexy and liberated. With a toned-down image of sex and sexuality, *Cosmopolitan Hong Kong* maintains the role of women's magazines as high priestess of women readers.

NOTES

1   This paper is part of my DPhil research thesis, which investigates the juxtaposition of cultural images in *Cosmopolitan Hong Kong* as a franchised edition. The objective of the thesis is to examine the different concerns in the production of the local edition: abiding by parent control, negotiating cultural differences, responding to social reality, and creating sales. The thesis also analyses the ways Hong Kong women's magazines shape local images of femininity.

2   Ballaster (1991) provides a detailed history of British women's magazines from the seventeenth century to today, while Janice Winship (1987a) and Cynthia White (1970) cite some earlier women's magazines in their analyses.

3   As Coward comments, women's magazines like addressing readers with the imperative 'you' in their articles. This is especially found in agony columns, where readers are answered/ given advice in a friendly tone (Coward, 1984, p. 36–40).

4   These examples can be found in any issue of *Cosmopolitan, More, Prima.*

5   For further details on the history of sexuality in Britain, see Weeks (1989, p. 121–38).

6   Mattelart (1979) has outlined a history of media internationalization, including magazines, films, and television.

7   Appadurai (1990) gives a detailed conceptualization of the movements involved in each of the different scapes.

8   *Cosmopolitan* British edition was the first among international women's magazines to be a franchised title (information provided in the brochure of the Hearst Corporation).

9   The comment is cited from an interview with Wong in October 1993.

10   Please refer to Edward Said's arguments on the stigmatization of foreign cultures (Said, 1978).

11   The series in the US *Cosmo* entitled 'Africa' (April 1994) and 'A Taste of Bohemia' (August 1993) are examples of the elements used in the parent edition to create the appeal of the 'exotic Other'.

12   In my thesis about the development of media in Hong Kong, I have analysed how Western images are commonly employed in television programmes and films.

13   Please refer to Endacott (1958), who provides a succinct account of the colonial government, and the establishment of colonial education in Hong Kong from 1841 to World War II.

14   According to Edward Said, colonialism values the colonialist culture over and above the colonized one, so that it becomes the superior 'Other'.

15   The comment is extracted from an interview with the sub-editor of *Cosmopolitan Hong Kong,* Lisa Lee. The interview was carried out in May 1993.

16   The comments in quotation marks are extracted from the interview with Wong, conducted in October 1993.

17   For details about Dr Ng's analogy between Hong Kong people's sex attitudes and Chinese traditional sexual mores, please refer to Ng (1989).

18   The comments are cited from an interview with Winnie Lee conducted in November 1993.

BIBLIOGRAPHY

Appadurai, Arjun (1990), 'Disjuncture and Difference in the Global Cultural Economy' in Mike Featherstone, *Global Culture*, London: Sage Publications.

Ash, Juliet (1989), 'The Business of Couture' in Angela McRobbie (ed.), *Zoot Suit and Second Hand Dresses: An Anthology of Fashion and Music*, London: Macmillan.

Ash, Juliet and Wilson, Elizabeth (1992), *Chic Thrills: A Fashion Reader*, London: Pandora Press.

Ballaster, Margaret et al. (eds) (1991), *Women's Worlds: Ideology, Femininity and the Woman's Magazine*, Basingstoke: Macmillan.

Barthes, Roland (1970), *The Fashion System*, London: Jonathan Cape.

Barthes, Roland (1991), 'Written Clothing' in C. Mukerji and M. Schudson (eds), *Rethinking Popular Culture*, Berkeley: University of California Press, pp.442–56.

Berger, John (1972), *Ways of Seeing*, Harmondsworth: Penguin.

Bergler, E. (1985), *Fashion and the Unconscious*, New York: Basic Books.

Campbell, Colin (1992), 'The Desire for the New' in Roger Silverstone and Eric Hirsch (eds), *Consuming Technologies: Media and Information in Domestic Spaces*, London: Routledge, pp.45–68.

Comfort, Alex (1963), *Sex in Society*, London: Gerald Duckworth.

Coward, Rosalind (1984), *Female Desire*, London: Paladin Grafton Books.

Craik, Jennifer (1994), *The Face of Fashion: Cultural Studies in Fashion*, London: Routledge.

Driver, Stephen and Gillespie, Andrew (1993), 'Structural Change in the Cultural Industries: British Magazine Publishing in the 1980s', *Media, Culture and Society*, Vol. 15 , pp.183–201.

Endacott, A. (1958), *A History of Hong Kong*, Oxford: Oxford University Press.

Faust, Beatrice, (1980), *Women, Sex and Pornography*, London: Melbourne House.

Featherstone, Mike (1990), *Global Culture*, London: Sage Publications.

Ferguson, Marjorie (1983), *Forever Feminine: Women's Magazines and the Cult of Femininity*, London: Heinemann.

Finkelstein, Joanne (1991), *The Fashioned Self*, Oxford: Polity Press.

Flugel, J.C. (1930), *The Psychology of Clothes*, London: Hogarth Press and The Institute of PsychoAnalysis.

Foucault, Michel (1979), *The History of Sexuality, Volume 1: An Introduction*, London: Penguin Books.

Hamelink, C.J. (1988), *Cultural Autonomy in Global Communications: Planning National Information Policy*, London: Centre for the Study of Communication and Culture.

Mattelart, A. (1979), *Multinational Corporations and the Control of Culture*, Brighton: Harvester Press.

McCracken, Ellen (1993), *Decoding Women's Magazines*, London: Macmillan.

McRobbie, Angela (ed.) (1989), *Zoot Suits and Second Hand Dresses: An Anthology of Fashion and Music*, Basingstoke: Macmillan.

Mukerji, C. and Schudson, M. (eds) (1991), *Rethinking Popular Culture: Contemporary Perspectives in Cultural Studies*, Berkeley: University of California Press.

Myers, Kathy (1989), 'Fashion n' Passion: A Working Paper' in Angela McRobbie (ed.), *Zoot Suits and Second Hand Dresses: An Anthology of Fashion and Music*, Basingstoke: Macmillan, pp.189–210.

Ng Mun-Lun (1989), *The Analogy of Sex*, Hong Kong: Shuang Mu Publishers.

Said, Edward (1978), *Orientalism*, London: Routledge.

Sreberny-Mohammadi, Annabelle (1991), 'The Global and the Local in International Communications' in James Curran, *Media, Culture and Society*, London: Edward Arnold, pp.118–29.

Tomlinson, John (1991), *Cultural Imperialism*, London: Pinter Books.

Tong Fang Publishers (1992), *The History of Sex and Marriage in China* (*Zhongguo Hunyin Xingai Shigao*), China: Tong Fang Publishers.

Weeks, Jeffrey (1989), *Sex, Politics and Society*, London: Longman.

White, Cynthia (1970), *Women's Magazines: 1693–1968*, London: Michael Joseph.

Wilson, Elizabeth (1985), *Adorned in Dreams: Fashion and Modernity*, London: Virago.

Winship, Janice (1987a), *Inside Women's Magazines*, London: Pandora Press.

Winship, Janice (1987b), 'A Girl Needs to be Street-Wise: Magazines for the 1980s' in Rosemary Betterton (ed.), *Looking On: Images of Femininity in the Visual Media and the Arts*, London: Pandora Press, pp.127–43.

8. On the Construction of Desire and Anxiety: Contestations Over Female Nature and Identity in China's Modern Market Society

Maria Jaschok

In this study of women consumers in Henan Province, an economically re-forming, but politically and culturally past- and native-oriented, society in the central plains of China, I am less concerned with the very real difficulties Chinese women experience in translating legal rights and ideological claims into practical economic opportunities for themselves.[1] This paper will instead attempt to trace certain aspects of the ambivalence women themselves feel as they contemplate their stake in China's development towards a market economy. I want to explore this problematic in several ways: (1) in terms of the traditional appropriation of women's bodies by an enduring Confucian morality and its residues in contemporary values; (2) through discussion of the interplay of cultural and commercial forces in the construction and main-tenance of an essentialized femininity (*suzhi*); (3) by exploring the complex cultural sources of women's identity in the wake of an increasingly gendered commercialization of images.

Two small-scale studies, both located in Henan Province, provide the data for microscopic explorations of two different generations of women consum-ers and their respective subjective responses and coping strategies, as tradi-tional norms, capitalist values and legacies from 40 years of state-sponsored egalitarian policies all press on the way women negotiate modernity.[2]

PATRIARCHAL APPROPRIATIONS OF WOMEN

When Ilse Lenz (1993) warns of the problematic which equates the struggle for personhood in a given society with so-called Western individualism, she cautions the student of Chinese society to recognize the historical embeddedness of cultural boundaries which constitute personhood for Chinese women, incorporating family and social networks, and reflected in values and conduct which are as much informed by the past as they are by an imagined modernity. At the same time, equal recognition needs giving to the fact that these uniquely 'Chinese' parameters of personhood are heavily contested by reflective voices from within the culture, with the tensions revolving around societal accessibility to, and patriarchal ownership of, womb and female sexuality.

The nature and persistence of this gender inequality in Chinese society exercises the minds of some of the more critical scholars from a growing, independent body of Women's Studies.[3]

Female identity in Confucian society lay in service as a reproductive tool to the patrilineage (embedded in the womb-centred life-cycle of women), cemented by strict codes of chastity and (female) monogamy; or it derived from her use as a sex object in the age-old tradition of prostitution outside the morality which underpinned the ideological centrality of the patriline. In either function, or identity, whatever the variations negotiated by individual life histories, women's sexuality and *suzhi* (disposition) were structured as outside and subordinate to male preserves of authority. 'Only within the family did she have a function, that of a tool, not of an embodied self; did she exist as a daughter, mother, wife, married woman, daughter-in-law, never as a female person (*nuxing*)' (Meng and Dai, 1989, p. 7). In this patriarchal order, femininity in its various manifestations within a woman's life-cycle fused nature (biology) with social identity (gender).

The moral code introduced by the Communist Party after 1949 with its progressive, pro-equal rights legislation and socioideological campaigns, so Du Fangqin (1990) maintains, carried the core seeds of a true sexual revolution by promising to overturn the Confucian dictum on feminine dependency, enshrined in the concept of *sancong* (the Three Obediences owed to father, husband and son). In place of an ideologically sanctioned captivity to the complicity of three generations of males (father, husband, and son), men and women together were setting out to destroy an oppressive patrilineal system (Du, 1990, p. 108). Women have in fact become legal subjects, with rights to economic and political participation; but enactment of their rights remains subject to their submission to the relatively benevolent control by the overarching patriarchal system of the Communist Party (and the state). The site of patriarchy has thus been enlarged beyond the past locus of family to encroach upon those spheres women entered into so as to 'join society'. In official institutions and at individual level a customary morality is seen to hold sway over women's ideas and conduct which manifests itself most saliently in an absence of a collective oppositional spirit (see Zhu, 1990; Li's argument, 1994; Spakowski's commentary, 1994). This lack of oppositionality has not surprisingly come to feature prominently in studies of women's prospects under the current transition from an economy which used to be almost exclusively under command of the state, to a system which is uneasily balancing socialist policy priorities with a flourishing private sector, increasingly only responsive to capitalist market laws (for example, see Rosen, 1993, 1994; Du, 1990).

Not unlike in Western societies, commercial advertisement motifs are tantalizing viewers with suggestions of *xing jiefang* (sexual liberation), in which liberation (so-called) culminates in a process of consumption of the feminized commodity. If, as Rubie Watson suggests, women's bodies and behaviour may be read as 'a metaphor, or perhaps in the Chinese case a surrogate, for control over the social order itself' (Watson, 1991, p. 360), a particularly complex theme of modernity can be seen to unfold: of Westernization and *kaifang* (openness in moral conduct) and its tension with customary constraints on women's public conduct and traditional domesticated personhood. However, this tension, so critical Chinese writers claim, may also resolve into a reincarnated patriarchy (whether represented by the state or the patriline) maintained on tradition and modernity alike. Today's Chinese women must challenge all-pervasive cultural dicta of *nanzun nubei* (privileging men, subordinating women), otherwise, whatever form the 'opening up' of society's mores may take, whatever the liberating potential contained in the current economic reform, modernity for women will turn out to be just another variation on a persistent theme of sexual inequality (Du, 1990 p. 87–123).

THE *SUZHI* OF WOMEN: ESSENTIALIZED FEMININITY IN A MARKET ECONOMY

In the author's interview with a group of women representatives of women workers in large enterprises and of Women's Federation officials in one of the more prosperous counties of Henan Province, Dengfeng County, introductory speeches celebrating the achievements of a 'socialist market economy' gave way in the heat of subsequent discussions to forthright expressions of indignation and anger over the fundamental disadvantages women face in a heavily male-dominated world (May 1994). Finally, exchanges centred almost exclusively on what was perceived to be the root of this severe disadvantage, the *suzhi* of women. An overused term in current official jargon, in this context *suzhi* denotes what participants considered to be 'the feminine disposition': to place themselves, as ever, wherever, in subservient stations in life. For many women competitiveness was not so much a competition with, but more of a competition for, men. Concern over the stability of marriage, a sense of powerlessness at work and acceptance of women's primary spheres of responsibility were seen as prejudicing women's efforts to take advantage of economic rights and thus opportunities.

The above debate came to strike at the heart of an intractable dilemma: is this contested 'feminine disposition', seen as pushing women into subordinate place, not also deeply inscribed by a neo-Confucianist patriarchy that infuses socioeconomic arrangements in state and private sectors alike? How likely are women to participate on equal terms with men, thus the Swedish sociologist Rita Liljestroem (1992) asked of her audience of Vietnam Women's Union members and entrepreneurs, in sites of modernity which are so heavily 'loaded with masculinist values' that women find themselves exchanging one set of ideological and social constraints on their body and mind with another – or find themselves (again) pushed into a domestic domain?

How do women, arrived at the mid-point of their life-cycle, view choices and opportunities in this new commercial culture? Which are the sources of their anxiety and uncertainty? In the following case study of middle-aged, married women, taken from the client list of an Avon saleswoman in Zhengzhou, the focus is on successful commercial probings and exploitation of unsettled psyches.

CASE STUDY: TARGETING ANXIETY

The American cosmetics corporation Avon[4] held its first training session for about seventy women candidates in Zhengzhou in February 1993. Would-be *Yafang Xiaojie* (Avon ladies) were given a history of the Corporation in the United States, an introduction to Avon products, their application and superior merits, and a concluding seminar on 'the psychology of the customer'. This session instructs students to differentiate among types of customers (speech, body language, background) and then hands out appropriate sales techniques: the 'gullible' client will need reassurance; the 'anxious' one will be comforted; the 'pragmatic' client (worried about the price) will be persuaded with reference to her 'entry' into the international (American) society of consumption. The 'parochial' customer will be soothed with reassurances that whilst ingredients are imported from the US, the mixture, concocted on native soil, in Guangzhou, will suit Asian complexions 'just so'.

Right now, about 250 *Yafang Xiaojie* are marketing Avon products to clients. The most successful saleswoman in Zhengzhou boasts about 150 clients on her list.

The motivation to do well by Avon is great. Not only do the saleswomen pay for their training, for 'the bag' (containing promotional materials and demonstration cosmetics), and for a booklet, but they also buy the cosmetics they are then to sell to their clients. Avon sales techniques are spectacularly successful. A most popular *Yafang Xiaojie*, Ms Yang, loves her job and the fact that she is suddenly a part of the wider world of fashion. An Avon award brooch was bestowed on her for bringing in sales of over 2,000 *yuan* per month out of which she netted 400 *yuan*. What makes Avon a success with both saleswomen and clients is the personal approach.

Because Ms Yang is known, is liked, is trusted, so Avon products are liked and trusted. The Avon personnel are havens of solidity in a commercial onslaught of products unsettling to consumers. Ms Yang listens with much sympathy to stories about husbands and frequent work trips, and she offers a panacea: lotions and gels and lipsticks from the same source which threatens to destabilize their lives – America as a symbol of a hopeful (but uncertain) future for which one prepares with much trepidation.

Ms Yang makes her thrice-weekly rounds of the *danwei* (work-unit) circuit and selected homes. Among her clients are professional women and, because she herself is the daughter of a university professor, a number of teachers. The best sales are made if she can arrive at a *danwei* after Political Studies sessions (still a weekly requirement) are finished. By then, so Ms Yang confided in me, the hunger to purchase even the most expensive items from her bag (around 120 *yuan* per item) is great. Ms Yang exudes faith in her products ('we are all believers') as she talks excitedly about the incomparable quality of a 'night gel' for about 120 *yuan* (the average salary of a teacher in Zhengzhou is 200 to 300 *yuan* per month).

There is increasingly pressure to go with fashion which makes it now imperative to spend too much money on cosmetics and clothes. Whereas formerly Zhengzhou was little affected by fashion trends, these last three years have seen annual changes in the public's appearance. It is important to appear well-groomed, to frequent hairdressers and beauticians, to look young and 'with it' even as traditional cultural norms applicable to women in their station in life (that is, over 30 years of age) disparage attention to fashionable appearance in favour of self-abnegation.

The background for this recent trend lies in the overwhelming domination by men of political and economic life. One dedicated Avon customer told me that her husband, an assistant bank manager, is rarely home at night. Socializing and business, one goes hand in hand with the other, are conducted often over dinner in expensive restaurants where attractive hostesses are a part of the service. These restaurants and bars are considered essential to a supportive business and investment climate. The job of a hostess is to provide comfort and entertainment. Wives and children stay at home, the price for their increased standard of living.

With many companies looking for attractive women to ornament reception desks and offices, wives are feeling the competition from young secretaries and hostesses. Indeed, the youthful models staring at passers-by from huge billboards must be reinforcing the dread older women feel when they contemplate their marriage. Again it is a status symbol to have a mistress, and it is no longer taboo even in the traditional climate of Zhengzhou to separate and divorce. (The fact that about 70 per cent of applicants for divorce in China are women does not give us the origins of a marital break-down.) The run on cosmetics counters and beauty parlours thus indicates increasing anxiety by these women over a loss of moral ground and societal support. In the past public opinion and ideological propaganda ensured at least stable, if not necessarily happy, marriages. The current alternatives in a society such as Zhengzhou are for most women still unacceptable. Divorce promises not so much independence as abandonment, economic uncertainty and social gossip. The purchase of anti-wrinkle creams and 'special' treatment plans is motivated not only by gullibility about consumerism but by acute anxiety over the future.

A 30-year-old university teacher, Ms Wang, one of the longest-standing Avon clients, admitted: 'Formerly we did not think of having to look a certain way, now we are all under pressure'. And the pressure is to look 'modern' and 'vital', ironically so as to be able to cling to past certainties of stable family relationships.

Ms Wang looks young and attractive. She is married to a middle-echelon business manager. Always most fashionably and expensively dressed, she prides herself on being a doting mother and a devoted wife. She also prides herself on her competence as a university teacher and popularity with students at the same time as she depends for every detail in her domestic life on her husband or parents-in-law. She has never travelled by herself on longer trips and would consider this a frightful prospect. Her husband is successful and, she thinks, loyal to her. He is also the unchallenged head of the family. She accepts this as a condition of female existence which moreover grants security and affection. Yet she too is wondering whether cosmetic surgery will ever come to Zhengzhou. For women like Ms Wang a central reality is that of essential identification with a domesticated existence and appropriate conduct.

Like Ms Wang, all clients on Ms Yang's list work outside the home, taking for granted the additional burden they carry. Work is less of a transcend-ence of domestic orientation than an extension of domestic boundaries to incorporate office, factory or classroom into its site of responsibility. If there is a breakdown in boundaries between public and private worlds it could be argued that women's traditional functions have expanded to serve in their sphere of work also; the implication is not that of a break from the primary sphere. At work, talks with other women focus easily on tasks for the family and domestic affairs; work hours are made to fit domestic schedules so that early departures from work or the taking of leave are too frequent to arouse comment. Women from the lower and middle echelons of university and business sectors who make up Avon's clients, live with each other more than with their (mostly male) superiors who (like husbands back home) do not attend too closely to the messier aspects of life's routine, here classroom teaching and office duties. Women's less close involvement with work is thus seen by both men and women as a 'natural' implication of primary duties and relationships. The success of Avon reveals itself to be a success because it appeals to the wife and the homemaker, because it makes its site of sale clients' familiar surroundings, thus providing a comforting alternative to modern, impersonal department stores and their unsettling advertisement images of seductive, anxiety-provoking women.

I took the issue of dependency to a further stage by inviting discussions with 52 young women of their responses to commercial advertisement constructs of femininity. Because their cultural processing also incorporates their mothers' presence in their lives, this following case study further serves to illuminate the background of those women (contemporaries of their mothers) who seek reassurance in consumption of Avon products.

SOURCES OF FEMALE IDENTITY AMONG THE YOUNG CASE STUDY: DESIRE AND DETERMINATION

These women are students of the first Women's College (as part of the university system) in China and recipients of a women-centred, confidence-nurturing education. About half of the students come from rural townships in Henan, the rest is equally divided between students from the countryside and from the capital of Zhengzhou. Positioned still as daughters, unattached, as yet without work and family obligations, their responses to commercial image-making accommodate the anxieties of their older contemporaries (see above), their mothers' generation, to generate a different amalgam of determination and desires.

Questions put to the young women (on average, 20 years of age) dealt with decisive heroic models, the impact of their mothers' life experience on their own values, perceptions of female models in advertising, and cultural norms applying to appropriate behaviour and appearance. It is suggested that all these different factors impinge upon the way the market's message is received and transcribed into a personal code of conduct.

DECISIVE ROLE MODELS

Which role models inspire the young women to emulate them? A surprisingly high percentage (35 per cent) reject role models altogether, seeing such a mainstay of Communist ideological inculcation as a sign of immaturity, of a vain search for perfection. 'We always think [that] a famous person is great, but their greatness is only because we didn't stand up. In fact, they are ordinary persons.'

Distrust of public persons and their pronouncements gave a more prominent place to persons from one's immediate family (father, mother, grandmother, brother) than to the predictable models, such as Mao Zedong and Zhou Enlai. Party-sponsored heroines such as the invalid Zhang Haidi only received one mention (as did the Tang dynasty empress Wu Zetian, a Confucianist anti-heroine).

The family emerges as of crucial importance in shaping women's aspirations and goals. But respondents also display a self-confidence mixed with a heavy dose of scepticism leading to rejection of *the* one model. Pride in one's uniqueness outweighs the patter of propaganda, whether ideological or commercial. Not one film star, singer, model or media personality was listed.

THE MOTHER'S PAST IN THE DAUGHTER'S PRESENT

Which are the sources of values transmitted by the person closest to the women, their mothers? How closely do they identify with their mothers' life-experience and expectations? And how might this shape a young person's experience of, and response to, the commercial marketing of femininity?

The *fangan* (tension) induced in a generation of 20-year-olds as a result of their parents' personal frustrations during the Cultural Revolution (1967–77) and subsequent years of subsistence-level living standards, is a recurrent theme in youth magazines, letters to the editors, and popular newspapers. Against this background, all the respondents saw themselves as heirs to their mother's dreams, aspirations and ambitions which the older generation, growing up during the Cultural Revolution, had never been able to realize.

This legacy instils determination to do well, to succeed in those areas where the mother had never been given a chance to prove herself; but it also engenders ambivalence. Typically, the mother is depicted as courageous, admirable, devoted, and a mainstay of the family. However, because her qualities are seen as having been appreciated only in an entirely familial context, she is also 'confined, narrow in her thinking, and traditional'. Thus admirable character traits, because at the service of the patriarchal institution, become devalued, even a source of anxiety to the daughter now encouraged through her education to consciously appropriate societal territory for the exercise of her talents and skills and for her personal growth. The invocation of the mother's dreams is at the same time a celebration of difference, of an optimism derived of youthful enthusiasm, a product of a positive educational environment. But within the larger political context, the euphoric refrain also suggests the continued working of what Lucian Pye calls 'the imperative of optimism' in China's political culture, whereby difficulties of societal transition are smoothed in a nurturing of collective faith in the imminent turn for the better, a faith kept alive through frequent enactments of 'ritualized enthusiasm' (Pye, 1988, p. 92–6).

Poverty, hunger (three respondents' mothers went begging as children), drabness of existence, monotonous daily routine, and, most prominently, an absence of control over one's life, an absence of choice, most impress respondents about their mothers. Most of the mothers come from peasant backgrounds; reared by traditional parents, very few mothers had more than rudimentary schooling. They were early on initiated into the duty of a daughter, looking after siblings, doing the housework and, at the marriageable age, agreeing to marry the man approved by the family. Two mothers married unknown men, the majority of the other mothers followed their parents' choice. The poverty of the 1970s made raising a family the central sole preoccupation. 'She [my mother] had no choice at all ... What was comfort? Eating rice was comfort, having a coat was comfort. This is my mother's life'.

The mothers' stories reflect their experience of being of little value. 'Mother said that a girl's value when she was young was no more important than a pig's. But if you feed a pig, you can get money for it.' The tales also tell of lives wasted and talent stunted. In recalling her mother's story as it has been told so often, the daughter interprets the underlying warning: not to continue the pattern of self-sacrifice. So in order not to break faith with her mother, the daughter must become what the mother has never been, a success both in a readjusted, or redefined, domestic function, and in society at large.

IMAGES OF THE DESIRED: THE 'PUBLIC WOMAN' AS A ROLE MODEL

The use of a famous person to advertise a commodity is intended to activate the consumer's faith in the efficacy of the recommended product, bringing into the commercial message fantasies which derive from public perceptions of the glamour of a famous star's life, and which make the act of consumption an act of consummation and transcendence (Williams, 1982, p. 354). From very early on, Chinese commercials have employed home-grown and overseas Chinese stars.

The commercial feminine construct appears either in the traditional mould of *jianqi liangmu* (virtuous wife and good mother) or in the guise of *xiandai huaping* (the modern flower vase). But this dichotomized tradition of femininity seems far less an issue than a perceived gulf of moral dimension which separates 'women for consumption' from 'women like us' (women as consumers and workers).

Like many others in this relatively new consumer society, the respondents like watching television commercials. They are fascinated by glimpses of high life as models move through luxuriously-appointed houses, enjoy the possession of expensive home gadgets and flaunt free time in five-star hotel coffee shops and bars. My question to the respondents was a direct test of their classification of the model as a woman in a public context (as the voice of seduction and source of identification with a modernized construct of self).

Above discussions have already described enduring traditional paradigms of virtuous womanhood as mistress of the inner realm (*neizhu*) and her sister without kin, the public woman as a commodity for sexual use. Historically, women's garments have always symbolized social status and a given stage in the female life-cycle in close adherence to the patriarchal code of appropriate feminine conduct (*side*). When women sought to challenge the social and sexual status quo, when dissenting notions of female fates and life-style were given expression, fashion has been a foremost vehicle for the signal for change. Different transmutations saw the early women activists and reformers around the turn of the century in severe, sometimes consciously mannish, clothing; they were succeeded by revolutionaries in functional worker-peasant garb and, since the early 1980s, by women in initially cautious but increasingly daring, sprightly, 'feminine' prints. Yet how much structural change in women's lives, thus of a change in the moral code which dictated women's proper place and appropriate conduct, can be inferred from a visible 'liberalization' of the fashion industry?

In conservative Henan, too much *nanfang* (southern) style awakens misgivings even in the heady 1990s. Too much red lipstick smacks of overturned barricades and absent authoritative (parental) voices and arouses social gossip. The fashion overkill which characterizes so many models in advertisements thus provokes, titillates, but also amuses and alienates and by its very public context also serves to negate some of the messages sent out to seduce.

The tone of voice in which the carriers of the commercial message are commented upon is highly moralistic; the women seen on television or on billboards are perceived as having come by their fortune through luck and good looks. Thus they are by cultural definition superficial, only serving pleasure and fashion. They are mere ornaments and lack inner life, education, ideals, and the will to work hard and diligently. Their life is glamorous but is also seen as characterized by transience and ultimate dissatisfaction because dedicated to the maintenance of outward appearance.

In other words, the boundaries that are drawn to distinguish between the models as public women and the respondents as consumers are boundaries of old: inner and outer worlds; life dedicated to cultivation of inner self and service to worthy causes contrasted with life in the public limelight and a shallow personality; the person of education in contrast to the woman as a 'vase' (a traditional representation).

The young students pondering advertisements on the whole understand their importance to the market economy, but are emphatic in not wanting to be confused with the women advertising the product. Women can hold up half of the sky and should not be in need of selling their smiles. 'These kind of commercials are old things. They were made by old thought. Women cannot be judged by a language [made] by men. It is an influence over [us] for sure.' The paraphernalia of beauty and fashion are not dismissed, but for many of the women students this represents part of a colourful, beautiful world to which access will be gained not by looks, but through education, knowledge, and learning from their mothers' past.

Most respondents are unable to articulate the contradictions which arise for them as they seek to reconcile puritanical rejections of the trappings of wealth, inherited from their parents' generation once steeped in a Maoist ideology of 'poor, but pure'; the indigenous patriarchal condemnation of 'public women' (which still taints women in the limelight of entertainment and the mass-media); and the desire to be modern, to conquer the world 'out there' with skills, in confidence and style. So they vacillate between at times outright and proud rejection of commercial propaganda, and a proud assertion of their essential difference, and at other times a wistful admission that a model's lovely appearance and the promise contained in the advertisement are a source of temptation.

But ultimately all the respondents are respectful of boundaries which separate what is 'reality' (the working women surrounding them) from the world of 'glamour' (of which the ads by the very fact of their representation of ways of life out of bounds for the majority of people are a part); what is constitutive of 'respectability' (education; professional achievement; hard and diligent work; contribution to society) from the milieu of commercial enterprise (with its still somewhat disreputable features developed in countless television series and articles); what is the mother's world, however confining, from that of the model as a commoditized image of women: substance as opposed to (male) fantasy.

There is little as yet of the blurring of 'fabricated' and 'hard' news that is

a feature of Western consumption of the mass media. The very contrast between the often gaudy, opulent world and its overdressed models as projected
by commercial advertisement and escapist entertainment, and the world of
news (constituted of production figures, model workers, soberly-dressed women
officials) makes the efficacy of the seductive message questionable. Many
respondents used the term *qiguai* (strange, weird) to characterize the role
models offered up for emulation by product advertisements; its connotation is
that of something 'alien', not readily assimilated into the world with which
they are familiar.

> They [peasant women in my home-town] must work in the fields from morning to
> night. They haven't time to beautify themselves. Most important of all, they don't
> need beauty at all. If a woman uses make-up when she works in the field, every-
> one will laugh at her.

There is thus a strong sense of rootedness in one's own environment – in
which solid norms govern identity, life-style, and expectations – and of concomitant constraints on individuals' experimentation with unsanctioned
forms of self-expression.

REFLECTIONS

My observations, however preliminary and tentative, suggest the importance
of foregrounding the given cultural process which intervenes between
commercial images and their women consumers. Legacies from women's
historical identities still inform gender-biased social norms and codes of
conduct; here the role of mothers as mediators between their own past
and present and their daughters' present and future has been considered
particularly crucial.

In the same way that the 'past' is crisscrossing the reception of modern
images – shifted, recast, but not erased – concepts of modernity are received
and adapted in endless, on-going transmutations. Representations and self-
representations of women as expressed in body and dress language, and in
the cultivation of the desirable feminine *suzhi*, are culture-specific phenomena of which only the close reading of a culture also in dialogue with itself
can begin to lay bare the complexity of the process at work.

Fashion, here understood as 'a network of meaning' (Barthes, 1967),
conveys differing connotations in Western and Chinese society. Elizabeth
Wilson defined fashion in a Western context as 'an aesthetic medium for the
expression of ideas, desires and beliefs' (Wilson, 1985, p. 9), and as an
enactment, both playful and serious, of an evolving identity (individual
or social), separate from an identity which is derived from membership

of a social stratum with its code of dress and decorum (ibid., p. 11–12). Transgressions and flights into liminal identities, such as Wilson discovers in current Western fashion, are irreconcilable with paradigmatic fashioning of identity particularly in the culture of China's inner provinces. A still solid social equation links body and dress language with social validation and identity, entailing significant repercussions for the individual woman: so that choice of a particular career in a private or public setting, of a style of fashion, of a certain conduct, are automatically choices within moral givens of which the arbiter continues to be society, rarely the individual. Thus here the context for modernity is not so much the assertion of individual autonomy against conformist pressures of a mass society, but a contestation over identification with different models of femininity which carry different legacies and moral connotations.

In the light of this interpretation, commercial messages which project glamourized, youthful, pouting, yielding femininity in modern settings of marbled hotel lobbies, luxurious kitchens, and glistening bathrooms, are seen as derivative of a paradigm which may evoke wistful dreams of comfort and raised consumer expectations, but which also reaches far back into the history of women's objectification as sex commodities. Confucian dicta on femininity and Communist puritan morality merge to infuse modern women's receptions of marketed female images with a detachment that may neutralize the intensity of commercial seduction.

The older generation of women, the mothers and their peers, the Avon clients, are perceived by their daughters as family-bound in their fundamental orientation and, compounded by the socioeconomic circumstances of the 1970s, deprived of personally fulfilling careers (career as understood in contradistinction to the performance of menial or unskilled work in urban occupations or physical labour in the fields) and material comfort. The daughters, whether rejecting or accepting of their mothers' aspirations for them, seek to widen the boundaries of their personhood. But they too rarely ever challenge the assumption that there is a larger moral authority to set the new delineations of personhood, even if this is cast in a spirit of self-affirmation. This is no less the case in the women-centred education of a Women's College where the defining paradigm of 'strong womanhood' is nurtured in a rigorous adherence to instructions from the leadership.

Anxiety over women's place in China's society now is awakening desires to change and adapt, but I have interpreted this more as a modernization of established patterns than as an experimentation with alternative life-styles. Even where critical voices contest representations of women as oppressively restrictive, where activists offer women-centred education and organization, these are all too often predicated on relational concepts which harbour the core dependencies of old and harbinger extra-familial dependencies no less confining. It makes for a poignant ideological statement that for influential Women's Studies scholars (for a recent exposition, see Li, 1994) the new consumer society's embryonic integration into the transnational commercial market is seen as posing less of a threat to women's self-representation, and social representation, than indigenous traditions (spanning pre-Communist society and the Communist era) of 'a properly constituted inequality' steeped in female dependency.

NOTES

1   For recent expositions of the impact of China's socialist market economy on women's economic, legal and social standing, see Rosen, 1993, 1994.
2   Formal interviews with Avon saleswomen and clients from Ms Yang's list of customers (December 1993– March 1994). Formal interviews with 52 women students of the International Women's College of Zhengzhou University (May–June 1994).
3   For recent publications on the new women's movement and Women's Studies in China, see Liu, 1991; Li, 1991, 1994; Spakowski, 1994.
4   Avon Corporation (*Yafang Gongsi*) started its business in China in 1990, one of the early foreign commercial success stories there. Based in Guangzhou, Avon is also represented in Shanghai and Beijing. In the first year of its sales campaign in Guangzhou, over one million units were sold. Trainers from Guangzhou are flown in to other cities to conduct training programmes. Ingredients and packaging are imported from the US, the actual product is mixed in Guangzhou to 'suit the Asian ladies' complexion' (*Yafang Xiaojie* Ms Yang's interview).

BIBLIOGRAPHY

Barthes, Roland (1983), *The Fashion System*, New York: Hill and Wang, originally published in 1967.
Braidotti, Rosi (1991), *Patterns of Dissonance*, Cambridge: Polity Press.
Du Fangqin (1990), 'Zhen yin daode zongheng tan' ('Discourses on Double Morality') in Li Xiaojiang (ed.), *Huaxia Nuxing Zhimi* (*The Enigma of Chinese Womanhood*), Beijing: Sanlian Shudian Chubanshe, pp.87–123.
Lenz, Ilse (1993), 'Neue Nachrichten von Nirgendwo? Zu neuen Perspektiven in der Geschlechterfrage' ('News from Nowhere? Concerning New Perspectives on Questions of Gender') in Brigitte Hasenjuergen and Sabine Preuss (eds), *Frauenarbeit Frauenpolitik* (*Women-Work Women-Politics*), Muenster: Westfaelisches Dampfboot, pp.96–110.
Li Xiaojiang (1988), *Xiawade Tansuo* (*Exploring 'Eve'*), Zhengzhou: Henan Renmin Chubanshe.
Li Xiaojiang (1991), 'Funu Yanjiu zai Zhongguode fazhan jiqi Qianjing Zhanwang' ('Developments and Prospects of Women's Studies in China') in Li Xiaojiang and Tan Shen (eds), *Funu Yanjiu zai Zhongguo* (*Women's Studies in China*), Zhishi Funu Jicong, Vol. 1, Zhengzhou: Henan Renmin Chubanshe, pp.3–22.
Li Xiaojiang (1994), 'Ein Rückblick auf die Frauenbewegung der neuen Zeit' ('A Review of the Women's Movement of the New Era'), *Frauen und China* (*Women and China*), 6, March issue, Berlin: Ostasiatisches Seminar der FU Berlin.

Liu Jinxiu (1991), '80 Niandai Funu Minjian Zuzhide Xingqi yu Fazhan' ('Rise and Development of the Women NGOs of the Eighties') in Li Xiaojiang and Tan Shen (eds), *Funu Yanjiu zai Zhongguo* (*Women's Studies in China*), Zhishi Funu Jicong, Vol. 1, Zhengzhou: Henan Renmin Chubanshe, pp.106–17.

Liljestroem, Rita (1992), 'Women and the Modernization Process', Paper given to the Conference on 'The Role of Women in Economic Transition in Southeast Asia', Hanoi, 10–11 September.

Meng Yue and Dai Jinhua (1989), *Fuchu Lishi Dibiao* (*Emerging from Historical Marginality*), Women's Studies Series, Zhengzhou: Henan Renmin Chubanshe.

Pollock, Griselda (1988), 'Modernity and the Spaces of Femininity' in Griselda Pollock (ed.), *Vision and Difference: Femininity, Feminism and the Histories of Art*, London and New York: Routledge, pp.50–90.

Pye, Lucian W. (1988), *The Mandarin and the Cadre: China's Political Cultures*, Ann Arbor: The University of Michigan.

Rosen, Stanley (1993), 'Women & Reform', *The China Review*, January issue, Hong Kong.

Rosen, Stanley (1994), 'Chinese Women in the 1990s: Images and Roles in Contention' in Maurice Brosseau and Lo Chi Kin (eds), *China Review 1994*, Hong Kong: The Chinese University Press, pp.17.1–17.28.

Spakowski, Nicola (1994), 'Wohin geht die chinesische Frauenbewegung?' ('What Future for the Chinese Women's Movement?'), *Frauen und China* (*Women and China*), 6, March issue, Berlin: Ostasiatisches Seminar der FU Berlin.

Watson, Rubie S. (1991), 'Afterword: Marriage and Gender Inequality' in Rubie S. Watson and Patricia Buckley Ebrey (eds), *Marriage and Inequality in Chinese Society*, Berkeley: University of California Press, pp.347–68.

Williams, Rosalind H. (1982), *Dream Worlds: Mass Consumption in Late Nineteenth-Century France*, Berkeley: University of California Press.

Wilson, Elizabeth (1985), *Adorned in Dreams: Fashion and Modernity*, London: Virago.

Zhonghua Quanguo Funu Lianhehui Funu Yanjiusuo and Jiangxi Shengfunu Lianhehui Yanjiushi (1991), *Zhongguo Funu Tongji Ziliao (1949–1989)* (*Statistical Data on Chinese Women 1949–1989*), Beijing: Zhongguo Tongji Chubanshe.

Zhu Qi (1990), 'Zhongguo Funu Canzheng yu Nuxing Canzheng Yishi' ('Chinese Women's Political Participation and Female Political Consciousness') in Li Xiaojiang (ed.), *Huaxia Nuxing Zhimi* (*The Enigma of Chinese Womanhood*), Beijing: Sanlian Shudian Chubanshe, pp.226–42.

Magazines consulted: *Jiating Shenghuo, Jiatingzhi You* (especially March 1994 issue), *Meirong, Nongjianu Baishitong, Nuyou* (especially the November 1993 issue), *Zhongguo Funu*.

Interviewees for the article included Avon saleswomen and clients in Zhengzhou (informal) and Avon *Xiaojie* Ms Yang (formal); students of the International Women's College of Zhengzhou University (formal); women worker representatives, Dengfeng County (Henan Province); All-China Women's Federation officials, Dengfeng County (formal); beauticians, cosmetics counter assistants, fashion store salespersons in major Zhengzhou department stores (informal).

PART FOUR

Crisis in Western Market Societies

9. Conflicts Between the Domestic and Market Economy in Britain: Past and Present

Eileen Janes Yeo

This chapter will weigh up the double burden that women of different social classes have carried from the past into the present. It will deal mainly with Great Britain which presents a case of international importance, as the first nation to develop a capitalist market system. Women's experience of processes long at work here need to be considered by women embarking on similar changes for the first time. Historical journeys, to be truly profitable, should illuminate problems as well as possibilities and uncover how apparently finished and immovable structures were created by human agency, in order to show their plasticity and capacity for change. What has been constructed can also be dismantled, no matter how hard the job may be. This chapter will focus upon the gendered construction of the modern market system and on two different class routes to the present, both of which devalued and concealed women's unpaid family and domestic work. Far from being outmoded in the present phase of globalization, these patterns with the addition of some new elements have become increasingly widespread and catch women both East and West in their tangled web.

FROM DOMESTIC ECONOMY TO DOMESTIC IDEOLOGY: THE MIDDLE-CLASS EXPERIENCE

To state the obvious, women have always played a significant role in the production of social life, but this role has changed from time to time. In the period preceding the economic 'take-off' into capitalist mass production and distribution, women had been active both in domestic and market economies and the two areas were more compatible than later was to be the case. This was partly because both production and retailing were often based at home and the whole household worked in the family enterprise. Even if the male head of the family acted as a kind of agent who 'took care of financial matters and contractual relations in the interests of all' (Scott and Tilly, 1982, p. 51), the wife had equally important and valued work in giving birth to and raising children and in managing the household tasks like cooking and cleaning. The family and household responsibilities amounted to her primary contribution to the domestic economy but she also contributed to the more narrowly economic marketing activities. In peasant households across Europe, while men tended to do the field work, women had responsibility for the animals and garden as well as producing clothing and processing food for family consumption and then taking the surplus to the local market. In the proto-industrial family system of production, where textile spinning and weaving was done at home, women along with children did the spinning while men did the weaving and then delivered the finished cloth to the middleman. Early retailing often involved the store being located on the same premises where the family lived and women being involved in a range of market and non-market activities at the same time. Crucially in these economic arrangements, while women contributed in a subsidiary way to market production, their labour was not usually independently priced.[1] The family as a whole created the product that went to market and the price it fetched went back to the family albeit through the male who was the interface between the family and the market.

Home-based work was demanding. In the case of the first generation of the family later to become one of Britain's biggest cocoa and chocolate manufacturers, life was not sweet for Elizabeth Cadbury. She served in the family shop in 1800, which sold silk, and ran the business when her husband Richard was away. She also managed the large household which included apprentices, shopgirls, eight surviving children, two household servants and her aging mother (Hall, 1982, p. 6). Nonetheless, if business was good, which put the allocation of time more within a family's control, the fact that all these various responsibilities could be carried out in the same physical space meant that a woman could integrate her domestic and market duties in a reasonably tolerable way. Ideal femininity was seen in terms of being a good manager of family, household and market tasks but in a setting which made such management more possible than impossible. Samuel Bamford described the rhythms of the day of a Lancashire silk weaving household during a short-lived golden age (Thompson, 1963, p. 304ff). Not only could his asthmatic aunt rise late and breakfast separately, but she could devolve the heavy housework to her daughter and concentrate on cooking and spinning. His uncle who wove in the adjoining loom shed would break his day at intervals of his choice to come into the house for a pipe and a chat (Bamford, 1848–9, p. 100, 104, 111–12).

For both middle- and working-class women, but in diametrically different ways, this equilibrium became destabilized as the modern market system developed. Middle-class women moved away from direct labour in the family enterprise and stayed in the increasingly separated home, although their activity was still strategic to economic development and class formation. An ideology of separate public and private spheres developed which still lingers on and has masked, until the recent revealing work of Leonore Davidoff and Catherine Hall (1987), the real contribution of middle-class women to market developments. Even women who stayed in the private sphere contributed their capital to the family business. Until the Married Women's Property Act of 1882, a wife's capital became her husband's property and even where marriage settlements and trusts kept her capital intact, it was often managed by male relatives and channelled into the family enterprise (Davidoff and Hall, 1987, pt. 2) As the banking system was so primitive, early capitalists relied heavily on family and friendship networks, not only to raise the initial investment for a business but to rescue it again and again when it failed. Women took on the task of cultivating these crucially important family and friendship networks. Women were also increasingly defined as the main arbiters of family consumption and constituted the home market to the extent that this was coveted by British merchants and manufacturers.

As importantly, women contributed to the positive image of the rising middle class. Class is always a cultural as well as an economic formation and rising classes especially need to project themselves as the embodiment, not of any sectional interest, but of the true good of all humanity. The middle class in Britain as elsewhere in Europe defined its identity in contrast to the landed (or aristocratic) classes above and the working class below. The bourgeoisie presented itself as more industrious, intelligent and especially more moral and religious than the brutal and sensual aristocracy or the ignorant and barbaric populace. Much of the virtue of the middle class was located in its responsible family life with a protector/provider husband and a pious wife and mother who made home into a haven of peace and love and a place of religious and moral redemption. The doctrine of separate spheres, which assigned the conflict-ridden public world of business and politics to men and allocated the private sphere of family, home, harmony and love to women, was integral to bourgeois identity and moral authority and was propounded by women writers of advice literature as well as by male authorities like ministers of religion.[2] This ideology, which equated true femininity with home and family and which turned public work into a contaminating activity, which was not only being pressed by powerful voices but being internalized by middle-class women themselves, would create large problems after 1850 for bourgeois women who wanted or needed to join the public labour market.

THE EXPERIENCE OF WORKING-CLASS WOMEN: FROM DOMESTIC TO MARKET ECONOMY

The early profitability of Britain's market economy rested on a foundation of low British wages, long working hours, a substantial pool of casual (intermittent) or unemployed labour and large export markets. This situation was achieved partly by a wide-ranging attack on the defences of labour, including trade union power in various industries and also legislative regulation of wages and working conditions. Trade unions became illegal as a result of the Combination Acts of 1799, passed in the panic around the Napoleonic Wars. When these acts were repealed in 1824, trade unions came under continual attack in a series of strikes and lockouts. Legislation regulating wages and hours stemming from Tudor times, like the Statute of Artificers, was systematically repealed in the 1810s by a government under the sway of a new political economy prescribed by free marketeers (Thompson 1963, p. 279, 284, 594–6). At the beginning of the Industrial Revolution women were key pawns or players in the achievement of a low-wage strategy. At the same time that middle-class women were moving out of the public labour process, working-class women were playing an increasingly exploited role within it, and experienced very acutely the contradictions between the demands of paid and unpaid work. Indeed women's value in the family economy did not translate into the discourse of political economy which did not recognize their unpaid family and domestic work as work at all. Only work which produced exchange value, that is, work which produced commodities or services for exchange in the market for profit, was considered value-creating by theories of political economy whether classical or Marxist!

Capitalists ignored women's value in the family economy but exploited their subsidiary role in market production in several ways. In some industries, like mechanized cotton and wool manufacture, capitalists directly introduced women and children to undercut the wages of men. Thus weaving, which had been the men's work in the domestic system, became the women's in the factory while the more auxiliary spinning, which had been women's and children's work at home, now went to men in the factory (Hall, 1982a).[3] In other instances, like that of the Leicester hosiery industry, a more protracted process of devaluing women's work took place. Here, according to Nancy Osterud, the domestic system of production was disrupted when men were taken into the workshops to do their customary job of knitting but now on wide frames while women were left at home to stitch the stockings by hand and defined and paid there as cheap and unskilled labour. When this definition had become firmly established, women were brought into the factory at the end of the nineteenth century as cheap labour first to do mechanized seaming then knitting (Osterud, 1986, p. 49ff., 63).

While the separation of home and factory, with both demanding long hours of work, was a less manageable situation in which to resolve the tensions between family and market demands, even home-based manufacture could produce insupportable strain. As state inquiries into the condition of hand-loom weavers (1836, 1841) and as Henry Mayhew's interviews with London artisan families (1849–50) make painfully apparent, employers and middle-men, also often caught in a competitive rat race, used a bewildering variety of 'systems' to force down production costs including: pushing work out of the public workshop into workers' homes where they would bear the overheads, moving from time rates of pay to piece rates for goods produced, lowering customary piece rates and imposing frivolous fines, subcontracting work to middlemen who would force piece rates down even more. All these systems led to oppressively long working hours; to use Mayhew's formula: 'under-pay makes over-work' (Yeo, 1971, p. 72–3). Longer working hours affected the whole family and in certain trades, like tailoring, artisans themselves drafted their wives and children into the work process for the first time to produce more goods in order to stay at their customary standard of living. They had continually to work much harder and longer to stay in the same place. One of the most unacceptable ways in which this strain was experienced both by men and women was in the undermining of traditional family roles and the sharp conflicts between work and family time. A tailor told Mayhew (1849–50, p. 209):

> It is six or seven years ago since I worked for the West-end shops. My wife did no work then. I could maintain her in comfort by the produce of my labour. Now she slaves night and day, as I do: and very often she has less rest than myself, for she has to stop up after I have gone to bed to attend to her domestic duties. The two of us, working these long hours, and the Sundays as well, can only get 15s ... now our wives and children must work as well as ourselves to get less money than we alone could earn a few years back.

Resistance to the capitalist strategy of using women as low-wage labour in public workplaces came from several directions. Labouring men were very aware that capitalists were forcing women into the labour market to under-mine the position of more organized male workers. But instead of standing for solidarity, that is entry for women into mixed trade unions and equal pay for equal work, male workers tended to oppose married women's full-time work, arguing that it interfered with women's primary family duties. Instead trade unions increasingly pressed for a family wage large enough to enable a male breadwinner to support a home-based dependent wife and children. They found unexpected allies in members of the evangelical middle class and gentry (ranging from the famous Lord Ashley through to state investigators like J.C. Symons) who championed the ideology of separate spheres and insisted that women belonged in the home where they would both civilize individual working-class families and tame the class as a whole by attracting their menfolk away from radical politics or pubs (Children's Employment, Mines, 1842, p. 35). Both parties supported the Ten Hours Act restricting the hours of employment for women and children in textile mills, while the Evangelicals got women banned from working underground by the first clause of the 1842 Mines Act.

Although different groups may have had different motives, working men, capitalist employers and the Evangelicals all helped create a situation where one or other half of the real lives of working-class women was rendered invisible, with the result that real contradictions could not be adequately addressed. Working men, while often appreciating women's family contribution, maintained the fiction of a non-working wife in their industrial demands and publicly underplayed their wives' necessary role as supplementary breadwinners if the family was to survive. Evangelicals and the state they influenced both assumed that women's rightful role was mothering at home and made no provision for childcare support to enable women more easily to undertake paid work either in the public sphere or based at home. Employers ignored the family duties of women, which were outside the remit of political economy, and never provided workplace nurseries on any scale. Unlike other Western European countries whether Catholic like France or Protestant like Sweden, childcare was never seen as a universal entitlement. Instead, nursery care was only provided from the first decade of the twentieth century, in a climate of eugenic alarm about the deterioration of the national race, specifically to deal with the 'pathology' of deprived or deficient mothers; the Department of Health took responsibility for children under five. Daycare became more widely available during the two world wars to free women for essential munitions work (Lewis, 1980, p. 80; Braybon and Summerfield, 1987, p. 106–7, 237–9). From 1951, with the advent of a Conservative government, state nursery schools offered only part-time sessions and Britain still lags behind all European countries except Portugal in its provision of daycare facilities for three to five-year-olds (*Women in the European Community*, 1992, p. 52).

Caught between different views which conceal one or other half of their lives, working-class women have often welcomed the chance to cut their working hours or leave the public labour market and concentrate their energies at home if an alternative source of income could be found. This was the case in the early nineteenth century where women supported movements like that for the ten-hour factory day and where the pattern increasingly became for unmarried women to work in public and for married women to retire into the home where they would, as need required, do paid work or exchange services with other neighbourhood women to continue fulfilling their primary role as good managers of family survival (Ross, 1983, p. 11). For complex reasons, which included their often temporary and intermittent appearance in the labour market, the fact that the attempt to organize them came from above, and the unsupportive attitude of organized male labour, the most effective forms of protection were not so much trade unions as state intervention especially via Wages Councils (first called Trade Boards when established in 1909), which set legal minima for notoriously low-paid occupations, together with legislation regulating hours of work and health and safety conditions (Hutchins, 1915, p. 183–4). Despite past and present surveys indicating that well-paid working mothers can provide more adequately for the welfare of their children than non-working mothers (Black, 1915, p. 7; *The Guardian*, 5 September 1994), the persistent ideology that women basically have no business in the labour market has meant that legislation in Britain has historically been geared to tackling the worst abuses rather than establishing an equal opportunities framework. Only recently, first with the Equal Pay Act 1970 and then with Britain's entry into the European Common Market, which entailed adopting European law, did equal opportunities legislation come into effect.

MIDDLE-CLASS WOMEN ENTERING THE PUBLIC LABOUR MARKET

No individual's entry into the labour market is ever 'free': it always is constrained by both class and gender pressures. In the case of middle-class women for whom legitimate femininity was so intimately tied to being a home-based wife and mother, it was particularly difficult to make the move into the market. The first women to challenge the ideology of separate spheres were unmarried women who wished to have regular public work or needed to earn a living to support themselves. To remain respectable, these pioneers allowed two characteristics to become attached to women's work which still handicap women today: lower pay and a concealment of family responsibility outside working hours.

Single women did not challenge the ideological supremacy of married motherhood: in fact they even extended the ideology of motherhood so that it would fit their situation and presented themselves as 'social mothers' who did self-sacrificing work in the public world by caring for others, often children among the poor, and by introducing a home influence into public life (Yeo, 1992, p. 75–6). Thus apart from visits to the poor in their dwellings, like those made by members of the Ladies' Sanitary Association, the forerunners of the profession of health visiting, incipient social work often took place in residential institutions called for the first time 'Homes' presided over by 'matrons'. They stressed that their work was even more sacrificial than married mothering. Although these pioneers developed the 'caring professions' such as nursing, social work and teaching on all levels, they also strengthened the idea that real caring could not be tainted with base money considerations. In many cases these women's professions began as unpaid voluntary service or, if paid, as in teaching, women earned significantly lower salaries for doing the same work as men (Morley, 1914, p. 43). Or else, as in the case of the Civil Service, women were kept at lower levels in jobs with specific responsibility for other women and children and legislation removing barriers to their career progress like the Sex Disqualification (Removal) Act of 1919 was ignored for the whole of the inter-war period (Zimmeck, 1984, p. 908–9, 921–2). Only in the case of medicine did the British Medical Association insist on equal pay regardless of sex, out of fear that women might be used to drag down the fees of men (Morley, 1914, p. 139).

So closely were respectable careers associated with single women that many professions operated a formal or informal marriage bar until after World War II (Zimmeck, 1984, p. 904–5, 922–3). Thus women school teachers (always the largest women's profession in Great Britain) had to give up their posts upon marriage in many places until the end of World War II (Lewis, 1984, p. 199). From the turn of the twentieth century onward some women did contest the splitting apart of professional and family ambitions and yearnings. The socialist Fabian Women's Group, for example, recommended university teaching and medicine as professions particularly compatible with marriage and childraising (Morley, 1914, p. 23, 162). They urged the establishment of nurseries where trained professionals could look after the children of other professional women (Fabian Women's Group, 1910, p. 7). On the whole, however, the concept of a woman's full-time career was developing which did not allow for the possibility of combining a profession with biological motherhood or other forms of unpaid family caring.

POST-WORLD WAR II PATTERNS: BACK TO THE FUTURE?

Although working- and middle-class women arrived at their twentieth-century position in the labour market by different routes,[4] similar disabling features historically became attached to their work: women were regarded as cheaper labour if they did paid labour at all and there was no publicly perceived problem about combining family and market responsibilities. The issue of conflict was not supposed to arise because women were ideologically positioned into an either/or choice between the two sets of demands. Working-class women were adjudged to be better mothers if they stayed at home and were only provided with childcare and communal services (including community restaurants) in wartime emergency or when perceived as defective carers. Professional women were assumed not to have family caring responsibilities, so again the issues of devising conceptions of a successful career which allowed room for these or of providing support services to family carers did not arise. Women were left to address these problems individually and privately and did so by hiring servants (until this became too expensive for the middle class after World War II) or by finding relatives or neighbourhood women willing to be childminders (still the predominant pattern, *The Guardian*, 6 August 1994; Meltzer, 1994, p. 22) or by trying to do everything themselves.

The end of World War II saw a new variation in an old pattern which has been the framework within which women have worked in Britain ever since. For many reasons which cannot be fully explored here, women's participation in the labour force became a more publicly accepted fact-of-life. Labour market demand for caring professionals to staff the expanded welfare state and to service the post-war baby boom, some women's determination to build on their wartime experiences of more social opportunities and some women's need for waged work in order to afford the new consumer durables which, paradoxically, were supposed to keep them happily at home, were among these reasons. The new resolution of 150 years of tension between family and labour force demands was now to be part-time work (Lewis, 1992, p. 72, 75–6). In theory this was supposed to allow time both for family tending and for paid work. In reality, as Jenny Shaw's chapter shows, this arrangement has further aggravated the contradictions which women feel of being pulled apart by 'greedy' demands from family and employers and yet feeling they should somehow be able to manage these and blaming themselves when they cannot.

Women are not to blame for the insupportability of these contradictions and we need deeply to recognize this. However it is also important to identify the new pressures which still hold the contradictions in place in order to try effectively to contest them. We are now in a particularly difficult situation where the conditions attaching historically to British women's work are not only being spread to the work of many more groups at home but also being exported abroad. Since the 1970s, the growth of the global factory has led to the exporting of the factory assembly-line phase of the manufacturing process to the Southern countries and especially to the Asian Rim. In the search for low-wage labour, this movement has involved the export of the oldest capitalist patterns of labour exploitation. Thus in the Southern countries, factory jobs involve long working hours, at very low pay in Western terms, with no 'career' possibilities or, perhaps a more accurate way to put it is with little opportunity for permanence and little by way of health and safety protection or social benefits. The exacting assembly of tiny computer circuits or meticulous machine sewing call for sharp reflexes, good physical stamina and the keenest eyesight. Fuentes and Ehrenreich (1984) called attention a decade ago to the preference for very young women who were taken on at age 16 and spit out as used up around age 25. At that time their wages of US$5.00 a day compared with average American factory wages of US$5.00 an hour indicated the source of their attraction for global capitalists. Another tactic is to push work back into the home and get the women workers to bear the costs of overheads. Industrial home-working (together with the most sophisticated computerized information flow to coordinate the production and distribution process) is a feature not only in more traditional areas like garment-making, as organized by a leading company like Benetton, but also now appears in the most sophisticated electronics industries, where, e.g., the assembly of semiconductors from kits is left to South Korean women at home.[5]

The current British experience of this process could arouse a frustrating sense of *déjà vu*, but the situation also contains contradictory potentials which could be mobilized towards new resolutions of old tensions. As in the early Industrial Revolution, although with significant differences, traditional 'masculine' occupations with powerful trade unions are being undermined while so-called 'women's work' is growing. The virtual collapse of shipbuilding, steelmaking and coalmining jobs has not only been caused by the movement of heavy industry to the Southern countries, but also by the unwillingness of the Conservative government to subsidize British companies along with its rush to privatize the nationalized industries (Hutton, 1995).[6] The cumulative statistics are staggering: since 1980, 5.6 million jobs, more than half the traditional jobs in British industry, have been lost (*The Guardian*, 16 January 1995) and male unemployment is running at 13.2 per cent compared with 5.3 per cent for women (*The Guardian*, 9 April 1994). The Conservative government, like the governments of the early nineteenth century, has also made a concerted attack on two of the traditional defences of labour: trade unions and regulatory bodies established by law. The severe handling of the Miners' Strike of 1984–5 has become emblematic of the government's attitude to working-class combinations. The Wages Councils were disbanded in 1993 which put an end to any mechanism for setting minimum wage rates.

For the first time in British history women with jobs almost equal men in the paid workforce: in December 1993, the figures were 10.85 million men and 10.53 million women (*The Guardian*, 9 April 1994). But this apparent parity conceals tremendous disparity in their terms and conditions of employment. Women are supposedly answering the call for 'flexible' workers in service industries, including financial and banking services, catering, health, retailing and secretarial work. But 'flexible' patterns often mean part-time, low-paid labour hired on a casual basis, on intermittent call arrangements or on fixed contracts. Also work is increasingly being 'outsourced' and contracted-out, as in the early industrial revolution, to be done at home (*The Guardian*, 14 January 1995, 'Careers', p. 3). Women fill over 80 per cent of part-time jobs and 77 per cent of part-time work is paid below the Council of Europe's decency threshold – currently £5.75 an hour. Since the demise of Wages Councils, which has hit women workers especially hard, much part-time work pays £3.00 per hour or less (*The Guardian*, 10 October 1994, Section 2, p. 10). Nonetheless, given the chronic inadequacy of public childcare facilities, it comes as no surprise that women reportedly 'want' these terms and conditions in order to have time to deal with family and household demands (*The Guardian*, 15 November 1994; 21 January 1995, 'Careers', p. 2). Where full-time work remains, the early industrial pattern persists with British women working the longest hours in the European Union in what is now being called the 'sweatshop of Europe' (*The Guardian*, 24 January 1995).

Perhaps a more accurate word than 'flexible' is insecure (*The Guardian*, 6 September 1994) since all of these arrangements preclude continuity of employment, never mind a career structure with a pension at the end or even, until very recently, basic employee rights. The absence of social protection is a cornerstone of current capitalist strategy. As a British industrialist, David Kerr, recently put it (*The Guardian*, 15 January 1994, p. 14), 'Central to attracting inward manufacturing investment into the UK have been flexible working practices, mobility of labour, competitive wage rates and, critically for firms, low social costs'. Even a majority of women executives, surveyed by the Institute of Directors, evidently feel that women's employment prospects are being hindered by the European directive giving all women workers the right to 14 weeks' maternity leave with pay! (*The Guardian*, 24 September 1994.)

The government has been staunch in its support of this attitude but the powerful alliance of capital and government is not having things entirely its own way. For example, the Government is currently embroiled in a series of disputes with the European Union and the British courts over social protection for part-time workers. While the Government exempted employers from having to pay National Insurance contributions for part-timers, in a case brought by the Equal Opportunities Commission, the British House of Lords decided that part-time workers are entitled to the same statutory rights as full-timers . Even though the British Employment Minister, Michael Portillo, vetoed European legislation to give part-timers statutory rights (including sick pay, redundancy pay, contracts of employment and protection from unfair dismissal), and was reportedly 'exuberant' that he had thereby 'saved' a large number of part-time jobs (*The Guardian,* 7 December 1994), he climbed down from this position later in the month and proposed legislation to put Britain back into line with the rest of Europe (*The Guardian*, 21 December 1994).

These contests indicate that the current situation contains possibilities as well as problems, openings as well as difficulties. Even the whole process of 'restructuring' needs to be read so that the possibilities of gearing it to the interests of the majority of women (and men) rather than to the interests of capital can be highlighted. The first huge change is in the nose dive in demand for 'male' full-time labour and upswing in the demand for 'female' part-time labour. This opens the way for a profound interrogation of gender roles and a renegotiation of the historically-created gender divisions of responsibility for tasks in family life. The old pattern of women shouldering double burdens needs to be shifted. This has to come partly through the public recognition that support systems are indispensable for childcare and household work no matter whether women or men do it. At the moment the government, in the most unsatisfactory way, only gives childcare allowances to lone parents which actually operate, like the Speenhamland poor relief system of 1795, to subsidize low wages.

The issue of employment 'flexibility', and the predicted death of the office and demise of the traditional 'career', opens space for more people-friendly discussions about the terms and conditions of paid work. Working at home can be exploitative or liberating. When professional men do it, it is called 'consultancy' and some women on administrative and executive grades, as in the Alliance and Leicester Building Society, are finding that home-working makes life more manageable for them (*The Guardian*, 21 January 1995, 'Careers', p. 2–3). But, as in the golden age of proto-industrialization, these workers can command high rates of pay and can therefore have more choice about their own working hours (although the pressure always exists towards cramming a full job into part-time hours and salaries). They are not so trapped in the vicious cycle that Henry Mayhew identified when he coined the adage that underpay makes overwork. How to provide effective employment protection for home-based and for part-time workers is clearly urgent.[7] Cressy Cannan's chapter opens the even more challenging question of how to provide a decent life for all without making employment the only access road to decent welfare benefits.

The break-up of traditional career structures needs to be mobilized by professional women for whom the issue of manageably combining paid and family work depends upon a wider acceptance of plural career models. At present, the idea of career progress still involves working in a full-time, continuous way and moving up the steps of the institutional hierarchy for a period of some forty years until retirement brings a good (occupational or private) pension. On this model women do badly, clustering at the bottom rungs of the promotion ladder and getting paid less than men who do the same job (EOC, 1993, chapters 12–16). In universities, for example, while women feature as nearly 50 per cent of undergraduate students, they comprise around 20 per cent of teaching staff and less than five per cent of professors (AUT, 1993, p. 1). The coming changes in career patterns could work for or against women. The increasing possibility of moving work away from an office situation and indeed of doing consultancy-type work by the project could be helpful. However, the emphasis on youthful productivity and on mobility between institutions as well as between geographical areas tends to disadvantage people who are primary family carers and are often tied to a locality. More realistic for women and men who choose to take on primary family caring responsibilities would be career models which allow for career breaks and for productivity in new rhythms especially later in life, as well as criteria which reward key activities that are also more manageable for people who are less geographically mobile. In university work, this would mean rewarding teaching and pastoral activity as well as research. Although this is a specific example, it serves to point out how the shake-up not to say break-up of old definitions, expectations and practices also needs to be seen as space to be seized for new thinking which could help women and men to resolve exhausting contradictions between their domestic and market lives.

NOTES

1   In women's trades like millinery, dressmaking, upholstery etc., women's labour would be separately priced although work would often be done at home.
2   Sarah Ellis wrote influentially in this genre: e.g. (1841), *The Daughters of England: Their Position in Society, Character and Responsibilities*, London: Fisher. Male authority included clergymen, e.g., Rev. Gisborne, Thomas (1797), *An Enquiry into the Duties of the Female Sex*, London: Cadell and Davies, and Rev. Close, Francis (1839), *A Sermon Addressed to the Female Chartists of Cheltenham*, London: Hamilton, Adams.
3   However, over time, with the help of increasingly complex machinery like self-acting spinning mules, trade unions succeeded in getting spinning redefined not only as male but as skilled work and cotton spinners actually joined the ranks of what has been called the 'aristocracy of labour' by the mid-century.
4   For an earlier analysis of the different routes and the political agenda resulting from them, see Atkinson, Mabel (1914), *The Economic Foundations of the Women's Movement*, Fabian Tract No. 175, London: Fabian Society.
5   For industrial home-working, see Rowbotham, Sheila and Mitter, Swasti (eds) (1994), *Dignity and Daily Bread: New Forms of Economic Organising Among Poor Women in the Third World and the First*, London: Routledge.

6 The privatized utilities have shed labour in what are now perceived as scandalous ways. For example, the British Gas chairman received a 75 per cent salary increase while the number of gas engineers was being reduced, their services being decreased and gas showroom workers getting pay cuts! (*The Guardian*, 7, 9, 24 January 1995; *The Observer*, 22 January 1995.) In privatized British Telecom, the staff of 32,000 maintenance engineers and 10,000 managers has decreased in ten years to 6,000 exchange engineers overseen by 1,500 managers; the estimate is that 90 per cent of redundant workers end up on the dole (*The Guardian*, 28 January 1995, 'Careers', p. 2).

7 Hewitt, Patricia (1993), *About Time: The Revolution in Work and Family Life*, London: Rivers Oram, chapters 6–7 makes constructive suggestions on these issues.

BIBLIOGRAPHY

Association of University Teachers (AUT, 1993), 'Discrimination at the Top', *Update*, 8, (7 June).

Bamford, Samuel (1848–9), *Early Days*, London: Frank Cass reprint, 1967.

Black, Clementina (1915), *Married Women's Work, Being the Report of an Enquiry Undertaken by the Women's Industrial Council*, London: Bell.

Braybon, Gail and Summerfield, Penny (1987), *Out of the Cage: Women's Experiences in Two World Wars*, London: Pandora.

Children's Employment, Mines (1842), First Report of the Commissioner, *Parliamentary Sessional Papers*, 15.

Davidoff, Leonore and Hall, Catherine (1987), *Family Fortunes. Men and Women of the English Middle Class, 1780–1850*, London: Hutchison.

Equal Opportunities Commission (1993), *Women and Men in Britain*, Manchester: EOC.

Fabian Women's Group (1910), *A Summary of Eight Papers and Discussion Upon the Disabilities of Mothers as Workers*, [London]: Fabian Women's Group.

Fuentes, Adrienne and Ehrenreich, Barbara (1984), *Women in the Global Factory*, Boston: South End Press.

Hall, Catherine (1982), 'The Butcher, the Baker, the Candlestickmaker; the Shop and the Family in the Industrial Revolution'; also (1982a) 'The Home Turned Upside Down? The Working-Class Family in Cotton Textiles' in Elizabeth Whitelegg (ed.), *The Changing Experience of Women*, Oxford: Basil Blackwell, pp.2–16, 17–29.

Hand Loom Weavers (1835), 'Report of the Select Committee', *Parliamentary Sessional Papers*, 13, pp.372–438.

Hand Loom Weavers (1841), 'Report of the Commissioners', *Parliamentary Sessional Papers*, 10, pp.273–414.

Hutchins, Barbara (1915), *Women in Modern Industry*, Wakefield: EP Publishing reprint, 1978.

Hutton, Will (1995), *The State We're In*, London: Cape.

Lewis, Jane (1980), *The Politics of Motherhood: Child and Maternal Welfare in England, 1900–1939*, London: Croom Helm.

Lewis, Jane (1984), *Women in England 1870–1950: Sexual Divisions and Social Change*, Brighton: Wheatsheaf.

Lewis, Jane (1992), *Women in Britain since 1945*, Oxford: Blackwell.

Mayhew, Henry (1849–50), *The Unknown Mayhew: Selections from the Morning Chronicle*, (eds) E.P. Thompson and Eileen Yeo, London: Merlin, 1971.

Meltzer, Howard (1994), *Daycare Services for Children: A Survey Carried Out on Behalf of the Department of Health*, OPCS Social Survey Division, London: HMSO.

Morley, E. (ed.) (1914), *Women Workers in Seven Professions: A Survey of Their Economic Conditions and Prospects*, London: Routledge.

Osterud, Nancy Grey (1986), 'Gender Divisions and the Organization of Work in the Leicester Hosiery Industry' in Angela John (ed.), *Unequal Opportunities: Women's Employment in England 1800–1918*, Oxford: Basil Blackwell, pp.45–68.

Ross, Ellen (1983), 'Survival Networks: Women's Neighbourhood Sharing in London before World War One', *History Workshop*, 15 (Spring), pp.4–27.

Scott, Joan and Tilly, Louise (1982), 'Women's Work and the Family in Nineteenth-Century Europe' in Elizabeth Whitelegg (ed.), *The Changing Experience of Women*, Oxford: Basil Blackwell, pp.45–70.

Thompson, E.P. (1963), *The Making of the English Working Class*, Harmondsworth: Pelican.

Women in the European Community. A Statistical Portrait (1992), Luxembourg: Eurostat.

Yeo, Eileen (1971), 'Mayhew as a Social Investigator' in E.P. Thompson and Eileen Yeo (eds), *The Unknown Mayhew*, London: Merlin, pp.51–93.

Yeo, Eileen Janes (1992), 'Social Motherhood and the Sexual Communion of Labour in British Social Science, 1850–1950', *Women's History Review*, 1 (1), pp.63–87.

Zimmeck, Meta (1984), 'Strategies and Stratagems for the Employment of Women in the British Civil Service, 1919–1939', *The Historical Journal*, 27 (4), pp.901–24.

10. Women, Time and Markets: The Role of Feminization and Contradiction in the New Forms of Exploitation

Jenny Shaw

In Robert Lane's (1991) *The Market Experience,* a monumental survey of the theory and implications of the market, there are only two references to women. The first, quoting T.P. Schulz, notes that as women's earning power increases, their time becomes more valuable, they have fewer children but invest more in them. The second, that market work by married women appears not to have a deleterious effect on their mental health. In six hundred and thirty pages of the most comprehensive Western book on the market, this is all. By contrast, this book views gender as critically shaping whatever benefits might accrue from the market and argues that while the market is theoretically indifferent to personal social characteristics, the societies into which it is introduced are not. They are deeply gendered, and this fact affects how market institutions bed down.

As Lane's overall purpose was to consider how the market might yield the conditions for happiness and well-being through forms of work, not gender, it is unfair to light on one point of omission. However, the assumption of an abstract and genderless person who might benefit from the market is unrealistic. Therefore, although I deeply respect Lane's work, this chapter queries both of his statements about women and suggests that the extension of the market is not indifferent to gender but runs in grooves made by it with consequences for women's use of time and psychic well-being. Men and women are not drawn into the market in exactly the same way or at the same rate. All over the world labour and capital markets are highly gendered and, inevitably, this has different consequences for each sex. Some of these may be expressed as psychiatric symptoms, but I interpret 'deleterious' mental health broadly to include the strain and stress of managing and internalizing the contradictory demands which accompany the articulation of market with non-market institutions.

In no part of the globe are there any wholly-market dominated societies; all are embedded within, and depend upon, social relations of a pre-market kind, and in most of these pre-market systems time is not treated as a commodity. Yet, whilst the progress of marketization is uneven and varies from country to country, it is usually women who remain in the pre-market structures for longer than men and/or have the job of mediating between the market and non-market sectors. When Lane commented that as women moved into market activities and their time became more 'valued', he meant 'value' in the sense that it is priced and belongs to the economic system. Although value in a broader, sociological sense cannot be equated with price, the tendency to rank paid work above any unpaid work or, to use Marxist categories, to rank exchange value over use value, is encouraged by the expansion of markets. However, behind the paid/unpaid labour distinction lies a gender division and the key point is that men's and women's time is not treated identically, even when both participate in the formal labour market at the same rates. Women are not free to control their time for themselves outside the market in the same way as men are, and the process of women being drawn into the market is far from straightforward. Women do not drop their familial or domestic responsibilities as they become full-time workers. 'Productive labour' is not substituted for 'unproductive labour' like looking after children or old people, but added to it. Somehow women have to find the time to do both sets of tasks. Effectively they have to manage the cultural contradictions of capitalism (Bell, 1979).

The time focus of this chapter is, of course, only one aspect of the market and in stressing that there are consequences for women of having to manage or straddle different temporal expectations I do not wish to imply that no other group has to manage contradictions or suffer the greater costs of doing so. Flexibility, restructuring and other related developments extract a heavy toll on many other groups too, but the general case about costs is easier to make for women as a group because their work experience is more uniform than that of men. They experience less social mobility and are concentrated in a narrower range of occupations and in part-time work which, paradoxically, is both a cause and an effect of their difficulties. Thus, in Britain at least, whilst work experience tends to divide men it unifies women (Heath, 1981).

Essentially, the chapter argues that those whose position demands that they manage contradictions pay a high personal cost: not only in raised rates of anxiety and depression, lower pay and self-esteem, but they are pushed towards constructing their identities around impossible and unrealistic ideals. Although the detail used to expand this point comes out of European experiences, the theoretical ideas stem from the development literature where the idea of women as managers of contradictions, often produced by 'structural adjustment' policies, is well established. In that domain the importance of attending to gender and women's subordination is increasingly recognized if desired goals such as 'sustainable development' are to be met. For example, disinherited or undercapitalized women may be obliged to farm in environmentally damaging ways. Such themes have been pursued in greater depth in the development literature, but the idea that women may bear the brunt of and/or have to manage the contradictions of change is not a uniquely development issue; it is a fundamental, lubricating feature of many complex societies, especially as they undergo rapid change. As hardly anyone foresees a slowing down of the rate of change, adjustment strategies and their consequences can be expected to persist for a good time yet.

FAMILIES, CONTRADICTIONS AND LABOUR MARKETS

Since Marxism has lost the popularity it once enjoyed in academia, the notion of contradiction as an analytical device for social scientists has lost some of its routine character. Yet this approach need not be tied to any one ideology: its value is that it helps identify flashpoints, growth points and crisis points. 'Look for the contradictions' is as useful a methodological hint as 'look for the function': neither should be rejected for fear that following them implies a commitment to either Marxism or functionalism. And families are quintessentially contradictory. They are what Lewis Coser (1974) calls 'greedy institutions', that is, they make unlimited demands on their members for commitment, effort and time. As such they are inevitably out of line with market institutions which are based on limited liability, contractual relations, measurable output and treating time as money. Still, the unlimited demands made by families are not shared equally by all family members and it is women who traditionally have had the job of maintaining family life and family values.

Even in countries such as Great Britain, which have been capitalist for a long time, many institutions remain which are not organized along market lines; of these family life and personal relations are the most prominent. For many, if not all, families represent a limit to market values and they operate as an important foil to the market in discursive or ideological terms. They are both opposed, and complementary, to the market. Without wanting to romanticize families as 'havens in a heartless world' (Lasch, 1977) it is clear that in most communities emblematic family values are not the instrumental or commodified ones of the market, but the expressive ones of love, loyalty, duty and caring. Yet, stark as the contrast between families and the market may seem, it is wrong to view them as utterly opposed; for family well-being is often interpreted in material terms, with the comfortably-off, well-knit family an essential to the buoyant market. We work hard and consume hard to enjoy goods with and in our families (Clayre, 1974; Wilmott and Young,

1973). For many, families are the motive for wanting to earn more.

Nevertheless, there are important incompatibilities between family norms and market norms and some family members experience these more intensely. The simplest example comes from the patterns of labour market participation of men and women. Almost universally women take time off from work to rear children and pay the price in terms of foregone wages and career development. Heather Joshi and Hugh Davies (1993) have estimated that in Great Britain, at early 1990s rates, an average mother 'lost' £240,000+ over a lifetime. No similar calculation exists in terms of days lost per year, but the stereotype of women as more unreliable workers than men and its consequences for their employment and promotion prospects is evidence of the price women pay for putting their families first, or of 'managing the contradictions' of paid and unpaid work.

Women largely accept that it is they, rather than their partners, who will have to work around school hours, illnesses and vacations, and they welcome part-time work as a way of doing this (Hakim, 1991; Hakim, 1993). That is, they accept their role as the managers of the contradictions. In a study of how willing workers might be to accept flexible or altered hours of work clear gender differences emerged. Men were perfectly happy to contemplate starting work earlier in the morning, but not working in the evenings or at weekends. Women, on the other hand, would contemplate evening and weekend work but not early morning starts. The implication of this is that men were keen to preserve their leisure and drinking time (evenings and weekends) whilst women, who had little or no traditional right to leisure, had to manoeuvre around getting children off to school (Fagan, 1994). Childcare came first, which is why they and not their husbands would consider working at weekends and in evenings.

As Arlie Hochschild and Anne Machung (1989) put it, women have to do a 'second shift'. Despite a real shift in values (Kiernan, 1992; Wilkinson, 1994) showing that a large proportion of both sexes agree with the ideal of sharing domestic labour equally, very few manage to do this. One part of the problem is that men and women have been changing at different rates. As the British M.P. Harriet Harman (1993) describes it, it is a problem of twenty-first century woman and twentieth century man. But the other side of the problem is that much of modern life and economic production is not as efficient as it seems. It creates an awful lot of 'shadow work' (Illich, 1981). This is the additional supplementary work such as housework, commuting, education and training, dressing well and even therapy, entailed by and deemed necessary to cope with modern life. This work has to be paid for or done by somebody and that somebody is more likely to be a woman than a man, although the problem of shadow work is not uniquely one of gender. Nevertheless the calculation that if women's domestic labour were to be included in national income accounting GNP would rise by 20–30 per cent – and this is only part of shadow work – is part of the lore of household economics.

Critically, the overload facing women in market societies is not solved once they enter the labour market. They are not released from the 'greedy institution' of the family, for much of the work which they take on within the labour market is itself of the service sector, 'people-work' or 'caring' kind. It is work that cannot easily be bounded by a four, six or eight hour shift. Those who do it either work extra unpaid hours because the client needed them or they take home the work with them in their heads, worry about it whilst cooking dinner, make telephone calls about it afterwards and lose sleep over it when they finally get into bed. Whilst the market works on clock time, much of women's labour, in and out of paid employment, is governed by process time (Davies, 1994). The overall effect is one of double time standards.

WOMEN AS MANAGERS OF CULTURAL CONTRADICTIONS

The idea of women structurally mediating or containing conflict and contradiction is a huge topic, initiated many years ago by the anthropologist Claude Lévi-Strauss (1949) who argued that exogamous, patrilocal marriage systems could be seen as ways of exchanging women and creating some kinship tie with groups or clans who would otherwise be viewed only as enemies. In this scenario the exchange of women performed a conflict-limiting function. The ensuing debate is far too great to review here, but the general point is that women are often located on margins and perform a structural role of resolving or internalizing systemic conflict or contradiction, and it is worth repeating. At the everyday level, and in societies far removed from those studied by Lévi-Strauss, women's lives are blighted as they have to 'make do', 'fit in' and make sense of a patchwork of demands and tasks; indeed their lives have been likened by Laura Balbo (1987) to the making of a crazy quilt.

If behaviour is the product of social position as much as individual inclination, women are caught in a trap which is the product of a multi-layered moral order. They are required to observe two opposing normative systems. They have to be available for their families, which largely means being willing to respond to unpredictable demands and, at the same time, if they are in paid employment, they have to be predictably and reliably available to do the work that they have contracted with their employers. At various points conflicts are bound to ensue. For simultaneous demands cannot be simultaneously met. This is the classic contradiction, the 'no-win' or 'double bind' situation (Bateson, 1973), in this case a cultural contradiction produced by superimposing market structures on non-market ones. The rules of each sector are incommensurate.

But tensions and contradictions are not simply flashpoints heralding breakdown or change, they are often structural features of complex societies. As David Lockwood (1976) comments in a discussion which draws a distinction between social and system integration, the two forms of integration are interdependent. The misalignment of institutional sectors may create the contradictions, but it is up to individuals to resolve and/or contain them: in other words 'to adjust'. Individuals have a flexibility which allows them to innovate, to 'make do', to solve problems; and it is those who are situated on the margins who have the most experience of mediating different systems and who are forced into developing these skills to the highest degree (Moser, 1989). Many of these are women and they develop these skills not just because of traditional gender subordination, or because the weak often have to use guile and their wits instead of material resources, but because the gender relationship itself is based on what might be described as a 'creative tension'. Something along these lines has run through much of the literature on marriage in the last twenty years but it has been formalized most succinctly by Amartya Sen (1989) for Third World households and by Gail Wilson (1991) for First World ones.

Sen uses bargaining theory to construct a model of gender relations based on a tension between cooperation and conflict and notes that conflicts of interest between men and women are unlike other social conflicts in that the two parties live together and conduct their conflicts in the context of considerable cooperation. All sorts of household resources are therefore not allocated in ways normally predicted by bargaining theory, that is according to interest, contribution or perceived legitimacy. Sen then suggests that the gender relation is a particular form of relationship, not of conflict or cooperation, but of cooperational conflict and that studying the allocation of any particular resource within a household should take this into account. For the data that he uses, Third World families and households, the base line is survival, and the option of exit is less easily available to parties who get a rotten deal, whereas in richer countries with richer households this option clearly exists. Though the First and Third World situations are substantially different in many respects, the physical non-expandability of time makes the use of the model equally applicable.

TIME ZONES, TIME MANAGEMENT AND WOMEN

Time is the ultimate scarce resource and has played an important part in the restructuring of social relations since the first Industrial Revolution. E.P. Thompson's (1967) classic essay on industrial discipline in Britain in the eighteenth century focused on time to show how successful factory production depended on a quite different set of attitudes towards time amongst labourers. However, whilst successful product manufacture demanded punctuality, the role of time in the second or IT-based industrial revolution is changing social relations in a different direction. Ways are now sought of exploiting time more intensively. Employers do not want to pay for 'down-time', only 'up-time' and, indeed, want to pay only for efficient contribution, not for the time spent at work – hence performance-related pay schemes, competitive tendering, out-sourcing and subcontracting. All of these are devices to shift the costs of time from employer to employee. Managing time is a taught skill and a minor industry (Whipps, 1994), whilst control over time is becoming a new form of cultural capital. Time is no longer a diffuse background factor, but a key variable in economic production, and in process production in particular (Von Tunzelmann, 1995).

As control over time is more contested in general it also enters into the negotiations between men and women. At the most general level time has become a commodity, the length of the working day has ceased what seemed to be its historical decline and there is a general sense of life as speeding up. Hours worked per day and per year are increasing (Roediger and Foner, 1989; Christopherson, 1991; Schor, 1992) and overall control over time determines success at the level of the individual, the firm and the nation (Toffler, 1990). In all these re-alignments there are losers as well as winners. The most obvious losers are the unemployed, but even those with jobs suffer for they work long hours under perpetual stress and strain with little or no time to enjoy their families. And, contrary to Lane's assumption that working mothers give more time to their smaller families, there is increasing evidence that children in the rich countries are neglected in important ways and get less, not more, of their parent's time and attention (Hewlett, 1991; Hewitt, 1993; Hewitt and Leach, 1993; Etzioni, 1994; Romer, 1994) whilst, at the other end of the life cycle, there is a global crisis over the care of the elderly.

Modern time management methods assume that time is a commodity like any other and that people will behave 'rationally' and allocate it according to neo-classical principles. But they do not and they daily demonstrate how important gender is and why Sen's model is better than the over-simplified one of marginal utility. Time management manuals tend to be gender-blind and ignore cultural norms and expectations which lead to men and women's time being treated unequally (Seymour, 1992; Shaw, 1994). Nowhere are women as able as men to delegate tasks as the manuals recommend, both because of their lower status and because men are generally reluctant to work for women. Their time is not valued in the same way as men's is. Studies of the distribution of labour-saving domestic appliances show both that time-using appliances diffused faster than time-saving ones and that it was men's discretionary time, not women's, which was the critical factor (Bowden and Offner, 1995). In fact, there are good grounds for seeing household labour and women's time as central to a form of fundamentalism which resists change. Rising standards, which mean that clothes get washed more often or fancier food is cooked, cancel out real and potential time gains for women. Another homely example of how marketization runs along gendered grooves is that the domestic tasks traditionally done by men in the West, such as window cleaning and car washing, have been extensively marketized whilst women's tasks, such as washing, ironing and the bulk of domestic cleaning, have not. Indeed, the process may even have gone into reverse: the advent of washing machines did not save women's time insofar as it led to the decline of laundries.

The net effect of the double time standards is that women have to be especially creative and inventive in managing contradictions at the everyday level. In all societies it appears to be women who go without food to make sure that there is enough for the rest of the family (Whitehead, 1981; De Vault, 1991), without sleep when that is squeezed by work and childcare (Biddle and Hammermersh, 1990) and without free time (Deem, 1986) when there is extra work to do. This pattern is not cost-free.

THE PRICE OF MANAGING CONTRADICTIONS

Measuring the costs, however, is not straightforward. The reason Lane believed market work for women did not have a negative effect on their mental health, despite the longer hours and the difficulty in reallocating domestic labour, was that in market societies it is unemployment rather than overwork which, hitherto, has been more damaging to mental health. Although he gives only one reference to support the point, the generally protective effect of work is well documented and applies to women as well as to men (Brown and Harris, 1978).

The costs occur in two forms, objective and subjective. In addition to the loss of pay, promotion, food, time and sleep mentioned earlier, women suffer higher rates of chronic illness because their caring and working roles leave them little time to look after themselves (Gove and Tudor, 1984; Bird and Freemont, 1991). Whilst the pattern of men's and women's health used to be markedly different, with women having longer lives and better health than men, mainly because they smoked less, the gap is closing. As women enter the labour force, they are beginning to produce disease patterns more like those of men: they smoke more and are rapidly developing stress-related illnesses. There is even evidence that, as women have less control over their work than men, the psychological strains on women are higher than those suffered by men (Karasek et al., 1987; Karasek, 1990). The combination of high responsibility but low discretion or control can be lethal and many women's jobs are of this order. As Karasek and Thorell (1990) warn, there is a major problem brewing for psychosocial and occupation-related health which may be made most visible through women's deteriorating health. The automated office revolution, the growth of communications work, flexibilization and the trend towards part-time work have all contributed to an increase in conditions of high responsibility and low recognition, all developments in which women have been in the front line.

The changing nature of work and the labour market are quite objective phenomena. What is less objective, but potentially as important, is the subjective fit between psychological characteristics or female personality and these structures. This, of course, is a tricky and speculative topic, but there are some striking parallels in work by feminists in the United States and Europe. The social psychologist Kay Deaux (1977) has demonstrated that men and women differ in the way they interpret their lives: women perversely but systematically interpret their successes as unpredictable and contingent but their failures as stable and certain, whilst men reverse this pattern. Another psychologist, Carol Gilligan (1982), has shown a further difference between the way men and women approach moral problems; with women prioritizing relationships and their consequences and men attaching greater importance to notions of objectivity and constancy. In Europe, Frigga Haug (1992) has suggested that women approach responsibility in an intrinsically masochistic way and Rosalind Coward (1992) that women's identities are characteristically formed around ambivalence and unrealizable goals. There is insufficient space here to do justice to these ideas but they add up to a picture of women as socialized into a pattern of accommodation, flexibility and instability, as core features of their identities.

The part-time option, when it is genuinely chosen by women, is a chimera: it appears to be a solution to overload and stress, but what it actually supports is the fantasy that a woman can do all the family work, reproductive and emotional, as well as paid work. It may be this, in combination with an inability to be realistic (Coward, 1992), that locks women into goals which are impossible to achieve, but for which they accept responsibility.

FEMINIZATION AS EXPLOITATION

For all women's willingness to endorse values other than competition and striving for success, the ideological message of the new workplace flourishes in their souls. Flexibility in time management appears to have thoroughly infiltrated housework, possibly because there are no institutional ways of 'protecting' women's work, and has led to ever greater numbers of women doing the 'second shift'. Flexitime is indeed the most important new mode of exploitation and one which is intrinsically linked to the rising rate of women in the labour market. It is frequently heralded as being in women's interests, but its main effect is to intensify their sense of responsibility. It makes adjustments to hours worked appear to be in the employees' interest when they are in fact as much, if not more, in the employers' interests.

In the early stages of an economic growth strategy it makes economic sense to employ more women, for they bring with them complex cognitive skills which can be paid for at the level of unskilled labour (Jenson, 1989). In the later stages of development, and especially where process work is taking over from manufacture, there are other broad advantages of feminization. It enables more effective work intensification in areas where efficiency is difficult to measure. This is most evident in the professions where the nature and rewards of work have changed substantially. Pay rates decline as women enter the professions so, in dual households, both adults have to work. As professionals and as mothers they work long hours and feel guilty about neglecting their children, whilst being fearful at the same time that their employers will think that they are spending too much time on their children and not enough at work. The 'inner life' of the professional middle class is built, as Barbara Ehrenreich (1990) terms it, on a 'fear of falling'.

Though 'child centredness' has clearly grown and childcare expanded to fill time theoretically 'liberated' by household technology (Vanek, 1974), the psychic consequences for mothers of this shift have been less discussed. The key concepts here are 'maternal guilt' and its flip side 'maternal duty', both of which are closely bound up with the changing nature and composition of the workforce. Stafford and Hill (1985) found the amount of time put into childcare varied significantly by educational level and that college-educated mothers put in more than double the amount of time on childcare than did less well educated mothers, whatever their labour market status – an average of 813 as against 231 minutes a week. The idea of the child's interest as equal to, or even overriding, that of the adult has also grown and adds to the sense of obligations to be fulfilled. When this shift in familial ideology is combined with the increase in 'people' work or emotional labour it is easy to see how a tendency to masochism, guilt and ambivalence becomes a highly exploitable seam.

Women generally remain grateful to have a job at all, and know that any criticism will be dismissed as 'whingeing'. They work ever harder to compensate and to demonstrate that they are not shirking. The important point here is that the intensification of work operates through norms which coordinate time, task and legitimacy. Capitalism, both early and late, exploits older non-market-based gender norms and expectations. Effectively this works through time expectations. Women are less unionized or protected than men, they work in process and people work more than manufacture and they are task- rather than time-oriented. Combined, these factors indicate that feminization of the labour force is an extremely important stage in economic growth and evolving patterns of exploitation.

CONCLUSION

Neal Acherson, a British journalist, wrote some years ago on the increase in the pace of life as he experienced it. Even journalists, who lead notoriously hectic lives, had noticed a change in their working conditions. No more boozy lunches at El Vinos's and a stroll back down Fleet Street to the office. In explaining the new patchwork existence of working from home, carrying in his head many tasks simultaneously, constant interruption, weaving domestic and paid work responsibilities together, Acherson noted both the pressure that this, teleworking life, brought and that it was not as new as it seemed. If we wanted to see the shape of the future, he urged, we need only look at our grandmothers. Far from women following the pattern of men's lives, it is women who are the vanguard and men whose lifestyles are now converging with women's as the growth of part-time work, no longer a specifically female phenomenon, demonstrates. Despite this convergence, there are signs that women continue to bear a disproportionate share of the costs of social change (OECD 1994). As competition intensifies, time itself becomes one of the areas where savings are sought and, in this phase, feminization of the labour force plays a crucial role.

BIBLIOGRAPHY

Balbo, Laura (1987), 'Crazy Quilts: Rethinking the Welfare State Debate From a Women's Point of View' in Anne Showstack Sassoon (ed.), *Women and the State: Shifting the Boundaries,* London: Hutchinson.
Bateson, Gregory (1973), 'Minimal Requirements for a Theory of Schizophrenia' in Gregory Bateson, *Steps to an Ecology of Mind,* St Albans: Paladin.
Bell, Daniel (1979), *The Cultural Contradictions of Capitalism,* London: Heinemann.

Biddle, Jeff and Hamermesh, Daniel (1990), 'Sleep and the Allocation of Time', *Journal of Political Economy,* Vol. 98, No. 5, pp.922–43.

Bird, C. and Fremont, A. (1991), 'Gender, Time Use and Health', *Journal of Health and Social Behaviour,* Vol. 32, No. 2, pp.114–29.

Bowden, Susan and Offner, Avner (1995), 'Gender, Class and the Diffusion of Consumer Durables in Interwar England' in V. de Grazia and E. Furlogh (eds), *Gender and Consumption,* Berkeley: University of California Press.

Brown, George and Harris, Tirril (1978), *The Social Origins of Depression,* London: Tavistock.

Christopherson, Susan (1991), 'Trading Time for Consumption: The Failure of Working Hours Reduction in the United States' in Karl Hinrichs et al., (eds), *Working Time in Transition,* Philadelphia: Temple University Press.

Clayre, Alisdair (1974), *Work and Play: Ideas and Experience of Work and Leisure,* London: Weidenfeld.

Coser, Lewis (1974), *Greedy Institutions,* London: Macmillan.

Coward, Rosalind (1992), *Our Treacherous Hearts: Why Women Let Men Get Their Way,* London: Faber.

Davies, Karen (1994), 'The Tensions between Process Time and Clock Time in Care Work: The Example of Day Nurseries', *Time and Society,* Vol. 3, No. 3, pp.277–303.

Deaux, Kay (1977), 'Sex: a Perspective on the Attribution Process' in J. Harvey et al. (eds), *New Directions in Attribution Research,* Vol. 1, Chichester: Wiley.

Deem, Rosemary (1986), *All Work and No Play? A Study of Women and Leisure,* Milton Keynes: Open University Press.

De Vault, Marjorie (1991), *Feeding the Family: the Social Organisation of Caring as Gendered Work,* Chicago: University of Chicago Press.

Ehrenreich, Barbara (1990), *Fear of Falling: The Inner Life of the Middle Class,* New York: Harper Collins.

Etzioni, Amitai (1994), *The Parenting Deficit,* London: Demos.

Fagan, Colette (1994), 'Who Wants to Work Nine to Five? Gendered Working Time-Schedules in Britain', Paper presented at 'Crossing Borders' Conference, Stockholm, May.

Gilligan, Carol (1982), *In a Different Voice,* Cambridge: Cambridge University Press.

Gove, William and Tudor (1984), 'Gender Differences in Mental and Physical Illness: The Effect of Fixed Roles and Nurturant Roles', *Social Science and Medicine,* Vol. 19, pp.141–49

Hakim, Catherine (1991), 'Grateful Slaves and Self-Made Women', *European Sociological Review,* Vol. 7, No. 2, pp.101–21.

Hakim, Catherine (1993), 'The Myth of Rising Female Employment', *Work, Employment and Society,* Vol. 7, No. 1, pp.97–120.

Harman, Harriet (1993), *20th Century Man. 21st Century Woman. How Both Sexes Can Bridge the Century Gap,* London: Vermilion.

Haug, Frigga (1992), *Beyond Female Masochism,* London: Verso.

Heath, Anthony (1981), *Social Mobility,* London: Fontana.

Hewitt, Patricia (1993), *About Time: The Revolution in Work and Family Life,* London: Institute of Public Policy Research/Rivers Oram Press.

Hewitt, Patricia and Leach, Penelope (1993), *Social Justice, Children and Families,* London: Institute of Public Policy Research.

Hewlett, Sylvia Ann (1991), *When the Bough Breaks: The Cost of Neglecting our Children,* New York: Harper Collins.

Hewlett, Sylvia Ann (1993), *Child Neglect in Rich Nations,* New York: UNICEF.

Hochschild, Arlie and Machung, Anne (1989), *The Second Shift: Working Parents and the Revolution at Home,* London: Piatkus.

Illich, Ivan (1981), *Shadow Work,* London: Marion Boyars.

Jenson, Jane (1989), 'The Talents of Women, the Skills of Men: Specialisation and Women' in Stephen Woods (ed.), *The Transformation of Work,* London: Unwin Hyman.

Joshi, Heather and Davies, Hugh (1993), 'Mother's Human Capital and Childcare in Britain', *National Institute Economic Review,* November, pp.50–63.

Karasek, Robert (1990), 'Lower Health Risk with Increased Job Control Among White-Collar Workers', *Journal of Occupational Behaviour,* Vol. 11, pp.171–85.

Karasek, Robert and Thorell, Tores (eds) (1990), *Health, Work, Stress, Productivity and the Reconstruction of Working Life,* New York: Basic Books.

Karasek, Robert et al. (1987), 'Work and Non-Work Correlates of Illness and Behaviour in Male and Female Swedish White-Collar Workers', *Journal of Occupational Behaviour,* Vol. 8, pp.187–207.

Kiernan, Kathleen (1992), 'Men and Women at Work and at Home' in Roger Jowell et al. (eds), *British Social Attitudes. The 9th Report,* Aldershot: Dartmouth.

Lane, Robert (1991), *The Market Experience,* Cambridge: Cambridge University Press.

Lasch, Christopher (1977), *Haven in a Heartless World: The Family Besieged,* New York: Basic Books.

Lévi-Strauss, Claude (1949), *Structures Elémentaires de la Parente,* translated by Rodney Needham (1969), *The Elementary Structures of Kinship,* London: Eyre.

Lockwood, David (1976), 'Social and System Integration' in George Zollschan and Walter Hirsch (eds), *Social Change: Explorations, Diagnoses and Conjectures,* New York: John Wiley.

McEwen, Alison Scott (ed.) (1994), *Gender Segregation and Social Change: Men and Women in Changing Labour Markets,* Oxford: Oxford University Press.

Moser, Caroline (1989), 'Adjustment from Below: Low-Income Women, Time and the Triple Role in Guayaquil, Ecuador' in Haleh Afshar and Caroline Dennis (eds), *Women, Recession and Adjustment in the Third World,* Basingstoke: Macmillan.

OECD (1994), *Women and Structural Change: New Perspectives,* Paris: OECD.

Roediger, David and Foner, Philip (1989), *Our Own Time: A History of American Labor and the Working Day,* London: Verso.

Romer, Paul H. (1994), 'Economic Growth and Investment in Children', *Daedalus,* Vol. 123, No. 4, pp.141-54.

Schor, Juliet (1992), *The Overworked American: The Unexpected Decline of Leisure,* New York: Basic Books.

Sen, Amartya (1989), 'Gender and Cooperative Conflicts' in Irene Tinker (ed.), *Persistent Inequalities: Women and World Development,* New York: Oxford University Press.

Seymour, Jane (1992), '"No Time To Call My Own": Women's Time as a Household Resource', *Women's Studies International Forum,* Vol. 15, No. 2, pp.187–92.

Shaw, Jenny (1994), 'Punctuality and the Everyday Ethics of Time: Some Evidence from the Mass-Observation Archive', *Time and Society,* Vol. 3, No. 1, pp. 79–97.

Stafford, F. Thomas and Hill, Martha (1985), 'Investments of Time by Men and Women' in F.T. Juster and F. Stafford (eds), *Time, Goods and Well Being,* Ann Arbor: University of Michigan Press.

Thompson, Edward P. (1967), 'Time, Work and Industrial Discipline', *Past and Present,* Vol. 39, pp.56–97.

Toffler, Alvin (1990), *Powershift. Knowledge, Wealth and Violence and the End of the 21st Century,* New York: Bantam Books.

Vanek, Joan (1974), 'Time Spent in Housework', *Scientific American,* Vol. 231, pp.116–20.

Von Tunzelmann, Nicholas (1995), 'Time-Saving Technical Change: The Cotton Industry in the English Industrial Revolution', *Explorations in Economic History,* January, pp.1-27.

Whipps, Richard (1994), 'A Time to Be Concerned. A Position Paper on Time and Management', *Time and Society,* Vol. 3, No. 1, pp.99–116.

Whitehead, Ann (1981), 'I'm Hungry Mum', in Kate Young et al. (eds) (1981), *Of Marriage and the Market: Women's Subordination in International Perspective,* London: CSE Books.

Wilkinson, Helen (1994), *No Turning Back: Generations and the Genderquake,* London: Demos.

Willmott, Peter and Young, Michael (1973), *The Symmetrical Family. A Study of Work and Leisure in the London Region,* London: Routledge and Kegan Paul.

Wilson, Gail (1991), 'Thoughts on the Cooperative Conflict Model of the Household in Relation to Economic Method', *IDS Bulletin,* Vol. 22, No. 1, January, pp.31–6.

11. From Dependence to Enterprise? Women and Western Welfare States

Crescy Cannan

INTRODUCTION

This chapter concerns the impact on women of the recent, interconnected, restructuring of welfare states and of labour markets. It will mainly be concerned with EU member states, and notably the UK, France and Germany, with some references to the USA. It will use experiences in these countries to make generalizations about social and cultural changes, resulting from economic policies, arguing that they have a particular impact upon women, although women are themselves a stratified group. I would like to link the material and personal consequences of these changes for women, as producers and consumers of welfare, and as workers in welfare states.

All developed capitalist economies are facing problems of slow or negligible growth, seemingly permanent unemployment, and changing family structures which have produced high proportions of lone-parent families. These factors have produced new kinds of marginalization, a new poverty, a growing dependence on social assistance, and conditions of precariousness in dualized labour markets which particularly affect women – as single parents, elderly people, young people, migrants (Room et al., 1990). These processes have affected women in declining regions or industries for some time, but flexible working conditions in new globalized industries and growing competition within the single European market will have great costs for those in precarious positions in the labour market, and are already creating a crisis in social assistance systems which have become ineffective in relieving growing poverty (Leibfried, 1993).

In the classic Western European post-war welfare states there is a common division between social insurance benefits (which derive from employment, or, via the family, dependence on an insured worker), and social assistance benefits, a more residual system providing benefits, often means-tested or discretionary, to those un- or inadequately insured. The great, and growing, differences between these first and second class systems have meant that it is often accurate to talk of dual welfare states in developed countries, with the social assistance system characterized by a high proportion of women claimants (Lewis, 1993, p. 14; Lister, 1993, p. 8–9). It is the social assistance system which has been most attacked in new right discourses, especially in North American theories of the underclass and the 'dependency culture'. Similarly, in the UK, while there have been increasing attempts to privatize and modify insurance benefits, it has been the assistance system (Income Support) which has been the object of restrictions and cutbacks, with parallel stigmatization of single mothers and welfare 'scroungers' and supervision of their private lives in ways which mark their social inferiority.

Within European Union (EU) social policy the poverty discourse is careful not to pathologize or to blame the poor in the way that underclass theory does, using instead the terminology of social exclusion and marginalization. These are understood as caused by mutually reinforcing processes in contemporary labour markets and now mismatched social security systems. The growing number of people in poverty and on social assistance has raised fears of breakdowns in social solidarity, a concept to some extent with origins in Catholic social thinking. Social policies have been explicitly connected to economic policies, for there is clearly a legitimation crisis for EU economic policies if growth (as well as the end of growth for some states) and human mobility cause a breakdown in traditional communities (Leibfried, 1993). The EU Social Charter will ensure social insurance and employment protection for skilled and professional workers, but for those in precarious parts of the labour market, or with a precarious relationship to it, the social assistance system may, Leibfried suggests, become more like the punitive and highly residual system of the USA as there is nowhere with a strong lobby for the poor.

As the new right discourse is the one that is making a strong challenge in Western Europe to both traditional conservatism (e.g. in Germany) and social democracy (e.g. in France), let alone in the former communist countries in East and Central Europe, it is that version of enterprise culture that I shall consider, though at points with reference to French Socialist Party enterprise policies. In all the debates the relationship between work, family and the welfare state is raised. As we shall see, these are very much women's issues, though the debates are not often conducted in a gendered form.

ENTERPRISE CULTURE

In the UK Conservative political thought began to distance itself from pure monetarism in the 1980s. In the first phase of neo-conservatism from 1974 the aim was conceived in negative terms – reduce taxes, cut spending, restrict benefits, control trade unions and so forth, and in so doing supposedly reduce state intervention and create the space for an expanded and more efficient market domain. In the second, Thatcherite, phase, from the mid-1980s, this move was seen in positive terms: there now needed to be a form of cultural engineering to promote the spirit of enterprise (Morris, 1991).

The two objectives of enterprise culture are to break the culture of dependence supposedly created by the welfare state and to create the new attitudes thought necessary to promote economic growth and prosperity (McCarthy, 1989). The culture of dependence is associated with a tendency to see others and especially the state as responsible for personal and social well-being. By contrast, enterprise culture denotes an active citizen characterized by autonomy, responsibility, initiative, self-reliance, independence, a willingness to take risks, see opportunities, and take responsibility for one's own actions. It is individualistic, and unemployment is a challenge to be met by actively seeking work.

British social policy, then, in the second half of the 1980s actively promoted values and principles, pre-eminently that of personal responsibility. In housing, health care, pensions, education, family matters and child welfare, personal responsibility and minimal state intervention are key principles. Citizens have rights as consumers (not as voters in a local democracy or as members of democratically elected organizations); they have rights of choice which become increasingly negative in areas where the private sector is unlikely to tread, such as social housing or long-term health or social care. This consumer, market 'democracy' is bound up with an attack on the powers and structures of local government and the National Health Service. Professional and administrative resistance to change has been met by the introduction of a new managerialism led by short-term economic, rather than service, goals (Keat, 1991; Newman and Clarke, 1994). Given that the post-war welfare state opened up employment for women, in the 'semi'-professions of teaching, nursing, social work, and in clerical, administrative and manual as well as supervisory positions, the managerialization of the welfare state and the challenge to professional authority have profound implications for women, for the conditions, content and availability of their work.

Enterprise discourse has origins in the USA under President Reagan, but continues with some modifications with President Clinton's empowerment agenda (stressing personal responsibility and parental discipline in teaching children respect for the law and American values). In France a socialist version has developed under President Mitterrand in which new urban and regional policies have emerged with the aim of regenerating the economy. The language of efficiency, competition, the free market and management predominates. The cooperation of universities, industry, social associations, public service professionals and city politicians has produced new plans for growth, new industries, advanced technologies and communications infrastructures. 'From 1985–1989 ... A new economy-oriented culture began to impose itself in the towns' (Biarez, 1993, p. 197). In France, however, there has been an attempt to combine such modern economic development with extensive policies to combat social exclusion and to promote solidarity (Cannan, 1995; Perrin, 1993). Yet while the policies of economic regeneration also aim to prevent social marginalization, they fail to challenge the model of economic growth, so they may actually speed it up.

These economic policies particularly rebound on women, though, as we shall see, in the French context social policies have protected them rather more than in other countries. First though I shall look more closely at how women are fitted into and affected by the range of welfare state regimes and by the social and economic changes which form the current contexts of those welfare states.

WOMEN AND WELFARE STATE REGIMES

All welfare states have, until now, incorporated two premises:

1. That there is or can be full employment – often conceived of as full male employment, though gender-blind in its dodging of the questions about whether employment means full-time, paid work, and continuous work.
2. That normal people live in nuclear families, with a family wage earned by the male breadwinner with dependent wife and children. The family is a private sphere, though different regimes place the boundary between public and private in different places.

We can define a welfare state as consisting of social security and social services (Cochrane, 1993), but the private sphere which also produces welfare (as do community and neighbourhood relationships, employment policies and family policies) is obscured in this kind of definition. Welfare can originate in the state, the market, non-statutory and/or informal relationships; it may be provided by the state or (indirectly) by firms, or via fiscal measures. In whatever kind of welfare state, rights through work, or derived rights through marriage or family, are fundamental – and were of course also so in the former communist countries of East and Central Europe. This was not a problem while everyone could find work but under free market policies more people will necessarily be without work or in precarious or lower paid work, so their welfare entitlements will be insecure. The extent to which this problem applies equally to men and women depends upon the varied employment promotion and protection policies which make the right to work more or less a reality and which regulate conditions of work.

The classic welfare states fall into different regimes or ideal-typical models. In each regime women experience a rather different welfare state from men. Comparing the regimes illuminates how welfare states impinge on women's lives, and how retrenchment is affecting women. Esping-Andersen (1990) has provided three much discussed worlds of capitalism. In the liberal, Anglo-Saxon regime means-tested benefits, and modest universal transfers and social insurance schemes are accompanied by benefits with strict rules and stigma. There is a traditional work ethic that limits state intervention and reform. It is typically to be found in the USA, Canada and Australia, and increasingly in the UK.

The conservative-corporatist or Bismarckian (Leibfried, 1993) regime links social rights to status and preserves status differentials. There is a strong influence of the church over social and family life, a subsidiarity principle which limits state intervention in the family to occasions when its resources are exhausted and which assumes that wives will provide unpaid caring services. Thus there are few services, but there are financial benefits which reward marriage and an uninterrupted work record. Typically this model is to be found in the Federal Republic of Germany, France, Austria and Italy.

The social democratic regime means universalistic state-run insurance benefits and services at middle-class standards. All contribute and all benefit. There is a commitment to high employment, to high levels of female employment and to a socializing of informal family care. This model is typically found in Scandinavia.

There is an absence of analysis of gender statistics, and in this respect Esping-Andersen fails to acknowledge that men's and women's labour are gendered commodities with specific relationships to the labour market due to their relationship to family life. The free services provided by women in the domestic economy find no place in the aggregate official social welfare statistics (Langan and Ostner, 1991). At the same time, different countries do more or less to help women in their caring roles (provision of nurseries, home helps, and so forth), so that the public and private spheres are always connected, but in subtly different ways in different welfare regimes. What I propose to do now is to consider the differential impact of these post-war welfare states on women, asking how current retrenchment is affecting women bearing in mind that welfare states are major employers of women.

THE SCANDINAVIAN OR SOCIAL DEMOCRATIC REGIME

The Scandinavian regime gives social rights based on employment rather than marriage; women in principle have equal access to the labour market, and have good entitlement to services (rather than monetary transfers) provided as means of assisting mothers, people with disabilities and so forth, into employment. But, as Langan and Ostner (1991) note in Sweden, women seem to have exchanged dependence on men for dependence on the state, and in practice the labour market is highly segregated. Women are much more likely to work in the public services than men, and to work part-time. With retrenchment in the welfare state, women will suffer disproportionately as their benefits and services, and the employment from which they derive, are cut. While the Scandinavian model presents the appearance that women have been liberated, it endorses a high degree of gender segregation in the labour market and in the home, and Langan and Ostner (1991, p. 135) characterize it as a 'universalization of a female social service economy', in which the power relationship between men and women has changed, but at women's expense.

Jane Lewis (1993) describes Sweden as a weak male breadwinner country. She argues that any development of the welfare regime concept must incorporate the gendered relationship between paid and unpaid work. The Swedish Social Democrats in the 1960s and 1970s aimed to create a dual breadwinner society, treating women and men as citizen workers, with social entitlements dependent upon employment status. But women – as under communism – were thus forced to work to gain their social rights as citizens. Because labour market segregation is among the worst in the Western world, Sweden in fact offered less to women than say France – which we will consider in the next section.

THE CONSERVATIVE-CORPORATIST OR BISMARCKIAN REGIME

Here we see a welfare regime typified in the Federal Republic of Germany; it has been a stable and long-lasting system which appears to be satisfactory to the major political parties and to the majority of men and women (Ostner, 1993). It pools risk only within certain groups of insured occupations, so that the egalitarianism and universalism of Beveridge's British model are absent. It emphasizes capitalist economic development and a traditional notion of the family, legitimated by the strong position of the Churches; its Catholic corporatism stresses social ties, subsidiarity, mutual obligations. Langan and Ostner (1991, p. 136) refer to it as a gendered status maintenance model; one aim of social security is to enable male workers to support a non-working wife and children as his dependants. The system, then, advantages the male 'normal worker' and the female 'normal wife', and it assumes long-lasting marriages. It serves poorly those who do not fit – divorced or never married mothers, the young and disabled who have not been able to work and gain insurance benefits, elderly people.

The post-war West German welfare state emphasized, using the principle of subsidiarity, the privacy of the family, and its right to freedom from state interference, conceived in negative ways and equated with Nazi or Communist policies. For this reason services to families are relatively few, and child benefits were introduced only in the 1980s – much later than in other European countries including East Germany. In both the former East Germany and West Germany women were controlled by the state. Chamberlayne (1994) refers to public patriarchy in the old state socialist system in which all citizenship stemmed from employment (and all were expected to work). East German women are now at greater risk of unemployment, because of economic collapse in their area, and they have been subsumed into a West German system which puts impediments to married women's employment, rewarding non-working wives through the tax system, having short school days and so forth. Paradoxically the West German system of private patriarchy based on the male breadwinner has produced a low birth rate: there are for most West German women high opportunity costs in having a child, in terms of foregone wages.

During the 1980s the Christian Democrats attempted to maintain the insurance/assistance divide despite overburdened locally-financed social assistance schemes (Chamberlayne 1991/2, p. 9). The Social Democrats and the Greens opposed this policy, calling for a common basic insurance scheme in order to remove the divide. The Greens went further, questioning employment as a basis for social protection because of the environmental costs of economic growth. They have raised the question of how we may begin to move away from an individual contribution system based on life-long employment to a concept of citizenship based upon social usefulness.

This could be an important policy shift for women given their less secure position in the labour market. French social policy over the 1980s began to move in this direction. RMI (*Revenu minimum d'Insertion*), introduced in 1988, is a benefit which integrates the insurance/assistance systems. It credits recipients with insurance contributions while helping them to become integrated through very broadly conceived work (because it could include unpaid work and informal caring or community work) or training (which can include personal development or engaging in self-help groups). There is an insistence in the large-scale urban social development programmes on participation of the excluded and of the need to promote social welfare and solidarity based upon membership of *le social* rather than employment (Cannan, 1995). And benefits which allow mothers to remain at home with children also credit them with insurance. There has thus been a policy of preventing the slide away from insurance benefits, an attempt to keep those at risk of marginalization in the first class welfare state, which should benefit women.

At the same time French women are markedly more likely than their sisters in other countries to be in full-time, continuous employment, and they are helped in this by generous childcare and family support services, and by extensive equality legislation. As Hantrais (1993) demonstrates, French social policy is distinctive in its accommodation of women's two roles, as workers and as wives/mothers, although the relative emphasis of these has changed under different governments. It is this characteristic that causes Lewis (1993) to call France a modified male breadwinner country as it recognizes women's claims as both wives/mothers and as workers: we can see the way French policies fit with Esping-Andersen's conservative welfare regime because its insurance system is not redistributive or egalitarian and because it emphasizes a strong place for the family, yet we also see, particularly but not entirely, under the socialists over the 1980s, a long tradition of promoting women in the workplace. Even so, French women conform to the trend in other countries: they are concentrated in the service sector, in the hotel and catering trades, and in the welfare state professions of primary school and nursery teaching, caring and social work, nursing and health care (Hantrais, 1993, p. 128).

THE ANGLO-SAXON OR LIBERAL REGIME

Here there is an emphasis on formal equality, but it is the equality of and in the marketplace in that equal opportunities and anti-discrimination legislation exists less to promote the collective rights of women (or black or disabled people) than to remove barriers to competition and individual freedoms. At the same time social policies encourage (or force through lack of alternatives) people to stay in the labour market because the state is only the provider of last resort. The state's granting of concessions to womens', black and disabled lobbies for equal rights in the workplace has been part of a process of turning the demands back on these groups: work, not welfare. Residual, and thus stigmatizing, services are reserved for the truly desperate and the 'deserving' poor. The family is a private realm, explicitly outside the reach of social policy unless it has failed.

The USA is the archetypal example of such a regime, yet we have to be careful as there is local variation of social provision in this federal system. Residual the welfare state may be, but nevertheless its health care, education, social services and social security systems are major employers, and as we saw in Sweden, employers of women. Again the labour market is highly segregated, with women disproportionately hit as workers by the public expenditure cutbacks of the 1980s (Ginsburg, 1992, p. 111), and by the further cuts in welfare programmes under President Clinton in 1994/5.

Gimenez (1989) has observed that, strictly speaking, what we are seeing in the USA is less a feminization of poverty (because the proportion of poor people who are women has not changed significantly over the last three decades) than a shift in poor women's dependence on poor men to dependence on the state (cited in Ginsburg, 1992, p. 114). Poverty has increased in the USA since the early 1980s, affecting a disproportionate number of mothers and children, leading Meucci (1992) to refer to a pauperization of motherhood in that country. Here we see the perverse effects of a welfare state which uses very low benefits as a work-forcing mechanism while creating more children with health and social difficulties who add to the numbers who become supervised in this system of public patriarchy. For both the USA and Britain have cut or restricted services to families, and drawn poor families who are seen as having behavioural problems, into the supervision of the social work and therapeutic system. In Britain an example of this is in the cuts in day nurseries which were transformed over the 1980s into family centres providing social work services to mothers who attended the centres with their children (Cannan, 1992). In both countries this has been part of a redrawing of the boundary between family and state, and a renegotiation of the social security contract, in which welfare dependency is castigated, and family self-sufficiency and privacy extolled. It is significant that the strength of the Anglo-Saxon new right discourse on the new obligations of citizenship has been such that the Democrats under Clinton and the British Labour Party, partly drawing on Clinton's message and on the report of the British Social Justice Commission (1994), have also emphasized responsibilities rather than rights of citizens.

Esping-Andersen, in passing, calls the UK a liberal regime; while this may be the direction of the Conservative government of the 1980s and 1990s, it has contradicted the egalitarian, universalistic system established following the Beveridge Report of 1942 (so Ginsburg (1992) prefers to call the British regime 'liberal collectivism'). While Beveridge emphasized universal social rights of citizenship, with a national insurance system, his model was based on full employment policies, family allowances and a national health service. He thus thought that National (social) Assistance would diminish as most people gained work or rights by marriage. His regime is also predicated on an assumption that most women would marry and once married would stop working and would perform the 'vital, unpaid services' without which 'husbands could not do their paid work, without which the nation could not continue' (paragraph 309, quoted in Meesor and Williamson, 1992, p. 62). While the new right claims that welfare states induce dependence, Beveridge was in fact most concerned with work incentives, personal and marital responsibility, savings and so forth, to promote the overall goal of economic growth (Harris, 1990).

This strong male breadwinner model (Lewis, 1993) has left a number of women in a vulnerable position – never-married mothers, divorced and separated mothers, elderly women who had worked irregularly, been married to a man with irregular work, or who had been carers for a disabled husband – and they have been increasingly represented in the social assistance system, being un- or poorly-qualified for insurance benefits. If the goal of a welfare state were equity it would lift lone mothers into a state comparable to two parent families. Sorensen (1989) found that while in Western Europe and the USA lone mother families are generally poorer than married couples with children, those in the USA are relatively worst off, those in the UK not far behind, with smaller but still significant differences in Holland and Sweden (and the Federal Republic of Germany – Ginsburg, 1992, p. 205). The isolation and poverty of lone mothers in Britain is compounded by poor mental and physical health (Popay and Jones, 1991). The benefit system in the USA then has an extremely limited impact, in contrast to Sweden, France and the Netherlands. This is not surprising given that it is the only developed country to have no universal child benefit, and that its principle benefit for lone and poor mothers, Aid for Dependent Children, has been restricted over recent years, with continuing cuts under the Clinton administration to welfare programmes such as school nutrition schemes.

The position of lone parents in France is better than in other countries, partly because generous universal child and family benefits and services pull lone parents into a state comparable with married parents, and partly because mothers are well supported as workers (Hantrais, 1993; Baker, 1991). The majority of British lone mothers are dependent on benefits, and as against the trend in other EU countries, the labour force participation rate of female lone parents in Britain fell during the 1980s (Moss, 1988, p. 3; Kiernan and Wicks, 1990, p. 33–4), and again unlike other EU countries, British lone mothers have a lower labour force participation rate than do their married counterparts (Room, 1993, p. 18).

Recently Britain has drawn closer to the American regime: the benefits system is being used more clearly as a work-forcing system, stigma and disincentives are attached more clearly to benefits, and despite the absence of support services such as childcare, the unemployed and lone mothers are increasingly castigated for not finding or creating work. Clearly this exerts downward pressure on wages – always an aim of enterprise policy which sees reducing wages as important for making industry competitive. Dominating this shifting discourse, especially in America, is the image of the welfare mother as promiscuous, lazy, ill-disciplined and a welfare cheat (Meucci, 1992; Fraser, 1993). In Britain the new Child Support Agency is being used to take women off benefits, forcing them either to return to dependence on the father of their children or to find work, though protest from fathers is halting a measure which does at least require fathers to acknowledge their responsibilities.

The different welfare regimes have varying encouragements and disincentives, helping or forcing citizens to work. This difference is an important one, and we have seen that in France or Sweden women are helped to work with employment protection legislation (such as rights for part-time workers, maternity rights, health and safety regulations) and childcare services, while in the USA women are forced to work by lack of services or by services used in such a way that there are deterrents to claiming. The simple feminist demand that women have equal rights to and at work has to some extent been hijacked by the new right: work in enterprise culture may not be liberating at all, because its conditions are not sufficient to provide the goods and freedoms which dependence on men or the state seemed to deny. It is with this question that I conclude, considering women as workers in welfare states.

WOMEN WORKERS AND ENTERPRISE CULTURE IN THE UK

I have argued that the vision of enterprise culture heralds policies that are disproportionately damaging for women. It is likely to reinforce gender (and perhaps other) divisions in its practical outcomes as it restructures the welfare state. But there may be wider cultural and environmental changes that we need to consider in terms of their impact on women's (and therefore children's) psycho-social well-being.

The attack on dependency culture is mainly directed at women, for it is women who are the single parents on social assistance, and women who are restigmatized in the public debates on whether single parenthood is an adequate form of family. The promotion of family responsibility is an attack on non-traditional family forms. The 'responsible' parent does not ask for support from the state and yet is advantaged by the state in hidden welfare states of fiscal measures, such as tax relief on private pensions or mortgages. The good wife is properly dependent on her husband; it is dependence on the state which is pathologized. The notion of personal responsibility has underlain the creation of the new image of public services and state benefits as undesirable for the 'normal' majority.

The introduction of internal markets in the health care system and of a mixed economy of welfare is fragmenting the community care services. The decline in the powers and resources of local authorities – a deliberate government policy – has meant that, despite the introduction of complaints procedures, citizen's charters and the like, users are not necessarily more empowered as consumers, and the services workers are not necessarily more accountable to their users. Women are greater users of these services as carers and as elderly people, and are disproportionately affected by local variation and restrictive services despite the needs-based rhetoric of the 1991 National Health Service and Community Care Act.

Sources of informal support – supposedly to flower under the freedoms of enterprise culture – may be eroded by it. As the decline in public transport takes people off streets and into cars, streets become less friendly and more dangerous. The growth of out-of-town superstores (by firms with strong links to the roads lobby) causes small shops and businesses in town and village centres to die, making it an even more isolated life for those without cars – predominantly the poor and women. Local networks are weakened and encounters between neighbours and kin decline, encounters which are important for mental health, and as sources of informal care and mutual aid. Together with the decline of small, local workplaces due to increased economic competition, the fabric of locality, of civil society is eroded. The EU model of growth is one that depends on mobility of workers, and it is already well known how patterns of migration and weekly commuting to work destroy the fabric of family and community life (for instance in Portugal, Room, 1993).

Performance-related pay, appraisal systems, and management-by-objectives are deliberately introducing masculinized organizational cultures which conflict with those of the welfare state professions (e.g. that it is more important to spend time with patients, pupils etc., than to improve throughput or reduce unit costs; that supporting and helping is more important than controlling social work clients). In hospitals, schools and social services there is greater supervision by managers – who may no longer be of the same profession – and a concomitant decline in professional autonomy (Clarke, Cochrane and McLaughlin, 1994). All this amounts to an attack on the 'semi'-professions, one of whose characteristics has always been that they have a preponderance of women, as workers and as clients or users. For women workers in restructured welfare state services there is a growing distinction between those on the periphery who find short-term contracts, competitive tendering and low pay, and those in the core. Here life is increasingly tough, especially for women who would be managers. While new managerialism seems to open opportunities for women, doing away as it does with old hierarchies, it makes extreme demands on workers' energies and commitment. As Newman (1994) has found, women in management have to make great personal sacrifices if they are to keep up with the pace, especially as the old securities of a life-long career with a single employer are disappearing fast.

As front-line workers of the welfare states, in health care, social services, the probation service, schools, in both statutory and non-governmental organizations, women have to face the consequences of the decline in long-term care services for mentally ill and elderly people, and the restrictions on social security benefits. These together are raising the levels of stress and violence with which professionals deal. Indeed, the culture of enterprise could be introducing a blend of hedonism which promotes an individualism associated with crime, divorce and child neglect, and a fear culture

> where life becomes a perpetual endeavour; where stress, guilt and fear of failure are likely to loom large; where the workaholic ethic threatens familial and personal relationships and leisure pursuits; where companionship in the workplace is constantly threatened by rivalry and suspicion; where the emphasis on responsibility and accountability exacts its toll. The subjection of human activity to the verdict of the market does not exactly encourage such human values as loyalty and integrity. (Heelas and Morris, 1992, p. 13)

CONCLUSION

The culture of enterprise uses a rhetoric of empowerment but is overwhelmingly individualistic. Enterprise literature emphasizes teamwork, but for specific, short-term purposes in flexible employment. The old solidarities of the workplace have gone, and as preparation, students' experiences of higher education are changing. Modular and credit accumulation systems encourage education 'as you go'; no longer part of a cohort which grows together in collegiate solidarity, mass education is now a lonely, private, individually negotiated affair, in which students are prepared for managing their own work without expecting to rely on others.

I have concentrated on the negatives of enterprise culture, showing that it underlies a restructuring of the welfare state with profound consequences for women who disproportionately inhabit its spaces as workers and as service users. On the other hand there are opportunities in enterprise culture. Old systems of domination are being broken up, with a new pluralism emerging in which grassroots groups and new cross-European networks are emerging (e.g. of women, of people with disabilities, around social exclusion). The basic income debate begins to challenge the social assistance/insurance divide and to look beyond employment as the basis of citizenship; this could offer women a way out of the current precariousness of marriage or work as a basis for welfare. Community care politics in the UK, involving new social movements and new partnerships (as in the social development of neighbourhoods in France), is beginning to create new solidarities which rest less in employment than in social participation. Women should – as in developing countries (Moser, 1989) – be able to take a lead in developing means of active citizenship, given their ingenuity and enterprise in managing to juggle benefits, children, precarious or low paid work, with informal care. There is no turning back to the classic welfare states with their stable Fordist labour markets, so the field is open for women to devise a socially just, environmentally sensitive basis for social rights which can take account of the varied needs and interests of women and which moves beyond a juggling act of dependence on men, the state or precarious employment.

BIBLIOGRAPHY

Baker, John (1991), 'Family Policy as an Anti-Poverty Measure' in Michael Hardey and Graham Crow (eds), *Lone Parenthood: Coping with Constraints and Making Opportunities*, Hemel Hempstead: Harvester Wheatsheaf, pp.110–25.

Biarez, Sylvie (1993), 'Urban Policies and Development Strategies in France', *Local Government Studies*, 19(2), pp.190–207.

Cannan, Crescy (1992), *Changing Families, Changing Welfare: Family Centres and the Welfare State*, Hemel Hempstead: Harvester Wheatsheaf.

Cannan, Crescy (1995), 'Urban Social Development in France', *Community Development Journal*, Vol. 30.

Chamberlayne, Prue (1991/2), 'New Directions in Welfare? France, West Germany, Italy and Britain in the 1980s', *Critical Social Policy* , Issue 33, pp.5–21.

Chamberlayne, Prue (1994), 'Women and Social Policy' in John Clasen and Richard Freeman (eds), *Social Policy in Germany,* Hemel Hempstead: Harvester Wheatsheaf, pp.173–90.

Clarke, John, Cochrane, Allan and McLaughlin, Eugene (eds) (1994), *Managing Social Policy*, London: Sage.

Cochrane, Allan (1993), 'Comparative Approaches and Social Policy' in Allan Cochrane and John Clarke (eds) , *Comparing Welfare States: Britain in International Context*, London: Sage/Open University.

Esping-Andersen, Gøsta (1990), *The Three Worlds of Welfare Capitalism*, Cambridge: Polity Press.

Fraser, Nancy, (1993), 'From Entitlement to Obligation? Shifts in the US Discourse of Social Welfare', Paper given at conference on 'Intellectuals in Political Life', Rutgers University, 12–13 February.

Gimenez, M. (1989), 'The Feminization of Poverty – Myth or Reality?', *International Journal of Health Services* 19(1).

Ginsburg, Norman (1992), *Divisions of Welfare: A Critical Introduction to Comparative Social Policy*, London: Sage.

Hantrais, Linda (1993), 'Women, Work and Welfare in France' in Jane Lewis (ed.), *Women and Social Policies in Europe: Women, Family and the State*, Aldershot: Edward Elgar, pp.116–37.

Harris, José (1990), 'Enterprise and Welfare States: A Comparative Perspective', *Transactions of the Royal Historical Society*, Vol. 40, pp.175–95.

Heelas, Paul and Morris, Paul (1992), 'Enterprise Culture: its Values and Value' in Paul Heelas and Paul Morris (eds), *The Values of the Enterprise Culture: the Moral Debate*, London: Routledge.

Keat, Russell (1991), 'Introduction: Starship Britain or Universal Enterprise?' in Russell Keat and Nicholas Abercrombie (eds), *Enterprise Culture*, London: Routledge.

Kiernan, Kath and Wicks, Michael (1990), *Family Change and Future Policy*, London: Family Policy Studies Centre.

Langan, Mary and Ostner, Ilona (1991), 'Gender and Welfare' in Graham Room (ed.), *Towards a European Welfare State?*, Bristol: SAUS, pp.127–50.

Leibfried, Stephan (1993), 'Towards a European Welfare State? On Integrating Poverty Regimes into the European Community' in Catherine Jones (ed.), *New Perspectives on the Welfare State in Europe*, London and New York: Routledge, pp.133–56.

Lewis, Jane (1993), 'Introduction: Women, Work, Family and Social Policies in Europe' in Jane Lewis (ed.), *Women and Social Policies in Europe: Work, Family and the State*, Aldershot: Edward Elgar, pp.1–24.

Lister, Ruth (1993), 'Tracing the Contours of Women's Citizenship', *Policy and Politics*, Vol. 21(1), pp.3–16.

McCarthy, Michael (ed.) (1989), *The New Politics of Welfare: An Agenda for the 1990s?*, Basingstoke: Macmillan.

Meesor, Lynda and Williamson, Valerie (1992), 'Vital Work To Do: The Implications of the Report for Women' in John Jacobs (ed.), *Beveridge: 1942–1992*, London: Whiting and Birch, pp.59–79.

Meucci, Sandra (1992), 'The Moral Context of Welfare Mothers: A Study of US Welfare Reform in the 1980s', *Critical Social Policy,* Issue 34, 12(1), pp.52–74.

Morris, Paul (1991), 'Freeing the Spirit of Enterprise: The Genesis and Development of the Concept of Enterprise Culture' in Russell Keat and Nicholas Abercrombie (eds), *Enterprise Culture*, London: Routledge.

Moser, Caroline (1989), 'The Social Construction of Dependency: Comments From a Third World Perspective' in Martin Bulmer et al. (eds), *The Goals of Social Policy*, London: Unwin Hyman.

Moss, Peter (1988), *Childcare and Equality of Opportunity*, Consolidated Report to the Commission of the European Communities: Brussels.

Newman, Janet (1994), 'The Limits of Management: Gender and the Politics of Change' in John Clarke, Allan Cochrane and Eugene McLaughlin (eds), *Managing Social Policy*, London: Sage, pp.182–209.

Newman, Janet and Clarke, John (1994), 'Going about Our Business? The Managerialization of Public Services' in John Clarke, Allan Cochrane and Eugene McLaughlin (eds), *Managing Social Policy*, London: Sage, pp.13–31.

Ostner, Ilona (1993), 'Slow Motion: Women, Work and the Family in Germany' in Jane Lewis (ed.), *Women and Social Policies in Europe: Work, Family and the State*, Aldershot: Edward Elgar, pp.92–115.

Perrin, Evelyne (1993), 'Traditional Industrial Cities in Europe and the Urban Policy Challenge, Conference, Lille, May 1992', *Journal of Urban and Regional Research*, 17(1), pp.129–31.

Popay, Jennie and Jones, Gill (1991), 'Patterns of Health and Illness Among Lone-Parent Families' in Michael Hardey and Graham Crow (eds), *Lone Parenthood: Coping with Constraints and Making Opportunities*, Hemel Hempstead: Harvester Wheatsheaf, pp.66–87.

Room, Graham et al. (ed.) (1990), *'New' Poverty in the European Community*, London: Macmillan.

Room, Graham (1993), *Anti-Poverty Action-Research in Europe,* Bristol: SAUS.

Social Justice Commission (1994), *Social Justice, Strategies for National Renewal,* London: Vintage.

Sorensen, A. (1989), 'Women's Economic Vulnerability: The Case of Single Mothers', Paper given at the EC Conference on 'Poverty, Marginalization and Social Exclusion', Alghero, April.

PART FIVE

Problematic Transitions to Market Societies
in the East

12. Confucian Ideology on Women and Married Women's Participation in the South Korean Labour Force

Kim Kyung-Ai

THE CONFUCIAN IDEOLOGY OF WOMEN'S SUBORDINATION: THE SEPARATION OF MEN AND WOMEN

Confucianism is a system of norms and values concerning the hierarchical relationship between people, focusing on the problem of how to establish moral right and harmonious relations (Kim Young-Ock, 1987, p. 33). The major teaching of Confucius on women was based on the Confucian definition of the relationship between men and women as: 'attention should be paid to the differences between husband and wife' (*Bu-bu-yu-byeul*) as one of the five human relations in society (Park Yong-Ock, 1976, p. 8). According to *Ye-ki*, a book of Confucian teaching, *Bu-bu-yu-byeul* was concretely regulated by *Nae-oe-bop* (the rigid rule of segregation) which specifies (1) separation in living and social space, and (2) the strict sexual division of labour between men and women (Han Myong-Sook, 1985, p. 5–6, 35).

According to the rule of separation in the living and social space of men and women by the *Nae-oe-bop*, women were defined as 'the person inside the home' (*an saram*), and men as 'the master outside the home' (*Ba-gat chu-in* or *Ba-gat yang-ban*), respectively. Women were supposed to spend most of their lives at home, entirely secluded from the outside world. Houses were divided into male sections (*Sa-rang-che* or *Sa-rang-bang*) and female sections (*An-che* – inner place, or *An-bang* – inner room).

The spatial segregation between women and men also entailed the sexual division of labour between men and women, who were assigned to different spheres of activity. Women were associated with the daily rhythms of domestic life as wives and mothers, while men were associated with the public sphere and also represented their household to the extra-domestic kin and in community affairs as breadwinners. Women were confined to their role of giving birth to their husbands' son(s) and rearing him (them) to perpetuate their family name. A woman should be a devoted wife, a dutiful daughter-in-law, and a self-sacrificing mother, providing every service to her children, her husband, and her husband's family, and preparing sacrificial rites for her ancestors at home.

Besides the sexual division of labour, the rule of segregation (*Nae-oe-bop*) confining women to the home was ultimately related to the segregation of women from men for the sake of chastity (Han Myong-Sook, 1985, p. 40). One of the most important reasons why women were strongly recommended to go outside the home as little as possible was to keep them away from other men, as expressed in the saying that 'both women and china should not be allowed to go outside the home' (the implication being that otherwise both would be broken). Even at home, women were recommended not to be together with men, even brothers and relatives from childhood, in the saying: 'men and women should not be together from the age of seven' (*Nam-yeo-chil-se-bu-dong-suk*). The purpose of keeping women inside the home and separate from men from childhood was basically to control women's sexuality throughout their lives. In particular, faithfulness to their husband was strictly demanded: during marriage, women were subject to being expelled from the home by their husband's family if they committed adultery, which is one of the seven evils (*Chil-geo-gi-ak*).

In contrast to this strict rule of sexual fidelity for women, a husband could have as many wives as he wanted, and was totally free to have extra-marital affairs with other women. *Kisaengs*, who were trained in dancing and singing in order to provide entertainment for men, were freely available to those who could afford them. For wives, being jealous of their husband's love affairs or concubines was another of the seven evils, as were disobeying their parents-in-law and failing to bear a son during the Chosun Dynasty. A woman's sexual fidelity to her husband had to be continued even after her husband's death. In the Chosun era, a woman had to serve (marry) only one man in her life, expressed as (*Bul-kyung-yee-bu* – 'women must not serve two husbands') according to *So-hak*, one of the books of Confucian teachings (Han Myong-Sook, 1985, p. 26).

Emphasis on a woman's sexual fidelity to her husband in Confucian ideology was implemented in traditional Korean society by coercion through legislation, inducements through various means of compensation from the state, and socialization by local community educational institutions (*Hyang-kyo*) and the family (Lee Ock-Kyung, 1985, p. 38–63). Firstly, the remarriage of widowed women became banned by the law on the prohibition of *Jae-Ga* (remarriage of widowed women), which was promulgated in 1477. The children of women who remarried suffered serious disadvantages: for example according to a law known as *Jae-ga-nyo-ja-son-gum-go-bup*, they were not entitled to apply for government examinations to become public officials, which were the most important jobs for the prosperity of family and kin among *Yang-ban* (aristocrats) at that time. The law was enacted in 1485 during the Chosun Dynasty. Women's remarriage or adultery not only destroyed the future of their children, but was also considered one of the most disgraceful forms of behaviour by their natal and their husbands' kin, and a source of great shame for their husbands.

At the same time, various rewards were given by the state to the kin and family of the *Yeol-yeo*, the women who did not remarry and were chaste even though widowed at a very young age, or who committed suicide in order to preserve their chastity. The families of women who were nominated as *Yeol-yeo* received prizes, mainly in the form of rice from the state and exemption from compulsory work for the state. For the families of the humble, nomination of one of the women in the family as *Yeol-yeo* could present a rare opportunity to enter the class of commoners. The state permitted the women's family thereby to enhance their status in society. Those were great compensations for people of all classes in the period and hence became a way for a kin to make a living based on the sacrifice of a woman's life (Lee Ock-Kyung, 1985, p. 45–8).

It might not have been the aim of the ideology itself to discriminate against women by segregating them from men. Nevertheless, the concept of segregation in early Confucianism was developed into, and closely associated with, the discrimination and subordination of women mainly through the control of women's sexuality by the group of people in power in the state.

At the end of the dynasty (nineteenth century), severe criticism of the Confucian ideology's subordination of women was followed by the introduction of the concept of equity for all men and women in front of God by Catholics and by the idea of equity in *Dong-Hak*, a Korean school of thought created by Choi Jae-Oo in 1860 (Kim Kyung-Ai, 1982). Finally, at the time of the Gapo Reformation a century ago (in 1894), the laws prohibiting women from remarriage and their offspring from applying for government examinations to become public officials were annulled, and support from the state for this was abolished. However, this did not completely destroy the ideology of the subordination of women, nor the double standard in sexual behaviour which controls women's sexuality by imposing fidelity to their husbands, while allowing men to enjoy free sex, or the sexual division of labour in Korea.

MARRIED WOMEN'S PARTICIPATION IN THE SOUTH KOREAN LABOUR FORCE[1]

The sexual division of labour based on Confucian ideology in pre-industrial society did not actually exempt women from productive work. Rather, women were expected to do not only reproductive work but also productive work in and around the home in the common and lower classes and even in the *Yang-ban* (aristocratic) class (Cho Haejoung, 1986, p. 160). Women did sewing, spinning, weaving, milling, domestic animal raising, vegetable cultivating and making soy bean paste and sauce, as well as preparing for the performance of Confucian rites. Middle-class and poor peasant women had to do field work as well, such as weeding, transplanting and manual irrigation even though their contribution was undervalued or considered as valueless (Kim Young-Ock, 1987, p. 35). Therefore, women's productive role in industrial jobs in urban areas is not a new role for most Korean women, who lost their traditional productive roles in farming as a result of industrialization and urbanization. It might be simply a recovery of their productive role within the new context of industrial work.

However, industrial work, particularly working outside the home, is qualitatively different in the sense that women come out from the 'inner place' (home) where they were supposed to remain. A chaste woman, devoted wife, and dedicated mother, who is confined spatially in the inner rooms of the house, now becomes a paid worker. The sexual division of labour in childcare and housework and the chastity of women could both be threatened by women engaging in paid work outside the home. However, the expansion of job opportunities along with economic development allows some women to take jobs outside the home despite the constraints of their traditional domestic responsibilities, the lack of childcare provision, and the behavioural culture based on traditional Confucian ideology. Meanwhile, others take jobs which seem compatible with their traditional role and norms, for example, home-based work, so as to resolve the dilemma women workers outside the home face.

LABOUR SHORTAGE AND THE INCREASE IN MARRIED WOMEN'S LABOUR FORCE PARTICIPATION

Recovering from poverty following the total destruction of the economy in the Korean War (1950–53), it is well known that the South Korean economy has shown an unprecedented growth since the first five-year economic plan was launched in 1962. The economic growth rate recorded 9.4 per cent on average during the period 1982–90, exceeding 12 per cent, the highest level in the world, in 1986, 1987, and 1988. South Korea's per capita Gross National Product (GNP) rose by nearly 23 times from US$243 in 1970 to US$5,569 in 1990.

The high growth resulted from a combination of import substitution and export-oriented growth strategies. Efforts were made initially to establish labour-intensive light industry, and later, heavy and chemical industries. This greatly expanded employment opportunities for men and women, absorbing large numbers of new workers. The total labour force increased from 10 million in 1970 to 18.5 million in 1990. Along with the increase in the total labour force, the number of economically active women increased by more than a factor of two, from 3.6 million to 7.5 million over the two decades. The rate of increase was greater than for the economically active male population, which only rose by 1.7 times, from 6.5 million to 11 million during the same period. The female share of the total economically active population has risen steadily from 34.9 per cent to 40.4 per cent during the last two decades according to the *1990 Annual Report on the Economically Active Population*. The female participation rate rose from 39.3 per cent in 1970 to 47.0 per cent in 1990, while the male rate slightly decreased from 77.9 per cent to 73.9 per cent during the same period, according to the Report.

However, the rapid increase in the number of both men and women in the labour force could not meet the demand for labour power. After the mid-1970s, labour supply shortages, particularly of unskilled young workers and of both single men and women, have been pre-eminent regardless of the state of the economy (Cho Uhn, 1990, p. 26). By the early 1990s, the shortages had not been replenished. According to the Survey on the Actual Conditions of Employment in the 14 major industrial estates carried out by the Ministry of Labour in 1991, the rate of labour shortages in clerical and production jobs was on average 5.3 per cent, the highest rate, 13.8 per cent, the lowest, 2 per cent. The rate for production jobs in the industrial estates was higher, reaching on average 6.1 per cent. By occupation, the labour-intensive manufacturing sectors were suffering severely from labour shortages, for example rubber and shoe manufacturing enterprises had shortfalls of 10.5 per cent and 9.5 per cent respectively.

The situation of medium-sized and small enterprises was even worse. Medium-sized and small labour-intensive industries, for example in textiles, shoes, and clothing, were suffering more severely, and some of them had to close down their factories either temporarily or permanently. Data collected by the Association of Medium and Small Enterprises indicated that the number of vacant jobs in firms in the manufacturing sector employing more than five workers was 198,000 persons and the vacancy rate had reached

15.2 per cent in 1991 (*Dong-A Ilbo* [daily newspaper], 9 July 1991).

The 1990s began with intense debates between the government, private enterprises, the labour unions, and women's organizations on how to resolve these labour shortages. First, the structural shift of the South Korean economy away from labour-intensive to more technology- and capital-intensive modes was considered as a solution. A second solution was that more labour-saving methods of production, such as factory automation, should be adopted. However, the overall weight of the labour-intensive manufacturing sector in such industries as textiles, garments and assembly-electronics in Korean industry will continue to be important; for example, even in the year 2000 the textile industry alone is projected to produce 9 to 19 per cent of total value-added in the manufacturing sector (Park Seil, 1988, p.102). Therefore, the demand for labour power will continue even if factory automation is introduced.

On the supply side, three means of raising the labour supply were suggested, including raising the level of married women's participation (*Dong-A Ilbo*, 1 August 1991; *Chosun Ilbo,* 30 March, 3 June, 20 July 1991). Recommendations were made to enhance married women's labour force participation, for example that daycare centres should be built both in the government-organized industrial zones and in urban low-income residential areas, and at the same time that private enterprises should gradually redesign their work schedules and their work processes in order to make it easier for married women to adapt to new industrial and factory work (Park Seil, 1988, p. 102). In 1991, the government announced the introduction of a part-time working system for married women in factories and service industries to solve the shortages in the labour supply. The scheme was criticized by women's organizations which argued that it would result in lower wages without fringe benefits, and instability in the employment status of women (*Chosun Ilbo*, 30 March, 3 June, 20 July 1991). The demand for married women's labour to fill vacant jobs seems to be of great concern to South Korea in the 1990s.

Married women who are seen as a 'reserve army of labour' always accounted for the absolute majority of the female labour force in South Korea. Around two-thirds of the female labour force in the 1970s were married women, rising to three-quarters by 1990. The economic activity rate for married women has drastically increased, exceeding that of single women by 1989 and reaching 47.0 per cent for all married women in 1990. The level of employed married women has increased drastically by 81.8 per cent, while that of single women rose by 15.4 per cent in the 1980s. The employment rate of single women had risen more rapidly in the 1970s.

The age bracket in which the largest number of married women in employment is concentrated, has become younger. The largest cohort of married women was in the age group 40–44 in 1983. In 1986, the 35–39 year old age group and in 1989 the 30–34 age group formed the largest cohort.

Amongst married women in employment, the age bracket from 30 to 34 increased by the largest amount between 1983 and 1986, and was the second highest rate, behind the over–60's between 1986 and 1989. Given that the average age of marriage was 25 years in 1988 (Korean Women's Development Institute, 1991, p. 86), it can be seen that women are working increasingly at an age when they could well still have young children. It seems likely that more women with young children are engaged in paid work than ever before. In short, it could be said that married women have been more actively seeking and taking employment over the past 20 years. Women with young children have engaged in employment more than ever before.

GENDER SEGREGATION IN THE LABOUR MARKET

It is said that the labour market vertically and horizontally segregates women and that it differentiates employment status by sex (Hakim, 1979). It has often been argued that the Korean labour market is also sex-segregated and that the female labour force is concentrated in a few specific industries (Chang-Mitchell, Pilwha, 1988, p. 104; Cho Hyoung, 1986, p. 164). As a result of occupational segregation by sex, women are concentrated in labour-intensive, low-skilled, monotonous jobs in so-called 'women's industries' like nursing, stenography and typing, domestic service, textile and garment production, (unpaid) farm labour, telephone operation and accounting (Cho Hyoung, 1986, p. 162), and situated on the lower rungs in the hierarchy of capitalism. These occupations are very much associated with traditional gender roles (Cho Hyoung, 1986, p. 159). Occupational segregation by sex intensified in the 1980s (Korean Women's Development Institute, 1991, p. 145).

By employment status, women are much more likely than men to be unpaid family workers, and less likely to be self-employed. In 1990 the absolute majority of family workers were female, while around three-quarters of the self-employed were male. The differential in employment status between female and male workers changed little in 1990 compared with Cho Hyoung's claim concerning the pattern in 1980 (1986, p. 162). It is clear that the sexual division of labour in the labour market, as the result of gender segregation by occupation and differentials in employment status, still persisted in South Korea in 1990.

MARITAL DIVISION OF LABOUR IN A SEXUALLY-DIVIDED LABOUR MARKET

Women have been integrated into the labour market differently from men as stated previously. In previous studies on trends in women's labour force participation in Korea, both married and single women have been generally categorized as a unitary group *qua* women compared to men in discussions on women's status in the labour market. However, it is not necessarily the case that single and married women participate in the labour market in the same way. Women's participation in the labour market varies according to their marital status. Women's occupation and employment status will now be explored by marital status.

Among women in employment, sharp occupational differences between married and single women have become evident in the past two decades. In different occupations, agriculture has been a typical area of employment for married women, accounting for 59.7 per cent and 46.5 per cent of all employed women in 1970 and 1980, respectively. Of these, 84.8 per cent and 90.7 per cent of the women respectively were married in 1970 and 1980. The number of married women in agricultural employment increased, compared to a decrease in the number of single women by 1980, showing a sharp contrast to the overall shift of the labour force to the urban sector. The population of married women in agriculture continues to form the largest source of employment of married women. For single women, agricultural employment fell by 32.1 per cent from 1970 to 1980. Married women in the rural areas took on the burden of farming as more and more single women, as well as men, emigrated to urban areas, filling the gap in agriculture which was given the lowest priority in economic development and therefore became the least developed sector. In 1990, 99.3 per cent of female farmers were married. However, in the 1980s, even the number of married women in agriculture fell by 23.8 per cent.

As the shift to industrial work deepened with economic growth, the demand for female labour in production became very high. The growth in employment for women has been dominated by expansion in production jobs, which grew by more than 3.6 times from 526,000 in 1970 to 1.9 million in 1990. In the 1970s, employment of single women in these jobs rose drastically to become the second largest occupation for females following agriculture. But in the 1980s, a different situation emerged. Firstly, this occupational category came to be the largest employer of female labour. Secondly, married women's participation in production rose rapidly by almost five times, taking the larger share of such jobs, whereas the number of single women in this occupational group fell by 42.4 per cent in the course of the 1980s. By 1990 the share of married and single women in this category had been reversed: that is, married women accounted for more than three-quarters of female workers in production jobs in 1990, whereas in 1980, two-thirds of women in such jobs were unmarried. The production sector is becoming the married women's workplace.

The other occupations dominated by married women were sales and service work, the third and fourth largest occupational categories. Even though their numbers did not increase as fast as in production and clerical work, the absolute number of female workers has increased by 3.6 times from 343,000 to 1.243 million in sales and by 3.2 times from 385,000 to 1.223 million in services over the past two decades. In sales, married women have constituted the majority of the workforce in the last 20 years. Services have shown the most drastic change in the labour force in the proportion of married and single women: single women occupied the majority of the female workforce in this sector in 1970. Twenty years later, the proportion has been reversed: in 1990 married women accounted for the absolute majority (85.6 per cent) of workers in this occupation and single women for only 14.4 per cent. Services in Korea have thus also firmly became married women's work during the last two decades. Married women provided large sections of the labour force in agriculture, production, and sales and services.

In contrast, clerical work, which includes typically female jobs such as typists, telephone operators, accounting clerks, etc., continues to employ largely single women. This occupation indicated the largest increase in the total number of women employed, by almost nine times during the past two decades. Married women increased their share of this market in the 1980s, but it has consistently been an occupation for single women, who still retained 80.7 per cent of these jobs in 1990. Single women preferred clerical work because they work using new technology in a clean environment in the centre of cities. Moreover, they enjoy higher social status than factory workers because according to the Confucian tradition, people who 'use a pen' are more respected than those who do manual work.

Professional, technical and managerial jobs have increasingly employed both married and single women, but single women have always been in the majority. Furthermore, amongst married women there were differences according to marital status. The distribution of widowed women showed a similar pattern to married women, but the participation of divorced women in the labour market was different: the most prominent differences were that the majority of divorced women were more likely to work in the service sector and less likely to be in agriculture than married women or widowed women. From the above, it is clear that women were sharply divided in their occupational status according to their marital status.

However, in addressing the problem of the relative occupational status of married and single women, it is not satisfactory to use broad occupational

categories. Such categories could conceal wide occupational status differences: for example in the same category of occupation, the status of the two
female working groups could be different.   Married women's participation
has increased in the lower sectors which single women avoided. For example, of the total number of women production workers in 1986, 97 per cent of
these workers in tobacco manufacturing, 66 per cent of those in furniture
manufacturing, 40 per cent in the food industry, and 37 per cent in shoe
manufacturing were married women (Cho Soon-Kyung, 1989, p. 100).
Married women were used to fill jobs in production work which single
female labour and male labour had left, substituting with unskilled, cheap
labour and hard work (Cho Uhn, 1990, p. 28), often suffering worse working
conditions than single women workers. Consequently, it can be said that
married women were situated in the worst working conditions and on the
lowest rung of the occupational hierarchy.

There is also a division between single and married women in terms of employment status. Married women predominate at all employment status levels
except as employees. Among employed women single women made gains in
the 1970s, whereas the number of married women increased in the 1980s.

Among the women in each group, the employment status of married
women was mainly as family workers in the 1970s, while the majority of
single women were in waged employment. The absolute majority of married
female family workers worked on family farms, and others worked in
services, e.g. in family-run shops. The distribution has changed as the result
of sectoral and industrial shifts. The shrinking of agriculture has reduced the
number of female rural workers and, consequently, also the proportion of
female family workers. By 1990 the share of family workers in married
female employment had fallen to 31.7 per cent among married women,
below the level of waged employment for this group.

The rise in paid employment for married women was due to an increase in
sales, services, and especially production work for this group. However, for
single women waged employment was consistently much more common than
for married women. Less than the half of married women worked in waged
employment in 1990, while for single women the figure was 93.1 per cent.
Even though the number of self-employed and family workers among married women has decreased, 20.0 per cent and 31.7 per cent respectively of
married women were still self-employed or family workers, compared to only
3.5 per cent and 2.4 per cent of single women in 1990. Furthermore, married
women without husbands were more likely to be self-employed and less likely
to be family workers than married women living with husbands. Among
married women without husbands, divorced women were more likely to be
employees whereas widowed women tended to be self-employed in 1990.

Clearly, the meaning of labour force participation differs greatly between married and single women in terms of employment status as well as occupational segregation. Among married women, differences were also shown. There was therefore division by marital status among women participating in the labour market. It can be called 'the marital division of labour among women'.

HOMEWORKERS MISSED IN THE STATISTICS

Even though statistics vividly show us the increasing number of women, particularly married women, in the labour force following the expansion of industry in South Korea, it is reported that a large number of women who would most likely be defined as 'economically inactive' by official labour statistics are earning an income through a variety of informal activities. Such informal activities are not restricted to urban poor families. Middle-class women are almost as economically active as working-class women in South Korea (Cho Uhn and Koo, 1983). Moreover, the number of married women in the labour force, particularly family workers, part-time workers, and domestic workers, is likely to be under-represented in official statistics. Male respondents might ignore their wives' contribution to their work and household income, or researchers might unquestioningly categorize women who stay at home as economically inactive when the survey is carried out (Suh Kwan-Mo, 1986, p. 50). Married women might under-evaluate their economic activities, regarding themselves as non-working housewives.

There are particular problems with homeworkers. It is impossible to calculate how many homeworkers are contained in the employed women category in official statistics. In 1990, the statistics on employment defined homeworkers as part-time workers. However, homeworkers were not likely to report themselves as employed. Almost all of the homeworkers in the sample taken for a study[2] said that they had categorized themselves as non-working housewives for the Population and Housing Survey carried out by the Economic Planning Board of the South Korean government in November 1990. Most homeworkers, like other informal sector workers, are thus likely to be missed in the statistics of the South Korean government.

Only an estimate can be made to grasp the size of the homework population using previous studies on married women workers in slum areas. Cho Uhn and Cho Oakla claimed that 'except the households which have extra money to spare (actually no household has it), almost all of the women in a squatter settlement in Seoul do homework' (1988, p. 78). They might exaggerate the number, but it shows how widely homework has spread in slum areas. Ahn Soon-Duk and Byun Wha-Soon (1988) reported the highest percentage of homeworkers in their studies in the slum areas of South Korea,

namely 41.4 per cent among 994 married women workers in a sample of the
areas. Park Kye-Young (1982) and Son Duksoo and Lee Mi-Kyung (1983)
also suggested approximately 40 per cent of married women in a slum area
in Seoul were homeworkers. In Cho Hyoung's research (1985), 36.4 per cent
of the sample of married women in a slum area in Seoul, 35 per cent of wives
of male factory workers in the research of Lee Hyo-Chae and Chee Eun-Hee
(1988), and one-quarter of the married women workers in the sample of Kim
Eun-Sil (1983) in a slum area, were all reported as homeworkers. Middle-
class women were also reported as homeworkers. According to the study of
the Hyundai Research Institute, 6.3 per cent of a sample of 500 middle-class
women in Seoul were found to do work at home for an income (*Dong-A Ilbo*,
12 October 1988). However, the nationwide survey on married women workers with the largest sample conducted by Roh Mihye et al. (1989) shows
9.4 per cent of the sample as homeworkers. The rates of homeworkers varied
in the previous studies. The rate might differ depending on the area even
though the mobility of work nowadays is much improved due to the development of transportation in South Korea. If an area is situated near an industrial estate, the job opportunities for homeworking might be much higher and
so the women in the area are more likely to become homeworkers.

With these varying results, it is very difficult to assess the number of
homeworkers in Korea. It can only be roughly estimated. A modest estimate
based on the rate (9.4 per cent) established by the latest and nationwide
survey (1989) with the largest sample size by Roh Mihye et al. of the Korean
Women's Development Institute suggests that there were approximately
1.1 million homeworkers in South Korea in 1990.

A PERSPECTIVE ON MARRIED WOMEN'S PARTICIPATION IN PAID WORK

Married women's paid work has increased as predicted, and the gains are
likely to continue. Some business firms are welcoming married women to
offset the shortages of young single women workers because they think that
married women are skilled,[3] but quit jobs less frequently, work hard (*Dong-A
Ilbo*, 1 August 1991) and have a low participation in labour movements
(*Hankook Ilbo* [daily newspaper], 3 February 1989).

However, one study claims that married women do not completely fill the
vacant jobs left by men or single women. Cho Soon-Kyung has argued that
married women did not fully substitute for men and single women due to
segmentation of the labour market. She also suggested that reproductive roles,
housework and child bearing and caring prevent them from responding to job

opportunities (1989, p. 117). Moreover, some industrial factory managers said that they would not consider employing married women because of their frequent absenteeism, even though they were suffering severely from labour shortages (*Dong-A Ilbo*, 1 August 1991); for example some textile industries which were seriously short of labour power, did not employ married women or elderly men who applied for the vacancies (*Dong-A Ilbo*, 20 July 1991).

Married women's employment in industry, both part-time and full-time, is likely to increase insofar as demand increases. However, occupational segregation and discrimination against women in the labour market seem to persist. Married women are unlikely to fill completely those jobs left vacant by men and single women either because of traditional Confucian ideology, or because of their roles as wives and mothers.

NOTES

1 This section is based on statistics from the Population and Housing Survey, 1970 and 1980 and the *Annual Report on the Economically Active Population 1990*, published by a ministry of the Korean government, the Economic Planning Board.
2 Author's PhD dissertation, 'Married Women's Labour Force Participation and Status: A Study of the Working Class in South Korea', Institute of Development Studies, Sussex University.
3 However, their skill is generally not recognized in employment.

BIBLIOGRAPHY

Ahn Soon-Duk and Byun Wha-Soon (1988), *A Study on the Child Care System in the Poor Area and the Environment*, Seoul: The Korean Women's Development Institute.

Chang-Mitchell, Pilwha (1988), 'Women and Work: A Case Study of a Small Town in the Republic of Korea', Unpublished DPhil Dissertation, Brighton: Sussex University.

Cho Haejoung (1986), 'The Transformation and Subjugation of Patriarchy: The Case of the Korean Family', *Hankook Yeosunghak (Korean Women's Studies)*, 2, Seoul: The Korean Association of Women's Studies, pp.136–201.

Cho Hyoung (1985), 'Women's Labour in the Informal Sector', *Korean Women and Labour*, Seoul: Ewha Women's University Press, pp.28–46.

Cho Hyoung (1986), 'Women's Labour Force Participation in Korea' in Chung Sei-Wha (ed.), *Challenges for Women*, Seoul: Ewha Women's University Press, pp.150–72.

Cho Uhn (1990), 'The Situation of Economic Growth, Inequality and Poverty in Korea: A Gender Perspective', The 20th World Conference of the Society for International Development in Amsterdam, 6–9 May.

Cho Uhn and Cho Oakla (1988), *A Study on The Characteristics of Residents in a Redeveloping Area*, Seoul: Seoul National University.

Cho Uhn and Koo Hagen (1983), 'Capital Accumulation, Women's Work, and Informal Economics in South Korea', Working Paper 21 on *Women in International Development*, Ann Arbor: Michigan State University.

Cho Soon-Kyung (1989), 'An Essay for the Analysis of the Korean Women's Labour Market', *The Women (Yeosung)*, Vol. 3, Seoul: Changjakguabipyongsa, pp.98-130.

Chosun Ilbo (daily newspaper) (1991), 30 March; 3 June; 20 July.

Dong-A Ilbo (daily newspaper), 12 October 1988; 20 July; 1 August 1991.

Hakim, Catherine (1979), 'Occupational Segregation: A Comparative Study of the Degree and Pattern of the Differentiation Between Men's and Women's Work in Britain, The United States and Other Countries', *Research Paper* No. 9, London: Department of Employment.

Hankook Ilbo (daily newspaper), 3 February 1989.

Han Myong-Sook (1985), 'A Theoretical Study on Confucian Views of Woman in the Yi Dynasty', Unpublished MA Dissertation, Seoul: Ewha Women's University.

Kim Eun-Sil (1983), 'A Study on the Character of the Urban Poor in South Korea: The Case of Squatters in Bongchun-dong', Unpublished MA Dissertation, Seoul: Seoul National University.

Kim Kyung-Ai (1982), 'A Study on Sexual Equality in the Thought of *Dong-Hak, Chundo-kyo*', Unpublished MA Dissertation, Seoul: Ewha Women's University.

Kim Young-Ock (1987), 'The Position of Women Workers in Manufacturing Industries in South Korea: A Marxist-Feminist Analysis', Working Paper – Sub Series on *Women's History and Development*, No. 6, Hague: Institute of Social Studies.

Korean Women's Development Institute, The (1991), *White Paper on Women*, Seoul: The Korean Women's Development Institute.

Lee Hyo-Chae and Chee Eun-Hee (1988), 'The Living Conditions of the Working Class in South Korea: The Process of Reproduction of Labour Power', *Hankook Saheehak (Korean Sociology)*, 22, Autumn, Seoul: Korean Association of Sociology, pp. 69–97.

Lee Ock-Kyung (1985), 'A Study on the Formational Conditions and Settlement Mechanisms of the *Jeong Juel* Ideology of the Yi Dynasty Through Reorganization of the Ideology Critique', Unpublished MA dissertation, Seoul: Ewha Women's University.

Park Kye-Young (1982), 'A Study on the Economic Activities of Squatters', Unpublished MA Dissertation, Seoul: Seoul National University.

Park Seil (1988), 'Labour Issues in Korea's Future', *World Development*, 16 (1), pp.99–119.

Park Yong-Ock (1976), *The History of Women in The Chosun Dynasty*, Seoul: Hankook Ilbo.

Roh Mihye, Kim Young-Mi, Yang Seung-Ju and Moon Yu-Kyung (1989), *A Study on Home-Based Work in South Korea*, Seoul: The Korean Women's Development Institute.

Son Duksoo and Lee Mi-Kyung (1983), *Poor Women in South Korea*, Seoul: The Christian Institute for the Study of Justice and Development.

Suh Kwan-Mo (1986), 'Social Statistical Study on the Structure of Social Class in South Korea', *Sanyupsahyeyeonku (Study on Industrial Society)*, Seoul: Hanul, pp.34–56.

13. Moving Towards the Market: Chinese Women in Employment and their Related Rights

Liu Bohong and Sun Rong

According to Article 4 of the Constitution of the People's Republic of China, 'Women enjoy equal rights with men in all spheres of life, political, economic, cultural and social, including family life. The state protects the rights and interests of women, applies the principle of equal pay for equal work to men and women alike, and trains and selects cadres from among women.' This fundamental law has, during the period of the centrally planned economy, provided a legal framework to ensure the employment of Chinese women, and has become a symbol for, as well as an important component of, women's liberation in socialist China. It was expected that, under the market economy, such a law would continue its function of protecting women's right to obtain employment, so that any deviation from equal opportunities for women in the labour market would be constantly controlled, and women could have the chance to develop their careers fully during the transition from a planned economy to a market economy.

Since the 1980s, changes in China's labour market, promoted by economic reforms, have taken place in the following respects. First, the widespread implementation of the Production Responsibility System (a kind of contract system) has increased agricultural productivity, causing the transfer of many surplus rural labourers to industry and cities. Secondly, urban reform of the economic system has gone deep into the reform of ownership forms, management mechanisms and labour employment systems.[1] As a result, it has brought about the practice of multi-ownership, realignment of enterprises and a variety of employment forms. Such changes require not only an alteration of the traditional planned employment system – which, strengthened by the state's administrative power, made a clear barrier between rural and urban development – but also a further reform of the labour employment system, especially the establishment of a labour market. It is under such circumstances that Chinese women have involved themselves in the movement towards a market economy.

Furthermore, Chinese market-oriented reform has its own special characteristics. First, the reform has been carried out steadily and prudently, with social stability as a prerequisite. The state has been more concerned about a stable development of society while working out strategies for the economic changes. Secondly, the reform of the Chinese urban employment system has focused on the introduction of market factors, such as competition, into the planned system, rather than its immediate replacement by the market system. Thirdly, China's labour market has not yet been fully developed, and therefore it can hardly become a major form of labour resource disposal in such a short period of time. Determined by these factors, Chinese women are having in some respects a different, in some respects a similar experience to Eastern European women in labour marketization. First, the movement towards the labour market in China is less radical, but rather a process of gradual change and steady development. Also, the movement shows its complexity because of the coexistence of the planned economy and the market economy. Moreover, this kind of a mixed performance of the two different systems has provided a certain kind of elasticity in the transition of the Chinese economy. This paper centres on the employment of Chinese women and the realization of their related rights in the process of China's economic reforms.

MARKET CHALLENGES TO WOMEN'S RIGHT TO WORK

The state-ensured model of urban women's employment has changed during the transition of the Chinese economic system, at a time when, surprisingly, the proportion and scale of women's employment are still rising, and women's right to work has yet to be realized fully.

Under the traditional planned system, urban women in China had enjoyed the privilege of a state guarantee of employment, but throughout the transition to a market-oriented economy, such a privilege has been challenged in the following ways. First, some work units refuse to take women applicants when recruiting employees, or raise the recruitment standards for women. Discrimination against female graduates from colleges and universities is becoming increasingly visible. Secondly, the reform and the system of labour optimization have made women workers the first to be affected as surplus labour. Thirdly, some enterprises force their female employees to take longer pregnancy and maternity leave. Finally, women employees are being required by some enterprises to retire five or even eight years earlier than the state-fixed retirement age (for women: 50).

Nevertheless, women's large-scale return to the home as a result of unemployment has not yet occurred in China, as they still have various ways of

implementing their right to employment, since the reforms have in fact expanded the demand for labour. For example, female graduates unable to
obtain good jobs can find less satisfactory jobs, and retired workers can
become self-employed. According to a census in 1982, there were 521.5 million employed people, of whom 227.8 million were female, making up 43.7
per cent of the total employed population. In 1990, the employed population
increased to 647.2 million, with 291.0 million being female, accounting for
45 per cent of the total. Over the same period of time, the growth rate of
the total employed population was 24.1 per cent; for the male employed
population this was 21.3 per cent, and 27.7 per cent for the female employed
population. Thus, the growth rate of the female labour force was 6.4 per
cent higher than that of the male labour force.[2]

GREATER OCCUPATIONAL CHOICE AS A RESULT
OF THE TRANSITION TO THE MARKET

During the transition of the Chinese economic system, women have played
an active role in both professional life and the transformation of occupations,
in order to realize their right to choose their jobs.

Comparatively speaking, under the planned system, women's role in their
professional lives had been thrown into passivity, because the state took complete responsibility for the distribution of employment. With the development of reform, women have acknowledged the differences between occupations, and have started to make conscious efforts to choose those vacancies
that can advance their social status. This is another key turning point for
Chinese women's entry into the marketplace. A survey conducted in Dalian
in 1986 showed that about 500 people had competed for 50 vacancies for
women in a commercial company known as Dalian Qiulin Superstore; and at
the Fulihua Hotel, there were 13 applicants for each job vacancy. In contrast
with this, the textile industry seems to be regarded with little enthusiasm by
women. In 1987, a big textile factory in Wuhan appointed only five female
workers, yet they had five hundred vacancies.

Furthermore, differentiation has appeared when occupational groups of
women take vigorous action to select jobs in the market. Those who were
first to enter into the labour market were young educated women with higher
professional skills, but lighter family burdens. They are often thought to be
in a strong position to deal with the dangers and insecurities of the market.
The next were women in economically-developed areas and some rural women,
who are eager to change their current status without caring too much about
what they may get in the job market. Another group of women competing
in the market are those who have already secured jobs, or are receiving a

pension, but still seek a second job. There are also a considerable number of women who lack confidence or the desire to participate in this competition. They are often middle-aged women with less education and skills but heavier family commitments, or who had better state protection in their positions. It is worth noting that the employment pattern of rural women has also been changing. If participation in agricultural activities enabled rural women to realize their right to employment, the transformation and division of occupations have made it possible for them to enhance further their initial right to select jobs.

The first channel that rural women use to transfer into non-agricultural activities is that of township enterprises. This type of transfer is described as 'leaving the land without leaving the village', and 'entering the factory without entering the city'. In the last ten years, people involved in such local transfers have formed the largest group transferring from agricultural to non-agricultural activities, and this specific mode of transfer has been seen as the easiest. The second destination of the transfer to non-agricultural activities is cities, where rural women appear to be the 'floating population', often engaged in dirty and heavy labour which urban people do not like to do. This is the so-called transfer involving 'leaving the land as well as the village'. According to a survey conducted by the Institute of Rural Development at the Chinese Academy of Social Sciences, between 1978 and 1988 a total of 130 million rural labourers transferred out of agriculture, of which 33 million or 25 per cent were women.

The transformation of rural women's occupations during the current social changes can be characterized as follows. First, the transformation has been led by women's own initiative. During the 1950s and 1960s, it was often through an external impetus that rural women would change their economic status or transfer from one occupation to another. They did not always have the awareness or motivation to make changes. However, since the 1980s, rural women have shown a degree of initiative in changing their occupations. They would now like to decide for themselves whether or not, how, where, and when, to select a job. This is also a sign of an independent awareness in rural women. Secondly, there are now varied modes of achieving such occupational transformation. In the 1950s, women could only take jobs in factories, while in the 1970s, they could also choose to study in the city, apart from being factory workers. Since the 1980s, more and more industries, areas, projects and departments have opened their doors to rural women, which has promoted occupational changes for rural women. Thirdly, women tend to have equal opportunities in choice of occupation. This has two facets: i) the improved external conditions, such as the development of the market, favourable government policies and the availability of credits, have helped to bring about relatively equal opportunities for women in employment; ii) the development of the economy has promoted women's liberation, and led to calls for the realization of equal opportunities in employment. During the 1950s, the young and educated had always been favoured in the labour market, and in the 1970s, 'old-boy networks' could determine chances in employment. However, the rural reforms in the 1980s began to break down these traditions: individual capabilities have become the first priority in the employment market. Rural women have thus been encouraged to pay attention to an overall improvement of their personal qualities in competing for jobs. Rural women's transfer to non-agricultural occupations has constantly consolidated their economic rights and interests. Women's right to choose jobs can be a significant sign of the expansion of their economic rights. The transformation of some women into urban professional citizens is surely an important movement towards the economic liberation of Chinese rural women (Huang Xiyi, 1991).[3]

STRUCTURAL CONSTRAINTS EMANATING FROM MARKET PRACTICES

In the economic reforms, the occupational structure of women's work has changed, and women's right to employment has been in the process of consolidation. However, some as yet underdeveloped and problematical factors have remained in the process of this structural change, most of which have in fact been generated by market practice.

According to censuses in 1982 and 1990, the occupational structure of employed women has changed in the following spheres. First, among the total figure of high-ranking professionals in science and technology, the number of women had increased sharply from 10.1 million in 1982 to 15.6 million in 1990, while the figure for men had increased by less from 16.3 million to 18.8 million. The proportion of female professionals in science and technology in the total employed population had risen from 1.9 per cent to 2.4 per cent in those eight years, while the figure for male professionals had decreased from 3.3 per cent to 2.9 per cent. In general, the growth rate in the female share in all kinds of professions was higher than that in the male share.[4] Secondly, the number of female employees in the civil service (including officers in government departments, the Communist Party and mass organizations, and the civil servants in state-owned enterprises and institutions) has also increased steadily. The number of female civil servants increased from 1.6 million to 2.8 million, occupying 0.3 per cent and 0.4 per cent of the total employed population respectively, although the growth rate was lower than the figure for male employment (*Chinese Statistical Materials on Women*, 1991, p. 260–5). The number of female politicians and managers went up from 844,223 in 1982 to 1.3 million in 1990, and its proportion in the whole population grew from 0.16 per cent to 0.2 per cent. Thirdly, the growth rate in both the number and proportion of female employees in services and commercial industries was higher than that for males. The censuses also showed that the ratio of female to male staff and workers in service industries was 51.6:48.4. Such figures indicated that, on the one hand, the development of the tertiary industry had provided more employment opportunities for women, yet, on the other hand, the tertiary industry was after all based on the employment of low-skilled and manual labour. Fourthly, the number and proportion of women workers had also grown faster than that of men in the fields of agriculture, forestry, husbandry and fishery. The number of working women in these sectors increased from 175.6 million in 1982 to 219 million in 1990, with the proportion in the total employed population rising from 33.7 per cent to 33.8 per cent (*Chinese Statistical Materials on Women*, ibid.). All these figures show that in these eight years women's occupational structure has improved. Nevertheless, under the guise of the high employment rate, the traditional structure of women's concentration in less-skilled occupations has remained unchanged.

In the early stage of the economic reforms, the promotion of tertiary industry as part of industrial structural adjustment has, to some extent, widened the gap in social status between the sexes. Unlike tertiary industry in the developed countries, which takes financial, electronic and high-tech businesses as its main areas of development, China's tertiary industry at this stage is composed merely of the service trades including stores, restaurants and hotels. The development of such a tertiary industry in China has reduced somewhat the unfavourable elements of women's occupations in agriculture and industry, but at the same time it has created a new pattern of less-skilled occupational conditions for women. For example, some sectors of this tertiary industry are nothing more than a social extension of women's role in the family. Instead of looking after their own family members, the women employed by some service trades would be employed to look after other people. Although the pay is reasonably high, these jobs are basically manual jobs which do not involve highly professional skills. Also, some service trades take only young, good-looking and educated women. Under this pressure of the market, those women who wish to return to employment, but are no longer young and pretty, have to take those jobs with relatively poor working conditions, high intensity of labour and lower incomes. This particular situation has resulted in an unbalanced pattern in women's employment.

Moreover, the rural working women transferred to cities and industrial sectors have been similarly influenced by such an underdeveloped employment market. They are often limited to the low-skilled or heavy labour jobs which urban women find hard to tolerate. If the rural labour force is considered as a reservoir for the entire industrial labour force, then rural women may be seen as the reservoir for the rural labour force (Jin, 1991, p. 38–40).

In general, the fact that rural women have played a role as cheap labour has maintained the structure of women's employment in less-skilled occupations. Finally, the sexual division of the labour market has been socialized in the reform, and has thus limited many professional and highly skilled women's ability to compete in a market seen to be particularly for men. Irrational factors have resulted from this division, such as 'gender isolation' in some female occupations, which may cause a degradation in women's occupational status.

EQUAL PAY FOR EQUAL WORK UNDER MARKET STRESSES

Women's right to equal pay for equal work has continued to be implemented throughout the economic reform, but under the influence of market forces, differences in overall income between men and women may come to be stressed. The principle of equal pay for equal work for men and women has been in place ever since the foundation of New China in 1949. Workers in the same industry doing similar kinds of work and having the same technical skills receive the same pay regardless of sex. However, due to current differences in cultural and professional competence as well as occupational composition, some real income gaps still exist between men and women. According to a survey conducted in 1990, average monthly incomes for male and female workers in urban areas were 193.15 *yuan* and 149.60 *yuan* respectively, with women receiving only 77.4 per cent of the pay given to men. In rural areas, the average annual incomes for men and women were 1,518 *yuan* and 1,235 *yuan* respectively, with women getting 81.4 per cent of the earnings of men *(General Survey On the Social Status of Chinese Women,* 1993, p. 86–9).

In October 1991, a sample survey on women's social status was conducted by a research group at the Chinese Academy of Social Sciences. The result showed that among 3,000 married couples from the following six regions: Shanghai, Shaanxi, Shangdong, Guangdong, Ningxia and Jilin, those from Guangdong had the highest monthly income, and at the same time, the income differential between husband and wife in this province was also the largest. On average, the husbands in Guangdong had a monthly income of 390 *yuan*, and wives had 320 *yuan* (about 82 per cent of their husband's income). Compared with Shandong, where the income differential between husband and wife was the smallest, Guangdong's figures were 5.5 per cent higher (Gu, 1993). Since Guangdong has been regarded as a developed area in the labour market, the above figures may to some extent be a reflection of market labour prices for workers of different sexes. Such transformations are seen, on the one hand, to break away the traditional egalitarian model of equal pay for different work, but on the other hand, to lead to a new employment pattern of different pay for equal work for both men and women.

MARKET EROSION OF STATE-ENDORSED LABOUR PROTECTION

During the period of economic reforms, women's right to labour protection has been better safeguarded by state-controlled organizations and enterprises, while in non-state enterprises controlled by market forces, such a right has been violated in varying degrees.

Since the mid-1980s, a number of laws and regulations have been promulgated. In order to protect female workers' legal rights and their labour safety, and to reduce discrimination against female workers with physical disabilities, China issued its first general law on women's labour protection in 1988 entitled *Regulations on Labour Protection for Female Workers and Staff.* Following this, in 1990 another law concerning women workers' treatment was passed by the state. According to this second law, women workers reserve the right to appeal to the department responsible for their work units or to their local government labour department when they feel that their rights to labour protection have been violated. However, the regulation is only applicable to women workers and staff in all government departments, mass organizations, and state-owned enterprises and institutions within the borders of the People's Republic of China. As a supplementary law to the *Regulations on Labour Protection for Female Staff and Workers,* the *Regulations on Prohibited Working Areas for Female Staff and Workers* were issued by the Ministry of Labour in China in March 1990. It laid down clear and specific rules on the areas and the intensity of labour permissible for female staff and workers. In 1992, the *Law of the People's Republic of China on the Protection of the Rights and Interests of Women* was published to provide an effective legal weapon for further enhancing the social status of women and guaranteeing their basic rights and interests.

In April 1993, five years after the publication of the *Regulations on Labour Protection for Female Staff and Workers,* a joint research group organized by the National Labour Union and the Ministry of Labour conducted a nationwide investigation into the implementation of the labour protection laws. The results of the research showed that 27 provinces and autonomous regions [of a total of 30, Ed.], in addition to four industries, had issued detailed rules and regulations on the implementation of labour protection for female staff and workers. It maintained that 83 per cent of the 2,000 selected enterprises had been able to carry out the *Regulations on Labour Protection for Female Staff and Workers;* 97.5 per cent of these enterprises had appointed full-time and part-time staff responsible for the labour protection of female staff and workers in an all-round way; 93 per cent of them had established a service for regular gynaecological check-ups; 87 per cent had arranged for pregnant workers to have ante-natal care; 96 per cent had offered paid maternity leave for 90 days or more; and 97 per cent had regulations facilitating nursing time according to the state regulations. Additionally, 16 provinces and 153 cities and counties have developed a system of 'maternity allowance'[5] in varying degrees, and 6 provinces together with more than 50 cities have proposed reforms of this particular system.

All these laws and regulations governing labour protection had been well implemented under the supervision of labour unions and the Ministry of Labour within the planned economic structure. Under the market mechanism, however, the above laws and regulations are found to be hardly ever put into effect, because the labour departments have little coercive force to control the enterprises practising the market system, and most private enterprises, joint ventures, foreign businesses as well as township enterprises do not have labour unions at all. In the development of a market economy, entrepreneurs tend to regard the costs and price of labour as vital factors in achieving economic targets. Under this circumstance, the violation of employees' rights and interests is occurring in some private and township enterprises, and particularly in foreign and joint enterprises. Female employees' rights are violated in various ways:

i) shortage of facilities for labour safety – in some chemical and light-industrial enterprises, conditions of ventilation and fire control are poor, facilities like fume and dust protection are in short supply, and a system of regular health check-ups for workers is completely non-existent;

ii) longer working hours and low pay – some women workers are forced to work overtime, with heavy labour intensity and quotas increased arbitrarily by employers – sometimes they are asked to work twelve hours without any extra pay;

iii) arbitrary discharge and punishment;

iv) no guarantees covering pregnancy, confinement and nursing – in some foreign and joint enterprises, female workers were dismissed because of pregnancy and confinement. Living conditions are poor for female workers, especially for casual workers. Moreover, the illegal employment of junior workers and the emergence of the sex industry have caused many social problems.

THE ROLE OF WOMEN'S ORGANIZATIONS IN THE TRANSITION

During the economic reforms, the decision-making and managerial powers of women and women's organizations have been given play to a certain degree, and women's sense of self-determination has improved.

Women's organizations at all levels have played an important role in promoting the participation of Chinese women in economic activities and management. Two organizations – the All-China Women's Federation and the All-China Committee of Women Workers – have proposed several measures to policy- and law-making bodies regarding the following matters: labour protection laws for women; maternity allowances; equal rights for women in housing and accommodation; land usage for women in rural areas; and an extension in retirement age for high- and middle-ranking administrative personnel and intellectual workers. Most of these proposals have been implemented as laws and policies by the state.

In 1987 there was a big decrease in the proportion of elected officials who were women at town and county level; and at provincial and city levels, no women were even selected as candidates for election. With the aim of changing this situation, the All-China Women's Federation and the Organization Department of the Central Party Committee issued a paper in 1988 putting forward some detailed requirements concerning the selection of political leaders and cadres during the economic reforms. In 1990 and 1991, these two organizations held two forums on the selection and training of women cadres, in which they expressed the opinion that it was essential for there to be women cadres at town and county levels. In the elections of 1992 and 1993, the relevant departments stressed that in every province, in both the Party elite and in government, there should be at least one female leader at the top level, and that if no suitable female candidate was yet available, a vacancy should be reserved (Zhang, 1994). After a series of effective measures, this problem of decreasing numbers of female candidates has been brought under control.

Women's organizations, labour unions, and committees of female workers have each played their own role in helping those women who have lost their jobs as a result of the changes brought about by the economic reforms. Take Liaoning province for example: in the past few years, the number of such female workers was 420,000, accounting for 56 per cent of those who had become unemployed. The women's organizations and committees of female workers in this province attempted to change women's ideas and to set up training for employment of various kinds and at various levels, suited to women's strengths and abilities. According to incomplete statistics, women's organizations in Liaoning have, through various channels, helped to arrange the re-employment of about 100,000 female workers in the past few years (Huang Shude, 1994).

The development of the market economy has promoted an awakening of women's sense of self-determination. Since the 1980s, a number of women intellectuals have organized the setting up of some institutions to provide research, education and services relevant to women. Women's organizations at all levels have published many newspapers and magazines to arouse women's sense of self-determination and to promote women's participation in the development of the economy. However, it should be appreciated that the liberation of Chinese women came about as a result of the Chinese Revolution and was implemented and safeguarded by the state. Consequently, Chinese women's sense of self-reliance and of their legal rights is very fragile: many women, especially women from poor rural areas, have a low standard of living and education, and many of them are illiterate. Thus, during the development of the market economy, it has been very easy for the rights of women to be violated. It should be stressed that this is an urgent problem that needs to be solved in order to achieve women's liberation in China.

Translated by Yao Lihua.

NOTES

1 See *Provisional Regulations on Socialist Competition*, a document issued by the State Council and the Central Committee of the Chinese Communist Party on 7 October 1980.
2 See *Chinese Statistical Materials on Women* (1991, p. 253) and also *Census in 1990* (1993, p. 297). The author documents, but does not highlight, the fact that increases in the quantity of female employment are being attained at the expense of its quality [Editor's note].
3 The author does not address until later in the paper the problematic aspect of this transformation embodied in the poor working conditions experienced by many rural women who make the transition to employment in the Special Economic Zones [Editor's note].
4 Calculated according to the censuses in 1982 and 1990; see also *Chinese Statistical Materials on Women* (1991, p. 260–5).
5 According to Lu Jimei (1993), the 'maternity allowance', proposed as a new system to be practised during the reforms, is a kind of economic subsidy offered by enterprises to women employees during their maternity leave.

BIBLIOGRAPHY

Chinese Statistical Materials on Women: 1949–89 (1991), Beijing: China Statistical Press.
Census in 1990 (1993), Vol. 2, Beijing: China Statistical Press.

A General Survey On the Social Status of Chinese Women (1993), Beijing: China Women's Press.

Gu Jiantang (1993), 'Regional and Age Variations in the Income of Chinese Married Couples', Paper presented at the Conference on Population and Women's Studies held at Nankai University.

Huang Shude (1994), 'Creating Opportunities for Women Seeking Re-employment', *China Women's News (Zhongguo Funü Bao* – a government newspaper), 18 May.

Huang Xiyi (1991), 'Changes in Rural Women's Economic Status in the Current Social Transformations in China', *Research on Chinese Women of Different Social Levels,* Government Publications, Henan People's Press.

Jin Yihong (1991), 'Chinese Rural Women's Outlet and the *Status Quo* in Economic Reforms', *Research on Chinese Women of Different Levels*, Vol. 2, Henan People's Press.

Liu Xiaoling (1993), 'New Social Divisions – Gao Xiaoxian's Talk on the Trend of Feminization in Rural Areas', *China Women's News (Zhongguo Funü Bao),* 3 December.

Lu Jimei (1993), 'Further Improvements in the Labour Protection of Women Workers', *China Women's News (Zhongguo Funü Bao)*, 23 July.

Zhang Xiaoyuan (1994), 'The Scenery Is Particularly Beautiful Here', *China Women's News (Zhongguo Funü Bao),* 5 January.

14. Economic Development and the Marriage Crisis in the Special Economic Zones of China

Zhao Weijie

One of the most important shifts of Chinese economic reforms was the transfer from a centrally planned system to a market economy. It has changed not only the economic existence of Chinese people, but also their political life, moral principles and mode of thinking. These changes are most evident where the practice of a market economy is briskest, as in the special economic zone (SEZ) of Shenzhen, where the most spectacular changes have taken place. However, the effect of the changes on men and women differs due to certain historical and cultural reasons. This article will examine how middle-aged married women are experiencing confusion at the mix of the old and the new mentality during market-oriented economic development, and how those successful men who are thought to have gender superiority have brought about a marriage crisis.

The category of middle-aged women discussed in this article are between 35 and 50 years of age.

THE PHENOMENON OF THE 'THIRD PERSON' IN SHENZHEN

Shenzhen is an immigrant city. Families there are divided into two types: immigrant and local. Both kinds of families are being influenced by a wave of 'third persons', which has caused considerable family disintegration.

According to a document from Shenzhen's Intermediate People's Court, among 547 cases of divorce which were put up for judicial decision in 1991, 187 cases (31 per cent) were initiated by women (the wives) about 35–50 years of age, of which 102 cases were a result of the 'third person' syndrome.

These figures are evidence of a marriage crisis among middle-aged women. When judiciary personnel at the People's Court in Shenzhen were discussing issues of marriage and the family, the problem of the 'third person' was always mentioned. I interviewed cadres from different levels of the Women's Federation in the Shenzhen area, and they recounted the problem most mentioned as being that of husbands who had love affairs outside the marriage. Labour contractors, for example, often 'contract' women who come from less developed areas seeking jobs to make money in the SEZs. Also, rich men tend to divorce their wives and marry women more than 20 years younger than them. The 'third person' who threatens someone's marriage becomes the subject of gossip. It is obvious that the phenomenon of the 'third person' exerts a tremendous influence on the married life of people in Shenzhen.

Why is this 'third person' syndrome now in the ascendant and proving such a strong cause of the marriage crisis among middle-aged women?

LOCAL FAMILIES

As is well known, Shenzhen Special Economic Zone has been given preferential treatment by the Central Government, and also has a special geographical location (near Hong Kong and Macao). Such advantages enable the local people to prosper in advance of other people in China. There were originally 80,000 inhabitants of Shenzhen, with 20,000 in the towns and 60,000 peasants in outlying districts. Before the reforms, the peasants were very poor and many male labourers ran away to work in Hong Kong. This left behind a population of mainly old people, women and children. There is a small town called Shatoujao in south east Shenzhen, for example, which is now nationally famous for its wealth. Geographically, Shatoujao and Hong Kong are joined by a single road, and the peasants on both sides used to cross the border to work on the land. During the Cultural Revolution, many people decided to stay in Hong Kong and not come back. In one small village, only the Communist Party secretary and his family were left.

Since the reforms began in the late 1970s, the peasants in Shenzhen have become rich, selling their land for factories, hotels and shops, and profiting from business deals. On plots of land given them by the government, peasants have built beautiful Western-style houses. Some have even built two or three houses, each of them about 200–400 square metres large. At the initial stage of the reforms, when the system was in transition from a centrally planned to a market-oriented economy, there was confusion between traditional principles and the new policies. This left loopholes which enabled the peasants to make money. Some even took to smuggling to get rich. Talking to some local women, they mentioned having bank accounts of several hundred thousand or even millions, but when asked how they had become so rich, they would smile and explain: 'We smuggled, and we called that *"Zouqiaotou"* (crossing the bridge between Shenzhen and Hong Kong)'. They regarded this as an open secret since everyone was doing it. Thus, the peasants in Shenzhen have become a rich class, and an earth-shattering change has taken place in their lives. Many peasants have given up farming as a result, and they describe this as 'washing the earth off their feet'. Their style of clothing and eating habits have also changed beyond all recognition. Today, many peasant families have cars and mobile telephones, and they often eat in expensive restaurants, smoke imported cigarettes, and drink expensive Western wines. Following all these changes, however, some peasants wanted to change their wives as well.

What about the situation of these peasants' wives? The women of those peasant families who have 'washed the earth off their feet' have become divided into two different categories. Some of them have become business women, entrepreneurs, or horticultural and poultry-farming specialists during the phase of economic development. These women's families are relatively stable with little opportunity for a 'third person'.

Another category of peasant women are almost isolated in their Western-style houses and gardens, and they become idle and lose contact with society. If it is true that Oriental women have heavier physiological and psychological burdens than Western women, then rural Chinese women carry an even greater burden. Their work as agricultural labourers is normally primitive and heavy. And at the same time, they bear three to six children according to the traditional Chinese concept that 'the more boys, the more good fortune'. They are also expected to take care of their parents and their in-laws as well as their husbands and children. They seem to age very quickly under such heavy burdens. They marry at the same age as their husbands, but as they approach middle age they begin to look old. Furthermore, due to poor education, they quite often find it difficult to understand the changes in society. So, even the wealthy material life resulting from the reforms has not changed them much. They seem to be satisfied with their life as it is, and the isolation of their home life keeps them ignorant about the new and exciting world outside. Those women who started off on an equal basis with their husbands (with both of them working in the fields) are now distanced from their men who have left the land and become involved in commercial activities.

Some men in Shenzhen want to swap their wives, and the women who come to Shenzhen from less developed areas are on the lookout for rich men. Such circumstances form the root of the 'third person' syndrome.

What kind of person is 'the third person', and what are the characteristics of the phenomenon of the 'other person' in the SEZs?

Shenzhen was the first region to be developed as a special economic zone, and was therefore both a pilot experiment and a display window for the reforms in China. The Central Government gave Shenzhen preferential policies for its economic development, which enabled the people in Shenzhen to enjoy a much higher standard of living compared to that of people in the interior of China. For these reasons, people in the interior started to yearn for the opportunities they saw in the special economic zones, and began to move into the SEZs including Shenzhen.

Shenzhen was a small town on the south coast of China, an area of only 300 square kilometres, compared with China's total area of 96 million square kilometres. Although many people wanted to move to Shenzhen, only a small number were able to get a permit. Nevertheless, the immigrant figures are growing every year, and there are now about two million people registered as temporary, working and living in Shenzhen alongside a permanent population of 800,000. Most people who come to visit Shenzhen or to do business there gain a good impression of it.

Many people want to live in Shenzhen but are prevented from doing so because of the residency restrictions. Generally, more women than men have applied for and received residence permits to live in Shenzhen. This is illustrated by the fact that there is an 8:1 ratio of women to men in the local labour force. If a man wanted to gain a foothold in Shenzhen, he would need to have some ability or skill. People with well-developed skills or a high degree of technical ability will find it easier to get into Shenzhen than those of poor education. Nevertheless, if women want to gain a foothold there, aside from the same rules applying as for men, they have the possibility of moving in through marriage.

Moreover, men and women have very different attitudes towards material wealth. Men may not notice another's clothes or possessions, whereas women can be very sensitive about these things. Women coming from the less developed interior will see the goods in shops and department stores, the modern furniture in other families' houses, and the fashionable clothes worn by Shenzhen women. All of these stir their desires. These women from the interior who want to become resident in Shenzhen often have very little education or few skills, but with youth and beauty they can compete with local middle-aged married women.

A typical example of the 'third person' may be found in the following case. A married man who used to be a peasant in the countryside became a contractor in Shenzhen in the course of the reforms, and now has a luxurious house and car, and is able to frequent expensive restaurants and hotels. One day he met a waitress from Sichuan province in a restaurant, and started to date her. This girl, although she had little education, was aware of how to get on. She knew that there was no comparison between her life in the province and her life in Shenzhen, and so she decided to stay there. They lived together for a while, but she soon put forward the idea of getting married. The man eventually agreed and divorced his peasant wife who had shared his life with all its hard work, but who was now old and out of date. In one year, this young girl had left her home town for the city and achieved her aim of marrying a rich man and having a comfortable life. This woman is 23 years younger than the man who is now her husband. Such 'third persons' can be found everywhere in SEZs.

One may ask how, in view of their isolated upbringing in the countryside, these young girls adapt so easily to the new life in the city, especially in terms of sexual openness (because in China, sexuality for women is traditionally the most deep-seated emotion). For this, we must refer to Marx when he says: 'Being determines consciousness, and the economic base determines the superstructure'. If this theory is applied to the 'third person', in the case of young women emerging from the isolation of simple village life, we see that when they come to the city their lives are changed by the material wealth around them, and they cannot help but want to be part of this wealth. In consequence, their moral beliefs and faith, which may not be so strong, collapse very quickly.

Benefiting from the economic reforms and particularly from the preferential policies for the SEZs, local families in Shenzhen have become the first wave of Chinese *nouveaux riches*. There is an explosion of material wealth in their life-style, but contrary to the young immigrant women, they find it difficult to change their culture and moral beliefs overnight. Before the reforms, the local peasants were extremely poor, and had little idea of modern life in cities. It seemed that their only hope for their future life lay in their children. Most peasant families in Guangdong province had three to six children. If they did not have a boy they might carry on having more children in the hope of getting a boy. The notions of 'having sons to provide care in old age' and 'more boys more good fortune' were very popular in rural areas. Such superstitions have remained unchanged in the minds of the local peasants living in the special economic zones including Shenzhen. Being the centre of their families, peasant men would like their wives to satisfy their physical needs, and to give them children to pass on the family name. This remains a strong part of their culture. Since the reforms, although these peasants have become rich very quickly, their traditional ideas about women and the family have resisted being changed at the same pace. Their deep-rooted culture has been revived in a new guise.

There has been a consumer bias towards material goods on the part of peasant families in the SEZs. For example, some peasants spend as much as 3,000–10,000 *yuan* in one restaurant, ordering large meals, much more than they can eat, and leaving most of the meal untouched. The purpose of visiting an expensive restaurant is not necessarily so much to enjoy the food as to derive satisfaction from showing off their wealth.

In their marriages, the peasants seem to have combined the traditional concepts of feudalism with the new concept of materialism. In Shenzhen, those rich peasants with feudalistic ideas would take the 'third person' and have an affair without giving up their families. For example, a rich contractor of labour bought several houses in different cities and installed a woman in each. He spent a large amount of money to buy the marriage registration for these women. In some cases where this is happening, the women (or concubines) would satisfy the physical and sexual needs of the men. If there were no sons in the original marriage, there is now a chance that the concubine may give him a son. Those wives who did not give birth to a boy for their families find themselves in a weak position to convince their men not to have concubines outside marriage, because they feel they have to face the fact of themselves growing old and becoming less attractive to their men. Some men may even move their concubines into the house to live together with their first wives, who would then be in the situation of having to share everything, including the bedroom. When a concubine was about to give birth to her baby, the wife would have to take care of her. This is basically the situation regarding the marriage crisis of local middle-aged women in Shenzhen.

IMMIGRANT FAMILIES

The marriages of women who are currently middle-aged in China can be seen as the outcome of the Cultural Revolution. During that period, an extreme left ideology dominated society. Having the correct parentage used to be the first consideration in getting married. What counted as good parentage was poor and lower-middle peasants, workers, or revolutionary cadres, and other requirements were records of schooling and social status. Alongside this strong political orientation, the women of that generation themselves maintained a very traditional ideology concerning marriage. They believed that as soon as a woman got married, she would became the property of the man for life. Almost none of the women of this generation had ever thought that something totally unforeseen could happen in their marriage. Therefore, many capable and intelligent women, once they married, gave up everything including their careers for their husband and children. Such a model was partly developed from the Chinese traditional culture of 'husband high, wife glorious'.

Prior to the reforms, immigrant couples were considered socially equal with each other under the centrally planned economic system. Also, compared

with local married couples, immigrant couples were more often better educated, and the women were sometimes even more educated than their
husbands. Generally, these people, who were young but felt depressed during
the Cultural Revolution, have by now reached maturity in the course of the
reforms. If they have the opportunity to build their life in Shenzhen in a
market-oriented economy, people tend to make use of all their personal
advantages such as experience, knowledge, physical energy, and intelli-
gence in order to realize their aspirations. Some people, who had a feeling
of obscurity before coming to Shenzhen, have now become very successful.
Some, who were well educated and from universities, have also successfully
developed their careers as businessmen and managers in this SEZ.

However, in this age group, men have achieved more than women. To
discover the reason for this, we have to look at history. It is a fact that,
throughout history, men have always been at the forefront of any dramatic
change in society. People simply accept that the man is the leader because of
his God-given strength. From way back into pre-history, humans have relied
on the physical strength of the male. Man has been the leader of his people
through war, fire, flood, and social and economic changes. Apart from these
natural characteristics behind gender bias, certain cultural and political
influences have also favoured men being dominant during the evolution of
human beings.

China is by no means an exception. For several thousand years, the
society has been male-centred. 'Men dominating society but women dominating the family' has long been considered as a social model for the Chinese
family generated from the culture. After the People's Republic was founded,
the symbol of a man and a woman holding the flag as equals did not alter the
deep-seated cultural roles of men and women. So, when the reforms offered
equal opportunities to male and female, many women were willing to leave
the opportunities to men. There are many examples of this in Shenzhen.

Married immigrant men then have more opportunities because of those
given up by the women. They become managers, contractors and businessmen. As their incomes increase and their careers become more successful,
their status changes, and the gap between men and women has been
widening. This gap is not just economic but also psychological and
behavioural.

These immigrant men from the interior have the advantage over local
men in that they are more educated and more easily absorb a different culture
and lifestyle, including different sexual behaviour. Their situations fit in
readily with those young single or divorced women who come to Shenzhen
for a new life. In particular, these women had hoped that they might be able
to play the card of youth and beauty to compete with the local women in
Shenzhen, and such a mentality just tallied with the needs of the immigrant

men. In speaking to the men from the interior about their poor quality of life, boring work, and suppression of their sexual feelings, one man said: 'I have suffered a lot during my life and now I want to enjoy what is left'. The suffering he mentioned was not only poverty but also lack of inspiration and sexual fulfilment. When these men moved to Shenzhen, they saw career opportunities and at the same time a means of breaking free not only from poverty but also from sexual repression.

While the men started to enjoy their new life in Shenzhen, their wives still stuck to the tradition of the man dominant outside the family and the woman dominant at home. They seemed to be used to the centrally planned system which had produced egalitarian economic conditions for everyone. So, when the opportunity arose, they gave way to their husbands without realizing that the outcome would be totally different under the market economy. They would never have imagined a situation where their men would be driving a Mercedes Benz and eating in expensive restaurants, while they would be left at home cleaning and cooking, or shopping for bargains in the market to save money.

The pressure on the wife of looking after the family and children means that, although husband and wife are the same age, the woman may begin to look older. In playing the role of wife, mother, daughter as well as a social role, it is often common for the wife to be the first to suffer hardship but the last to enjoy comfort. Any wealth is distributed first to the husband, second to the children, and then to the parents. This has a biological effect: the wife ages earlier, and even at 40 years of age can experience the menopause.

Single women moving to Shenzhen are quite different. Apart from being young and attractive to men, they are normally well educated with degrees or diplomas. There are also single women who are divorced and want to escape their hurt and emotional bruising. Other single women, generally from the lower class who want to do better, may get jobs as nightclub singers or dancers. Most single women become unskilled workers, and when they get to Shenzhen, no matter what their original intention, only a few decide to return home.

These single women are usually sensitive to new ideas, they want to stay in Shenzhen and are not too bothered about how they can achieve this. For example, a young single woman asked a middle-aged female doctor to help her find a job, and the doctor did. However, after being refused several jobs, the young woman turned to seducing the doctor's husband. This became a tragic incident in the doctor's life. She said about the young woman that:

> She thinks everything about living in Shenzhen is good. She feels liberated and has never wanted to go home. She had a lot of difficulties finding a job and some-where to live, but I would not have thought that she would have done these things. Now I am getting old, and she is just 30 years old. How can I compete with her?

As already stated, this young woman's ambitions and needs coincide with the physical and psychological needs of immigrant men in Shenzhen. When these men were young, they looked for wives in the traditional way, expecting wives to care for the family and to support the husband competing in society. Now that they have become successful, they want younger women, just for pleasure. This is the problem for middle-aged married women, and the 'third person' crisis in their marriage seems to be unavoidable. Here is another example: one of the pioneers in the development of Shenzhen was a happily married family man in every way. A month before his 50th birthday, he divorced his wife and married a woman of 32 years old. He said: 'Frankly, I am ashamed to say it, but at only 40 my wife became menopausal, and was no longer interested in the sexual side of our marriage'.

THE PHENOMENON OF THE 'THIRD PERSON' AS A FORM OF 'POLLUTION' IN SOCIETY

Married life in Shenzhen is like a boat capsized by the waves. This has made many middle-aged women angry and puzzled. One of the wives, who has kept her looks, says:

> Husbands have changed their standards in judging their wives. They used to demand not only our ability to look after the family, but also our devotion to a career. Now, however, they have turned their attention to sexuality as a result of the country becoming more open. The advantages we used to possess have now become our weak points. It seems clear that we have little chance to compete with young women in that respect, but do we have to leave our families?

Another woman spoke to the 'third person' who had an affair with her husband, and asked her: 'Why do you want to destroy my family by taking away my husband? We have children, he is 40 years old and you are only 20'. The woman was then told: 'Your husband does not love you any more, and he wants to live with me. You can do nothing about this but divorce him'. Some 'third parties' even threaten the wife, telling her to leave and claiming that the home is theirs.

Some single women in Shenzhen have involved themselves in families in Hong Kong. The Women's Federation of Shenzhen once received a letter from a married woman in Hong Kong. The 36 year old woman wrote in her letter that:

> I write this letter to ask your organization to help. I live in Hong Kong. I married my husband in April 1978, and we now have five children. We used to be a happy family, but my husband recently met another woman, Miss Wang. She comes from

Hubei province on the mainland, and is now working in a clothes factory in Shenzhen. She quite often makes a date with my husband, and wants me to divorce him so that they can get married. My husband has now asked for a divorce. I would like you to do something to stop her destroying my family.

The Women's Federation of Shenzhen has received many letters of this kind.

The phenomenon of the 'third person' is the biggest 'polluter' in Shenzhen. Young women are using their looks and youth to get money and residency, but have caused unrest in many families. Such 'social pollution' creates a big psychological problem for some married women. One wife, who was at one time very self-confident, has become anxious and says: 'I would not like him (the husband) to become a manager or get rich'. Another woman said: 'When we were poor we wished we could be rich; now that we are rich, I am afraid that he will give me up'. A woman becomes very suspicious if her husband comes home late. She even worries when her husband makes love with her twice during one week, suspecting that he might be losing interest in her. In such families, the wives live in fear and suspicion, and they are always worried that their husbands are having an affair even though it may not be happening.

At a forum on the subject held in Shenzhen, several women participants asked questions like: 'If your husband gave you up, how would you cope with it?'; 'If a "third person" became involved with our family, how should we respond ...?'; and: 'If my husband was having an affair with another woman, should I divorce him or not; do I lose anything by staying silent?'

From the above analyses, we may draw the conclusion that it is middle-aged women in Shenzhen in particular who are most likely to have a crisis in their marriage. Older marriages suffer less from this crisis, and are thus more stable. The younger generation influenced by modern life has a new concept of marriage. Even in divorce, younger women would get less psychologically hurt. Middle-aged women, who got married in the traditional way, tend to devote themselves to their husbands, children and parents. They have to face not only the double burdens of the family and society, but also the conflict of Eastern and Western cultures found in Shenzhen as a special economic zone more open to the West. All these pressures are exaggerated when the phenomenon of the 'third person' comes into the family. They are besieged with both internal and external difficulties. Some of these women, after experiencing the break-up of their marriage, have tried to start a new life, but other women find it hard to change their beliefs or traditions. Neither are they able, because of women's often emotional nature, to face up to the trauma of the 'third person'. The Women's Federation in Shenzhen has done a great deal to help these women overcome their marriage crises.

THE SEZ'S CULTURAL AND ADMINISTRATIVE MODEL AND ITS IMPACT ON THE CONDITION OF MARRIAGE AND FAMILY

With the emergence of a large number of joint enterprises, foreign-owned and private businesses under the market economy, competition has intensified in Shenzhen. This has brought about a change in the traditional administrative model, in which the Communist Party's organizations previously played the most powerful role in handling all kinds of business.

For the past 40 years, the unitary planned economic system has created a unitary marriage model. This has been determined by the nature of public ownership as well as by the Communist Party's supreme power. Under this model, every single marriage had to obtain permission from a government registrar; then the couple would be entitled to be put on the waiting list for a flat or room distributed by their work units. This would mean that they might have to live in the same building with their colleagues and bosses with whom they were familiar. Under the centrally planned economy, the work unit was like a small society, and therefore the leadership of this society had a large say in people's lives. If there was a problem with someone's marriage, the unit leader would normally turn up to intervene. If the wife found her husband was having an affair, she would go to the husband's work unit to complain, so as to have an assurance that her husband would not be able to divorce her. This could sometimes damage the husband's career prospects, because the unit leader had the power to judge and control his team members' private life. Therefore, men became extremely careful not to make any mistakes in their marriage.

The practice of establishing a market economy in Shenzhen, however, has altered this model of marriage. Today, if the husband had an affair and the wife tried to get help from his boss, the manager would say: 'My job is to look after the company and make money, and your job is to take care of your family. If your marriage is in crisis, you should go to court. It is not my business'. In the meantime, due to the commercialization of housing and accommodation, the small community commitment no longer exists.

Looking at the cultural aspects of life in Shenzhen, we may find that, as the economy develops and the society offers more opportunities, people's ideology has changed a great deal. In the less developed areas where the planned economy has not yet been seriously challenged by market practices, people may still be interested in other people's private lives, and would gossip. Here in Shenzhen, people have become more interested in making money, and society itself has become more tolerant. At the same time, the increased income enjoyed by individuals has produced more independence

in people's lives. Issues of sexuality are becoming more and more private.
So, now, if a husband and wife have a marital problem, they prefer to sort it
out on their own. With less unitary control, society is becoming more relaxed.
However, people's sexual behaviour sometimes goes too far now, and there
are less social sanctions on it.

In Shenzhen, the women who have affairs are usually ten, 20, and even 30
years younger than the men. So the question arises, why do these young
women want to have an affair with, or marry, men who are in some cases
as old as their fathers?

The answer to this is that, besides the huge temptation of material well-
being to these young women, another reason is the development of the
market economy with its concept of the exchange of commodities which has
its influence everywhere in Shenzhen's society. This concept of exchange
has become a part of marriage. Some women use their youth and attractive
looks to get husbands, and then through money and the right to residence in
Shenzhen automatically come to lead a much more comfortable lifestyle.
These women see the exchange as of equal value. Since those men's wives
have lost their ability to compete in the sexual market, the young women feel
justified and at ease in replacing them.

In summary, there are many reasons for the marriage crisis among the
middle-aged population, but the major one is the development of the economic
conditions of society as well as the family. This being the case, we argue that
women's liberation and equality between men and women must rely on economic changes as a first step. When men and women become economically
equal to begin with, women's liberation can possibly be achieved.

Translated by Min Dong Chao.

15. Ironies of History: Citizenship Issues in the New Market Economies of East Central Europe

Barbara Einhorn

Women's rights have sometimes been described as basic human rights. A more specific and nuanced approach, I would argue, is to try to define what kind of rights would enable women to become equal citizens in a society character- ized by social justice and gender equality. Furthermore, since citizenship is always conferred by the state, it is fruitful to compare the theory and practice of two different sociopolitical systems with regard to women's citizenship. This chapter will therefore look at differences in women's access to citizen- ship rights in East Central Europe under the former state socialist regimes and during the present transition to democratic market-based systems.

Gender can be regarded as an appropriate lens through which to view the process of social change and its contradictions. What happens to women as citizens, and to gender relations both in the workplace and in the family, pro- vides a sensitive set of indicators of change. Historically, liberal democratic definitions of citizenship posited a universal category of membership. Recent feminist analyses (Anthias and Yuval-Davis, 1989; Vogel, 1991; Lister, 1993) have pointed out that citizenship is never uniform; rather it is always mediated by gender, class and race. Indeed, as Ruth Lister argues, 'the classical status of citizen was explicitly defined so as to exclude women' (Lister, 1993, p. 3). In nineteenth century Britain, for example, citizenship was confined to prop- erty-owning males. Women were relegated to the private sphere, with indirect access to citizenship rights, mediated by their husbands who played an active role in the public spheres of work and politics.

State socialism drew women into the public sphere of work and politics. But although their obligation to work also gave them rights as mothers, the contradiction for women in East Central Europe was that their 'emancipation' as citizens depended on their membership of the labour force without, how- ever, unequal gender relations within the spheres of paid or unpaid work being addressed. Now, market pressures are retrenching women, sending them back to hearth and home, where a conservative and/or nationalist discourse tells them that their primary responsibility is to 'produce babies for the nation'. Within the family, traditional patriarchal gender roles are being reinforced. Once again, women are to be deprived of citizenship rights in the public sphere of work and politics. Nor is their relegation to the private sphere necessarily matched by the right to claims on the state in their role as mothers. Indeed in many of the countries in East Central Europe, as in Western European countries involved in the process of restructuring, marketization is linked with the withdrawal of state welfare provision of the kind earlier seen as an integral part of the entitlements deriving from citizenship (T.H. Marshall, 1949, referred to in Vogel and Moran, 1991, p. xi).

What are the prospects now for women's citizenship rights in East Central Europe? In contrast to the traditional notion of women as simultaneously the signifiers of the nation and its objects, over which men go to war, the suffrage achieved by the first wave feminists ushered in the era of women as political subject citizens in their own right.

To this conception, the role of the state as provider of entitlements is central. In the socialist experiment in East Central Europe, women's right to social welfare provision such as maternity leave/childcare/pension rights was tied to their labour market participation. Now, however, in the neo-liberal market democracies, society's responsibility for reproducing and caring for the workforce is devolved onto individual families, for which in turn the woman is made responsible. This means a return to dependence on women's unpaid labour, on informal networks, with state support only in cases where the family fails rather than as a matter of right, as an entitlement.

This chapter will use a theoretical frame focusing on entitlements as a basis for citizenship in order to compare the gender impact of state socialism with that of the new market-based democracies.[1] Within this frame, it will explore several areas of change: private property rights; women's opportunities in the labour market; the role of the state and the function of legislation in influencing the family and the public/private divide; reproductive rights and the impact of political discourse on women's role. This analysis of what is happening to women's citizenship in the process of social transformation in East Central Europe will help to illuminate more generally related issues of theoretical significance and of policy relevance.

ENTITLEMENTS AS A BASIS FOR CITIZENSHIP RIGHTS

The principal entitlements under capitalism arise from the ownership of property on the one hand and the capacity to sell labour power on the other. The latter is modified by the individual's capacity to accumulate human capital, or skills. Property can be broken down into natural resources and command, in one way or another, over reproducible capital, as in ownership of buildings and equipment versus shares or other financial instruments.[2]

These entitlements are modified by the intra-household distribution (of labour and resources) on the one hand, and state provisions affecting reproduction of the household and regulation of the labour market on the other. In addition, the prevailing political discourse helps to shape both state policy and individual options and choices.

Under state socialism, entitlements arise from state ownership and distribution of the benefits from natural resources (land) and reproducible capital, in combination with the individual sale of labour (human capital).[3] These entitlements too are modified by intra-household distribution and by state provisions affecting the reproduction of the household and regulating the labour market.

Systemic differences mean entitlements in each of the two systems vary as a result of the following four elements:

1. Private vs. state ownership of the means of production;
2. The degree of state regulation of labour markets;
3. The degree of state intervention in household reproduction – for example through legislation and provision of welfare;
4. The nature and role of the dominant discourse.

In this chapter I discuss the way these four differentiating factors affect women. The following sections investigate the question of entitlements and citizenship rights by focusing in greater detail on property ownership; women's opportunities in the labour market; the way legislation and official rhetoric affect the relationship of private and public spheres; and political discourses in the context of the East Central European transition from state socialism to market capitalism.

PROPERTY OWNERSHIP

In the newly marketized economies of East Central Europe, the redistribution of, and the benefits from, property ownership are switched from being an entitlement apportioned to individual citizens by the state, to being subject to the vagaries of both private property rights and redistribution within the household. Particularly with regard to the latter, there is ample literature showing that this leads to gendered and unequal outcomes.

The restoration of private property rights – the first feverish activity in legislative change in most East Central European countries – will be likely to mitigate against women's opportunities to act as autonomous economic agents. The chance to establish private businesses has thus far tempted far fewer women than men to take entrepreneurial risks (see Kostova, 1994, p. 105 on Bulgaria; Paukert, 1993, on the Czech Republic). This unwillingness to take risks is less attributable to some essentialist notion of women's timidity than to the material disadvantaging of women via occupational segregation in the labour market under state socialism. This form of discrimination has also ensured that, in the new situation, women have less access to capital, influence, information and the 'old-boy' networks by means of which many former *apparatchiks* have become the managers and entrepreneurs of the new market economies.

Former owners of land whose property is being returned are almost always male. Cooperative household and village patterns of involvement in socialist agriculture (apart from Poland, where the traditional peasant culture endured throughout the state socialist period) will revert to a patriarchal – often semi-feudal – peasant family farming system with its accompanying strict division of roles within the family (see Pine, 1992; 1994). This patriarchal family unit will be the rural economic unit in the newly marketized societies.

It can therefore be said that while gendered role divisions persisted in the state socialist period, they did so within and in contradiction to a culture whose discourse favoured gender equality. Now, the patriarchal family as an economic unit provides a material base for perpetuating or exacerbating gender inequalities while exemplifying and being in tune with the conservative values which form the currently dominant discourse in much of the region.[4]

Indeed Mežnarić and Ule (1994, p. 155–6) unwittingly espouse such gender hierarchies within a newly entrenched public-private divide when they define a modernized society, which they see as belatedly emerging in Eastern Europe, as being 'based on private property, which is protected by law' and praise as 'the strength of modernized Western society' its 'separation of private (household, family) and public (market)' spheres (although, to be fair, they do also recognize 'the state's role as provider of services for the community').

WOMEN'S OPPORTUNITIES IN THE LABOUR MARKET

Most theories of gender equality, whether bourgeois or socialist in origin, have focused on women's labour force participation as a key factor in the achievement not only of economic independence from men, but of personal autonomy and self-esteem. State socialist societies achieved unprecedentedly high levels of female labour force participation, but did not resolve problems of occupational segregation at work (Nickel, 1993, p. 139; Kostova, 1993,

p. 94–9). Further, the model of women's emancipation to be achieved through labour force participation actually exacerbated gender inequalities because of women's far greater responsibility for the family (see Einhorn, 1993a). Now, by contrast

> the economic function of the family is being restored through property rights and inheritance. This makes it very likely that the family could turn from a predominantly consuming unit into a more comprehensive economic unit, especially given the development or re-emergence of small firms and farms. This could lead to changes in family roles and thus in the role of women. (Kostova, 1994, p. 95)

The state has historically been the largest employer of women in both capitalist and state socialist societies. It has also been the standard setter and monitor of minimum standards – in wages, equality legislation and compensatory measures for women's reproductive role (ILO, 1994a). Removal of this role through the physical contraction of the state sector in favour of the market as sole regulator means that the principles of redistributive justice and gender equality are subsumed under the need for economic efficiency.[5] In East Central Europe, labour mobility, the need for rationalization and cost-cutting combined with the reintroduction in some countries of an economic base for the family unit translate into disproportionately high and involuntary (see Funk, 1993; Nickel, 1993) female unemployment rates.

The high rates of female unemployment have multiple causes. The compensatory legislation left over from the previous regimes allowed and allows women to be perceived as 'unreliable' workers (high absenteeism for children's illnesses; lengthy maternity leave entitlements requiring temporary replacement).[6] The structural shifts of the transition to the market, which might be expected – involving as they do the shift from heavy to light industry and expansion of the service sector – to stimulate the demand for female labour, are in fact disadvantaging women workers.[7] In newly marketized sectors such as banking and insurance, which were female-dominated under state socialism, women are being ousted by men, especially in middle management where they were previously well represented. There is much evidence that joint ventures and foreign investors are particularly guilty of openly expressing preferences in job advertisements for male workers and especially male managers (see Einhorn, 1993b; Fong and Paull, 1993, p. 233; Paukert, 1993).

The trend is towards substituting male for female workers in East Central Europe as there ceases to be compensation for absenteeism caused by the needs of household/population reproduction in favour of unbroken service by purportedly unencumbered male workers. In this region, therefore, marketization tends to shrink women's employment opportunities.[8]

The 1994 *World Labour Report* of the International Labour Organization

(ILO, 1994b) identifies globalization as one of the two powerful forces shaping employment worldwide. The other is liberalization. Increasing capital mobility as a symptom of these processes is illustrated by the flight of capital – not only from Western Europe, but also from Eastern Europe, to Asia, in search of ever-cheaper labour.[9] This is an additional factor mitigating against women's employment opportunities in East Central Europe.

In Western Europe and the newly industrializing Asian economies, restructuring and structural adjustment respectively have introduced the concept of 'flexibilization'. Ostensibly, this enables women better to combine their productive and reproductive roles. 'Flexibilization' can mean different things in different contexts, but West European experience indicates that the type of flexible employment favoured by post-industrial, recession-hit economies is 'female-friendly' precisely because it involves a shift to insecure, part-time and home-based work under unprotected job conditions. The shift to part-time jobs may be welcomed by overstretched East European women as an opportunity better to mesh their two roles. However, existing evidence suggests that the advantages of 'flexibilization' accrue to firms rather than to women workers, since it is a process accompanied by the casualization of labour contracts, and thus a lack of: employment protection; social security provision, minimum wage legislation; access to training, career prospects and trade union representation (ILO, 1994a). 'Flexibilization' can sometimes mean cheaper female labour (with lack of social protection) being used to undercut men, especially in the newly industrializing economies of Asia, but in the context of global marketization this tends to mean a quantitative increase in female employment opportunities at the cost of quality in terms of working conditions.

A recent ILO global study of women in productive employment maintains that 'equality of opportunity and treatment for women and men in employment has yet to be achieved anywhere. The relationship between family responsibilities and work is increasingly seen as a serious obstacle in attaining this basic human right' (ILO, 1994b, p. 3).

THE RELATIONSHIP OF PUBLIC AND PRIVATE: THE ROLE OF LEGISLATION AND THE STATE

While state socialism treated citizenship as universal, based on the rights of a class – its workers – it simultaneously addressed the issue of special needs in compensatory legislative and social measures which treated women as a sub-group (for example in protective legislation, or maternity leave entitlements which were only belatedly made available to men or grandparents). A contentious approach to gender equality, many Western theorists have argued that protective legislation should apply to all workers, not just women (Fong and Paull, 1993, p. 242), or even, as did Helsinki Watch in its 1992 analysis of the situation of women in Poland (Helsinki Watch, 1992, p. 4), 'that gender-specific laws have no place in modern society' if the goal is gender equity as a basis for citizenship. This argument rests on the view that 'even when meant as a protection, in effect they provide an opportunity for discrimination' (ibid.).[10] And certainly during the state socialist period such measures served more to entrench existing gendered role divisions than to 'compensate' women and enable them to act as equal citizens – largely because the primary site of gendered power relations – the family – was exempt from scrutiny.

Both under state socialism before 1989 and in the newly marketizing democracies since then, there is a sizeable gap between rhetoric and the reality of women's role. State socialism's construction of women as workers *and* mothers has quite simply been replaced by a vision of women as mothers. Both systems instrumentalized women's needs in order to fulfil primarily economic, but also demographic imperatives. The industrialization process in state socialist economies was marked by labour shortages and thus a demand for female labour. The state was therefore prepared to socialize reproductive labour to a certain extent in order to underwrite women's primary role as producers.

By contrast, the newly market-based economies in East Central Europe need to shed labour; and in many cases, this need is reinforced by a felt need to boost the falling birthrate. Both birds can be killed with the same stone by defining women as 'natural' mothers (the neglect of which fact has been retrospectively made a scapegoat for all manner of social problems). It is a phenomenon not confined to East Central Europe that the neo-liberal market-led paradigm aims to pare down the role of the state and facilitates this by propounding a renewed central role for the family as the basis of society.

The contraction of the state sector also means a cut in public social provision, devolving responsibility for reproducing the labour force and wider caring roles onto individual families (viz. the principles of subsidiarity and 'care in the community'; see Crescy Cannan's chapter in this volume).

In reality as opposed to rhetoric, women are now, as they were then, stuck with the two roles of worker and mother, since their earning capacity is as fundamental to the family's survival in the new market-led economies as it was in the old centrally-planned ones. The sole difference is in the signifiers, or in the way those roles are ideologically marked: where state socialism prioritized women's productive role, with motherhood achieved on the side, the new market-led economies sanctify their reproductive role, and categorize them as secondary earners (a 'reserve army of labour'?).

How women are able to synthesize these two roles, or mediate between their role in the public sphere of paid work and the private sphere of unpaid domestic labour, differs in different types of society.

Much has already been written on the fact that 'the concepts of private and public (in East Central Europe) have meanings and functions different from those of Western countries' (Havelková, 1993, p. 68–9; see also Einhorn, 1993a, p. 59–68). As a consequence of state socialism's control, not only over the command economy but of the public sphere more generally, the private sphere of the family 'assumed a special function as the refuge of moral values. ... [It] substituted for the public sphere. ... As the private sphere became more important, so did the role of women' (Havelková, ibid.).

However, state socialist compensatory legislation, combined with the Kádárist concession of a private sphere free of interference from the state, in effect served to entrench patriarchal patterns of gender roles within the family. And in the resulting 'us' (the people) versus 'them' (the state) dichotomy (Marody, 1991, p. 112–13) which fostered a gender-neutral solidarity within the family, women were prepared to endure whatever inequality or indignities they suffered behind the closed doors of the private in order to maintain this sphere of individual (male) autonomy.

Now, by contrast, while conservative discourses (from the Church, nationalist ideologues and the state) reinvest the family with the rhetorical value it lacked in state socialist practice, in reality the locus of the private sphere has lost its halo. Former dissident men for whom the private sphere of family and informal networks acted as a kind of substitute civil society are leaving this site to become citizens, subject-actors in the public spheres of the marketplace and mainstream politics.

Meanwhile, the new conservative discourses cast women as primarily responsible for the family, as mothers rather than workers, reinforcing even more firmly the public/private divide and signalling a return from public (socialist welfare state) to private (women dependent on a male breadwinner) patriarchy (see Dölling, 1991; Einhorn, 1993a; Chamberlayne, 1994).

The revival of traditional attitudes and gender role models allots to women a life of sacrifice 'taking comfort in the Virgin Mary's example' (see Harsanyi on Romania, 1993, p. 40). They are cast as heroic women coping with the burdens of transition, in the mould of strong Polish women during the 150 years of partition (Titkow, 1993, p. 253), icons of motherhood sacrificed to their 'symbolic mission' (Lissyutkina, 1993, p. 282) as saviours of the nation.

And although the model of liberal democracy being followed by the formerly state socialist countries is based on individual rights, 'the economic model that is expected to develop' is one which 'emphasizes the family rather than its individual members' (Kostova, 1994, p. 131). The outcome of this is that the individual rights ascribed to citizens in liberal democratic discourse will tend in this context to be male.

THE INFLUENTIAL ROLE OF POLITICAL DISCOURSE

The dominant political discourse is extremely influential in the construction of women's roles and the scope for or contraction of their options in different social paradigms. Official state socialist rhetoric constructed women as workers and proclaimed women's 'emancipation' (although some critical opinion – for example Buckley, 1985, p. 50 – has suggested that this was a purely instrumental way to underwrite the demand for labour in the then industrializing economies of the Soviet Union and much of East Central Europe, particularly once central planning began). By contrast, most Western market economies have constructed women first and foremost as mothers, with their wage-earning activities seen as a secondary role.

Now, newly emergent conservative and nationalist discourses in East Central Europe claim it was precisely the 'emancipation' of women under state socialism that was the undoing, not just of women, but of social cohesion in general. There is also a shift from a universalist egalitarian approach to one which espouses gender difference, yet fails to address women's special needs in the way that state socialist compensatory legislation attempted to do. As Dobrinka Kostova puts it, writing of the Bulgarian context: 'whereas socialist ideology proclaimed that women as a group should be advanced, the special conditions and problems of Bulgarian women are now ignored' (Kostova, 1994, p. 117).

Thus there is a contrast in the basis for entitlements regarded as central to citizenship rights in different socioeconomic paradigms and their accompanying political discourse. For women this boils down to being entitled to goods provided by the state on the basis of their roles as worker, as mother, or simply as an individual citizen of a particular state.

Understandably the ideology of egalitarianism espoused by state socialism is now perceived as the imposition of uniformity and lack of choice. However, the rejection of hated stereotypes of the uniformed party official, drab mother or exhausted female worker has led to the revival of essentialist notions of femininity and masculinity, with a celebration of women's 'naturally' nurturing role in terms which, in effect, equate femininity with maternity. Further, there is a political attempt common to most of the former state socialist countries to control women in this role. A clear expression of this attempt has been the attacks on abortion rights in several countries.

Nationalism, especially in former Yugoslavia, appears as the most extreme form of the new conservative discourse in which Renata Salecl claims that 'national identity serves as a support for the formation of a specific version of the "moral majority" (in Poland, Slovenia, and Croatia, etc.) which conceives Christian values as the ideological "cement" holding together the "Nation"' (Salecl, 1994, p. 20).

This form of national-conservative discourse is used to manipulate ideo-logically sanctified motherhood in contradictory ways. So, for example, the Serbian media has urged Serbian women to have more children in order to overcome the extremely low birthrate, described as the 'white plague', while vilifying Albanian women in Kosovo who tend to have large families as 'prisoners of the patriarchal family', or as 'baby factories' too ignorant to know better (Bracewell, 1995). Who is entitled to become a mother? The sanctity of motherhood in the name of the nation is relative, it appears, depending on whether the ethnic group women belong to is positively identified with or marked as 'undesirable' by the ethnic group dominating legislation and policy. In Croatia, a legislative draft proposes to foster 'the profession of mothering' (by banning abortion and introducing pro-natalist measures) as 'the most sublime profession in Croatia' (*Proposal for Demographic Renewal*, 1992, Section 38.1a), with rewards and preferential treatment for families of three or four children. The *Proposal for Demographic Renewal* simultaneously voices explicitly the cynical ulterior motive of such policies which intend to withdraw working mothers with children from 'unsuitable jobs': 'In that way thousands of jobs would be vacant' (ibid., 38.1b).

Nationalist discourse may appear as an extreme form of the new 'moral majority's' ideology, but it is in fact a simple extension of the conservative discourse on the family within the nation-state which is emerging in most Eastern European countries. Andjelka Milić (1993, p. 110–20) distinguishes between patriotic nationalism as a movement from below for the recognition of cultural identity, and state nationalism, a political project with an ideology which is 'internalized by the individual when times are confusing and society is in crisis'. The latter, she claims, 'approaches individuals as objects' and 'instrumentalizes their feelings' in establishing a strict hierarchy of roles whereby 'women are given a strictly limited sphere of action – to reproduce the nation – and men are instructed to defend it' (ibid., p. 120).

If the family is seen as the social and economic basis of the new market society, it has also come to fill the vacuum left by the demise of the state socialist project. The search for a collective identity has invested itself in the notion of the ethnic or national 'family'. Just as state socialism required individual rights to be subsumed under the collective goal of 'building social-ism', now individual women's rights are to be subordinated first to the good of their individual family, and beyond that to the wider ethnic or national family. Yet we see here a gender-differentiated appropriation of the individual rights upon which the model of liberal democracy espoused by these coun-tries is based. For men, it seems, are to inherit citizenship rights, including the right to determine which women shall exercise reproductive rights, while women are given the goal of duty to the nation.

Even within their newly circumscribed role, women-as-mothers acting as political subjects can be manipulated in the name of the nation. At the outset of the conflict in former Yugoslavia women mobilized to oppose the war. Invading the parliament in Belgrade in July 1991, they demanded the return of their sons from the Yugoslav army. However, when after the army's occupation of Slovenia Serbian women went there to bring their sons home from the front line, they were defeated by political manipulation which led them to identify first as members of their ethnically defined national grouping of which the Slovenes were portrayed as the national enemy, rather than as simply mothers with a collective interest in protecting their son's lives and opposing war (see Drakulić, 1993, p. 129; Salecl, 1994, p. 14).

Women – and more specifically female bodies – are often projected as the embodiment of the nation, over whose (territorial) integrity men are prepared to lay down their lives. Far from being safe on the 'home front' away from the site of hostilities, however, in modern wars 'women apparently always find themselves in the front line' (Seifert, 1995). Rape in war on the scale[11] suffered by Bosnian women at the hands of Serbian men is thus no chance 'by-product' of battle, but rather, claims Ruth Seifert, has the 'strategic function' of destroying the enemy's cultural identity (Bracewell, 1995; Salecl, 1994; Seifert, 1995). In deeply patriarchal traditional cultures such as those of Serbia and Bosnia a pre-twentieth century conception of citizenship is based on individual property-owning males, whose women, confined to the inner sphere of the home, belong to them. Thus the violation of the enemy's women destroys not only his cultural identity, but also his property (Salecl, 1994, p. 17). His property is 'polluted' by being impregnated with the seed of the enemy: what could be seen as the normal inter-breeding of a once multi-cultural society now becomes, in the perversions of this nationalist conflict, the worst shame and desecration it is possible to inflict on one's enemy.

If the egalitarian project of state socialism produced a society characterized by gender inequalities, conservative and nationalist discourse serves as an extreme illustration of the ultimately gendered (male) nature of individual liberty in the neo-liberal democratic model adopted by the formerly state socialist countries of East Central Europe. As Dasă Duhaček puts it, 'the egalitarian layer cracked and revealed an almost untouched patriarchy' (Duhaček, 1993, p. 136). However, a reaction which rejects the goal of gender equality in the name of recognizing differences among individual women or groups of women runs the risk of falling into the kind of situation where women lose entitlements and become pawns in a game of nationalist political manipulation. In the former Yugoslavia for example, 'women renounced ideology and egalitarianism and in doing so renounced themselves and fell, with rare exceptions, into the nationalist trap' (Duhaček, 1993, ibid.).

The moment is ripe for a re-examination of feminist theory in order to reformulate the pre-conditions for gender equality in the wake of a failure to achieve equal citizenship rights for women by either state socialist or Western market societies. Zillah Eisenstein (1993, p. 314–15) sees 'the feminist challenge now' as being 'to address a radicalized democracy that unsettles the gendered structures of statist socialism and '"free" markets'.

The need is to define citizenship in a manner which, while respecting, indeed celebrating, difference and women's multiple identities – of profession, family, ethnic group, sexual preference, culture – yet does not fall into the essentialist trap, and gives fundamental rights of endowment to all women, including those in ethnic minorities, and particularly migrant and refugee women. Pointing to 'the tension between individuality and collectivity' as the starting point for such a redefinition, Zillah Eisenstein distinguishes 'a liberal individualism that pictures an atomized and disconnected person in competition with others from a post-patriarchal individuality that recognizes the capacities and diversity of individuals as a part of a community that can either enhance or constrain their development' (Eisenstein, 1993, p. 315). In this process Western feminists have much to learn from women in East Central Europe with their experience of the subordination of individual aspirations to one or other of the two collectivities – the building of a socialist society, as opposed to duty to the family as the basic unit of an ethnically defined nation – described in this article. What survives may just be an antenna for social justice and a sense of solidarity across differences.

ACQUIRING OR RETAINING RIGHTS AS CITIZENS

What are the mechanisms for getting women's needs and aspirations heard and translated into policy? Do they reside in the mainstream political institutions, or in the informal networks and organizations of a revived civil society? Will women organize to defend the right to work, access to adequate levels of political representation to ensure that women's needs are addressed, the right to reproductive choice and to social welfare provision, in other words their economic, social, political and reproductive rights?

Current trends suggest that they will do so. The notion that a swift sleight of hand would resolve all at once both the economy's need to shed labour and the social needs of families by relieving women of their dual role as workers *and* mothers, has been shown to be a myth. On the one hand it is still the case that in Poland, for example, 2.6 salaries are required to enable families to survive (Hauser et al., 1993, p. 269). On the other, surveys in East Germany (Nickel, 1993, p. 147), Poland (Titkow, 1993, p. 254), Czech Republic (Havelková, 1993, p. 70; Paukert, 1993), Bulgaria (Petrova, 1993, p. 26), and Russia (Bodrova, 1993, p. 182–5) all show that despite their initial inclination to accept this relegation to a private existence with a sigh of relief, women derived more from their jobs than mere money. Employment provided them with their sense of identity and self-esteem, their social status and support networks. Although in the Bulgarian and East German cases it seems that some women may be prepared to accept a later start to their career (Bulgaria) or the 'three-phase model' (East Germany), 'they could never accept being economically inactive' (Kostova, 1993, p. 103). Consequently, although one Hungarian survey (Tóth, 1993, p. 220) claimed that 35 per cent of women *would* choose to stay at home if their husbands earned enough for a 'family wage', the figure for Russia (Waters, 1993, p. 292) and for East Germany (Engelbrech, 1993) was less than ten per cent. These surveys showing women's desire to uphold their right to work even were it not financially necessary, may form the basis of resistance to the domination of purely market mechanisms.

On the issue of reproductive rights, spontaneous groups were formed in Poland, Slovenia, Hungary, East Germany and elsewhere to defend women's rights to legal abortions. Fuszara (1993, p. 251) sees it as an ironic unintended outcome of the Polish government's attempt to ban abortion that they have spawned women's activism as citizens acting on their own behalf. In former Yugoslavia, women's self-organized counselling of refugees and rape victims is central to the maintenance of dignity and identity of ravaged peoples.

However, the issue of their citizenship rights is not one for which women alone are responsible. Regardless of whether women begin to self-organize to defend existing or to demand new rights, there is an irreducible need for the state to play a central role in guaranteeing gender equality. In this regard, it is significant that, after the initial urge to abandon all state socialist legislation and social provision, there is now a sober rethink of the magic of the market in East Central Europe in the light of its effects in the first five years. A Council of Europe recommendation of 3 February 1995 urges the countries of East Central Europe to 'retain some achievements of the communist system "to combat the poverty caused by the market economy"' (Riols, 1995). This statement provides stark evidence of the need to redefine the relationship between state and market in order to discover the balance between them most likely to produce social justice and gender equality.

NOTES

1   This framework is developed, with his help, from one used by David Evans (1993).
2   The ethical justification for the distributive outcomes of capitalism vary. The untrammelled version of neo-liberalism (see Sen, 1981, p. 469–71, on Hayek, Nozic) holds that as long as the process by which property is acquired is legitimate (competitive market), then the holding of property and its disposition, including between generations, is just. It does not matter what the *outcome* of the market system is; as long as it is a competitive process, the system is seen as *just*.

3　The ethical justification for this system arises from the Marxian principle that all citizens under socialism are entitled to the rewards, i.e. to their per capita share of natural resources and physical capital. Roughly speaking, this was achieved under state socialism. The aspects that were probably most modified from the ideal conception arose through *Nomenklatura* misuse of the system.

4　It is important to distinguish here between liberal and conservative definitions of citizenship. Liberal and even neo-liberal discourse is ostensibly gender-neutral; it is the restoration of patri-archal traditional peasant culture which makes for the conservative version of it expressed in many of the countries of East Central Europe.

5　The assumption is made within these market-led strategies that the state or public sector is by definition inefficient, an assumption which is now being widely challenged (see for example ILO, 1994a).

6　Fong and Paull (1993, p. 235–6) distinguish here between the 'real and perceived cost of　female labour'.

7　A sector which merits further research in this respect, since it was peripheral to state socialist planned economies, but is central to a market economy, is that of banking, insurance and fin-ance. For early case studies, see Nickel (1993, p. 143–4) on the East German state insurance company and Maier (1993) on East German savings banks.

8　The resulting scenario is bizarre: the notion of individual enterprise in the marketplace, com-bined with involuntary and disproportionately high female unemployment, has spawned in Russia an image of the prostitute as 'the pioneer of the market economy' (Lissyutkina, 1993, p. 284). Larissa Lissyutkina describes the shift in images of female workers and femininity from state socialism to market eloquently when she states: 'Without skipping a beat, the image of the woman worker was overthrown by the ideal of the woman as prostitute or beauty queen' (ibid., p. 275).

9　A good example of this is the textile and garments industry, where international firms first moved from Europe to the newly industrializing economies of Asia (NIEs), but more recently have made a second and in some cases even a third move, from South Korea and the Philippines to Indonesia and Malaysia, Thailand and Sri Lanka, China and Vietnam. Women workers in the collapsing textile industry in East Central Europe have been acutely affected by this competition on the world market, despite their relatively low wages when compared with Western Europe or the USA (ILO, 1994a).

10　Fong and Paull (1993, p. 242) argue rather for what they call 'pro-active measures' which 'may be desirable to support the position of women during the period of transition'.

11　While reports on the numbers involved vary from 20,000 to 50,000 (Einhorn, 1993a, p. 106), the scale and enormity of the rapes is beyond question.

BIBLIOGRAPHY

Anthias, Flora and Yuval-Davis, Nira (eds) (1989), *Woman-Nation-State*, Basingstoke: Macmillan.

Bodrova, Valentina (1993), 'Glasnost and the "Woman Question" in the Mirror of Public Opinion: Attitudes towards Women, Work and the Family' in Valentine M. Moghadam (ed.), *Democratic Reform and the Position of Women in Transitional Economies,* Oxford: Clarendon Press, pp.180–96.

Bracewell, Wendy (1995), 'Women, Motherhood and Contemporary Serbian Nationalism', *Women's Studies International Forum*, Special issue on 'Gender, Ethnicity and Nationalism', Issue 18, Nos 5–6, Autumn.

Buckley, Mary (1985), 'Soviet Interpretations of the Woman Question' in Barbara Holland (ed.), *Soviet Sisterhood: British Feminists on Women in the USSR*, London: Fourth Estate.

Chamberlayne, Prue (1994), 'Women and Social Policy' in Jochen Clasen and Richard Freeman (eds), *Social Policy in Germany*, Hemel Hempstead: Harvester Wheatsheaf, pp.173–90.

Dölling, Irene (1991), 'Between Hope and Helplessness: Women in the GDR After the "Turning Point"', *Shifting Territories: Feminism and Europe*, Special issue No. 39 of *Feminist Review*, Winter, pp.3–15.

Drakulić, Slavenka (1993), 'Women and the New Democracy in the Former Yugoslavia', in Nanette Funk and Magda Mueller (eds), *Gender Politics and Post-Communism: Reflections from Eastern Europe and the Former Soviet Union*, London and New York: Routledge, pp.123–30.

Duhaček, Daša (1993), 'Women's Time in the Former Yugoslavia', in Nanette Funk and Magda Mueller (eds), *Gender Politics and Post-Communism: Reflections from Eastern Europe and the Former Soviet Union*, London and New York: Routledge, pp.131–7.

Einhorn, Barbara (1993a), *Cinderella Goes to Market: Citizenship, Gender and Women's Movements in East Central Europe*, London: Verso.

Einhorn, Barbara (1993b), *The Impact of the Transition from Centrally Planned to Market Economies on Women's Employment in East Central Europe*, Consultancy paper for the ILO, Brighton: Institute for Development Studies.

Eisenstein, Zillah (1993), 'Eastern European Male Democracies: A Problem of Unequal Equality' in Nanette Funk and Magda Mueller (eds), *Gender Politics and Post-Communism: Reflections from Eastern Europe and the Former Soviet Union*, London and New York: Routledge, pp. 303–17.

Engelbrech, Gerhard (1993), 'Zwischen Wunsch und Wirklichkeit: Einstellungen ostdeutscher Frauen zur Erwerbstätigkeit zwei Jahre nach der Wende – Ergebnisse einer Befragung' ('Between Desire and Reality: East German Women's Attitudes to Paid Work Two Years after Unification – Results of a Survey'), *IAB Werkstattbericht*, No. 8, June.

Evans, David (1993), 'Domination and Exploitation in the World Economy in the 1990s', *IDS Bulletin*, Vol. 24, No. 3, pp.36–48.

Fong, Monica and Paull, Gillian (1993), 'Women's Economic Status in the Restructuring of Eastern Europe' in Valentine M. Moghadam (ed.), *Democratic Reform and the Position of Women in Transitional Economies*, Oxford: Clarendon Press, pp.217–47.

Funk, Nanette (1993), 'Feminism East and West', in Nanette Funk and Magda Mueller (eds), *Gender Politics and Post-Communism: Reflections from Eastern Europe and the Former Soviet Union*, London and New York: Routledge, pp.318–30.

Funk, Nanette and Magda Mueller (eds) (1993), *Gender Politics and Post-Communism: Reflections from Eastern Europe and the Former Soviet Union*, London and New York: Routledge.

Fuszara, Małgorzata (1993), 'Abortion and the Formation of the Public Sphere in Poland' in Nanette Funk and Magda Mueller (eds), *Gender Politics and Post-Communism: Reflections from Eastern Europe and the Former Soviet Union*, London and New York: Routledge, pp.241–52.

Harsanyi, Doina Pasca (1993), 'Women in Romania' in Nanette Funk and Magda Mueller (eds), *Gender Politics and Post-Communism: Reflections from Eastern Europe and the Former Soviet Union*, London and New York: Routledge, pp.39–52.

Hauser, Ewa, Heyns, Barbara and Mansbridge, Jane (1993), 'Feminism in the Interstices of Politics and Culture: Poland in Transition' in Nanette Funk and Magda Mueller (eds), *Gender Politics and Post-Communism: Reflections from Eastern Europe and the Former Soviet Union*, London and New York: Routledge, pp.257–73.

Havelková, Hana (1993), 'A Few Prefeminist Thoughts' in Nanette Funk and Magda Mueller (eds), *Gender Politics and Post-Communism: Reflections from Eastern Europe and the Former Soviet Union*, London and New York: Routledge, pp.62–73.

Helsinki Watch (1992), 'Hidden Victims: Women in Post-Communist Poland', *News from Helsinki Watch*, Vol. IV, Issue 5, March.

ILO (1994a), *Productive Employment: Women Workers in a Changing Global Environment*, ILO Contribution to Chapter II of the *1994 UN World Survey on the Role of Women in Development*, Geneva: International Labour Organization.

ILO (1994b), *World Labour Report*, Geneva: International Labour Organization.

Kostova, Dobrinka (1993), 'The Transition to Democracy in Bulgaria: Challenges and Risks for Women' in Valentine M. Moghadam (ed.), *Democratic Reform and the Position of Women in Transitional Economies*, Oxford: Clarendon Press, pp.92–109.

Kostova, Dobrinka (1994), 'Similar or Different? Women in Postcommunist Bulgaria' in Marilyn Rueschemeyer (ed.), *Women in the Politics of Postcommunist Eastern Europe*, New York and London: M.E. Sharpe, pp.117–32.

Lissyutkina, Larissa (1993), 'Soviet Women at the Crossroads of Perestroika' in Nanette Funk and Magda Mueller (eds), *Gender Politics and Post-Communism: Reflections from Eastern Europe and the Former Soviet Union*, London and New York: Routledge, pp.274–86.

Lister, Ruth (1993), 'Tracing the Contours of Women's Citizenship', *Policy and Politics*, Vol. 21, No. 1, pp.3–16.

Maier, Friederike (1993), 'The Labour Market for Women and Employment Perspectives in the Aftermath of German Unification', *Cambridge Journal of Economics*, Vol. 17, pp.267–80.

Marody, Mira (1991), 'On Polish Political Attitudes', *Telos*, No. 89, Fall, pp.109–13.

Mežnarić, Silva and Ule, Mirjana (1994), 'Women in Croatia and Slovenia: A Case of Delayed Modernization' in Marilyn Rueschemeyer (ed), *Women in the Politics of Postcommunist Eastern Europe*, pp.153–70.

Milić, Andjelka (1993), 'Women and Nationalism in the Former Yugoslavia' in Nanette Funk and Magda Mueller (eds), *Gender Politics and Post-Communism: Reflections from Eastern Europe and the Former Soviet Union*, London and New York: Routledge, pp.95–108.

Moghadam, Valentine M. (ed.) (1993), *Democratic Reform and the Position of Women in Transitional Economies*, Oxford: Clarendon Press.

Nickel, Hildegard Maria (1993), 'Women in the German Democratic Republic and in the New Federal States: Looking Backward and Forward (Five Theses)' in Nanette Funk and Magda Mueller (eds), *Gender Politics and Post-Communism: Reflections from Eastern Europe and the Former Soviet Union*, London and New York: Routledge, pp.138–50.

Paukert, Liba (1993), *Women's Employment in East-Central European Countries during the Period of Transition to a Market Economy System*, Geneva: ILO, Working Paper.

Petrova, Dimitrina (1993), 'The Winding Road to Emancipation in Bulgaria' in Nanette Funk and Magda Mueller (eds), *Gender Politics and Post-Communism: Reflections from Eastern Europe and the Former Soviet Union*, London and New York: Routledge, pp.22–9.

Pine, Frances (1992), 'Uneven Burdens: Women in Rural Poland' in Shirin Rai, Hilary Pilkington and Annie Phizacklea (eds), *Women in the Face of Change: The Soviet Union, Eastern Europe and China*, London: Routledge, pp.57–75.

Pine, Frances (1994), 'Privatization in Post-Socialist Poland: Peasant Women, Work, and the Restructuring of the Public Sphere' Cambridge Anthropology, Vol. 17, No. 3, pp.19–42.

Proposal for Demographic Renewal (1992), Legislative draft, Croatia (English translation by the Zagreb Autonomous Women's Centre).

Riols, Yves-Michel (1995), 'Unease Sweeps East', *Le Monde*, reprinted in *The Guardian*, 9 February.

Rueschemeyer, Marilyn (ed.), *Women in the Politics of Postcommunist Eastern Europe*, New York and London: M.E. Sharpe.

Salecl, Renata (1994), *The Spoils of Freedom: Psychoanalysis and Feminism after the Fall of Socialism*, London and New York: Routledge.

Seifert, Ruth (1995), 'The Second Front: The Logic of Sexual Violence in Wars', *Women's Studies International Forum*, Special issue on 'Gender, Ethnicity and Nationalism', Issue 18, Nos 5–6, Autumn.

Sen, Amartya (1981), 'Ethical Issues in Income Distribution: National and International' in Sven Grassman and Erik Lundberg (eds), *The World Economic Order: Past and Prospects*, London: Macmillan, pp.464–94.

Titkow, Anna (1993), 'Political Change in Poland: Cause, Modifier, or Barrier to Gender Equality?' in Nanette Funk and Magda Mueller (eds), *Gender Politics and Post-Communism: Reflections from Eastern Europe and the Former Soviet Union*, London and New York: Routledge, pp.253–56.

Tóth, Olga (1993), 'No Envy, No Pity' in Nanette Funk and Magda Mueller (eds), *Gender Politics and Post-Communism: Reflections from Eastern Europe and the Former Soviet Union*, London and New York: Routledge, pp.213–23.

Vogel, Ursula (1991), 'Is Citizenship Gender-Specific?' in Ursula Vogel and Michael Moran (eds), *The Frontiers of Citizenship*, Basingstoke: Macmillan.

Vogel, Ursula and Moran, Michael (eds) (1991), Introduction to *The Frontiers of Citizenship*, Basingstoke: Macmillan.

Waters, Elizabeth (1993), 'Finding a Voice: The Emergence of a Women's Movement' in Nanette Funk and Magda Mueller (eds), *Gender Politics and Post-Communism: Reflections from Eastern Europe and the Former Soviet Union*, London and New York: Routledge, pp.287–302.

Index

abortion 225–6, 229
Academy of Social Sciences (China)
  196, 199
Acland, Alice 33, 41n4
Addams, Jane 15, 17, 19
advertisement(s)
  China 86, 116, 120, 123–5
  France 52–5
  Hong Kong 97, 104, 108, 110
  Italy 68, 77–8
agriculture
  China 193, 196, 198, 207
  Eastern Europe 220–21
  France 48, 50, 56n
  South Korea 185–8
Ahn Soon-Duk and Byun Wha-Soon
  189
All-China Committee of Women
  Workers 202
All-China Women's Federation, see
  Women's Federation
America, see United States of America
  (USA)
Anderson, Lindsay 72
anxiety, cultural 48, 53, 71, 114,
  118–20, 122, 126, 147
Appadurai, Arjun 101, 108, 110
appropriation(s), cultural, see cultural
Archibald, Mary 24
L'Art Ménager 49
authenticity 85–7, 90–91, 93–4
autonomy, female 71–2, 162, 171, 220,
  224
Avon cosmetics corporation 5, 117–20,
  127n4, 128

Baker, Ella 27
Balbo, Laura 150
Bamford, Samuel 132
basket power 30–43 (esp 34–5)
beauty, notions of 99–100, 108–9, 124
Bellamy, Edward 14
Bernège, Paulette 49, 52–3

Beveridge Report (1942, UK) 165, 168
birth rate
  Eastern Europe 226
  France 50–1
  Germany 166
bodies, women's 100, 114–17, 125–6
Boris, Eileen 19
'Bread and Roses' strike (USA, 1912)
  23
breadwinner, male 75–6, 82, 135, 163,
  165–7, 169, 180, 224
Britain 2, 4, 6, 30–46, 47, 50, 67,
  131–45, 147–9, 160–61, 164,
  168–72, 217
Brown, Elsa Barkley 19
Brown, Helen Gurley 102
Buckley, Mary 225
Bulgaria 225, 228–9

Cadbury, Elizabeth 132
Cameron, Ardis 23
capital 1, 3, 31, 133, 141–2, 146, 152,
  184, 218–19, 220, 222
capitalism 13, 68–9, 72, 74, 89, 116,
  133–6, 140, 147, 156, 164, 185,
  218–19, 221, 229n2
capitalist
  cultures 110
  economies 1, 135, 141, 160, 165
  exploitation 139
  ideology, see ideology
  market system 131
  societies (Western) 3
caring (work) 138–9, 143, 148, 150,
  152–3, 162, 164, 166–7, 169–73,
  190, 218, 223
Chamberlayne, Prue 166
Chee Eun-Hee 190
Chen Kaige 81, 89
child benefit(s) 166, 169
childcare 2, 12, 17, 25–6, 68, 78, 136,
  138–9, 141–2, 149, 153, 155,
  167–70, 182, 184, 218